of related interest

Children as Citizens
Education for Participation
Edited by Cathie Holden and Nick Clough
ISBN 1 85302 566 6
Children in Charge 5

Children in Our Charge
The Child's Right to Resources
Edited by Mary John
ISBN 1 85302 369 8
Children in Charge 2

Educational Citizenship and Independent Learning
Rhys Griffith
ISBN 1 85302 611 5
Children in Charge 6

The Participation Rights of the Child
Rights and Responsibilities in Family and Society
Målfrid Grude Flekkøy and Natalie Hevener Kaufman
ISBN 1 85302 489 9
Children in Charge 4

Young Children's Rights
Exploring Beliefs, Principles and Practice
Priscilla Alderson
Forewords by Save the Children and Mary John
ISBN 1 85302 880 0
Children in Charge 10

Children's Rights and Power in a Changing World
Mary John
ISBN 1 85302 659 X
Children in Charge 9

Traveller Children
A Voice for Themselves
Cathy Kiddle
ISBN 1 85302 684 0
Children in Charge 8

Children in Charge 11

Children's Rights in Education

Edited by Stuart N. Hart, Cynthia Price Cohen, Martha Farrell Erickson and Målfrid Flekkøy

Jessica Kingsley Publishers
London and Philadelphia

First published in the United Kingdom in 2001 by
Jessica Kingsley Publishers Ltd,
116 Pentonville Road,
London N1 9JB, England
and
325 Chestnut Street,
Philadelphia, PA 19106, USA.
www.jkp.com

Library of Congress Cataloging in Publication Data

A CIP catalog record for this book is available from the Library of Congress

British Library Cataloguing in Publication Data

A CIP catalogue record for this book is available from the British Library

ISBN 1 85302 977 7

Printed and Bound in Great Britain by
Athenaeum Press, Gateshead, Tyne and Wear

Contents

Introduction

Stuart N. Hart

Children's rights in education is a theme that has the potential to increase the meaning and power of both rights and education. Arguably, a well-developed foundation of children's rights to, in, and through education can help assure that the short- and long-term best interests of individuals and their societies will be served. The chapters of this book consider many of the critical issues and sub-themes that clarify and give direction to these possibilities. To help set the stage for what follows, this introduction describes emerging conceptualizations of human beings and children and the recent history that led to the development of this book, and it provides brief comments about the book's contents.

This is quite an exciting time for the human race. The meanings and possibilities of humanness are being expanded. Experts within the science of cosmology have recently begun seriously to doubt theories that postulate randomness or chance factors as being central to the nature of the universe and its history. Much to the surprise of many scientists, substantial evidence has been found indicating that the development of the universe has been designed from its earliest recognizable beginning and fine-tuned throughout its evolving progress to produce human beings. The label 'anthropic principle' has been given to the theory formulated to describe these findings, findings that contradict the notion that the universe does not have direction or purpose and that human beings simply represent one of its by-products. It strongly suggests that maybe, just maybe, there is a something very special about human beings in the larger scheme of things (Barrow and Tipler 1998).

What is it about human beings that is so special? Our opposable thumb and extensive use of tools set us apart from most of the other living creatures. The power of our extensive language capabilities appears to be a key difference between us and other life forms. There is a characteristic, however, while somewhat related to these, that seems to be of far more significance – it is our capacity for existential choice. There is no other living thing known to be able consciously to step out of the time stream and, thereby, consider the past, present and possible futures in dealing with issues and choices. Weighing issues across time and the awareness of doing so and of the associated evolving meaning of self appear to enable us to choose and act beyond instinct and, at times, beyond any but the most abstract conceptions of self-interest.

What are the life purposes or goals of this very special creature we call 'human' to which existential choice might be applied? Certainly individual survival and collective survival through protection and procreation are strong drives or needs. Psychologists worldwide have accepted the relevance, if not in purist forms at least in general forms, of the basic needs identified by Maslow (i.e., physiological, safety, love and belonging, esteem and self-actualization), the stages of psychosocial developmental postulated by Erikson (i.e., trust, autonomy, initiative, industry, identity, intimacy, generativity and integrity), and progressive achievement of Kohlberg's stages of moral development (i.e., pre-conventional, conventional and post-conventional). Recent research evidence has identified three needs or goals of human development that are compatible with these dimensions, appear to respect and incorporate them, but which are at an integrative and somewhat higher overarching level. They are the needs for competence, connectedness and autonomy (Ryan and Deci 2000). Predating this research, the closely related goals of independence, social responsibility and self-actualization had been proposed as the major goals or directions for human development and human rights support by Hart (1991), and labeled collectively as 'responsible autonomy'. Additionally, it is important to recognize that whatever human beings have the potential to become and do, our newly advanced knowledge of brain development indicates that the period of human life with the greatest potential is childhood, when some 100 billion neurons are at a stage allowing for trillions of connections if, during this period, experience supports their establishment (Nash 1997).

It is against this background that the human rights of children and their relationships to education become particularly meaningful. Certainly, most persons would agree that the development and use of tools and language can strengthen the capabilities and rights of humans, and that education, broadly defined, can foster these conditions. Agreement might also be easily achieved regarding rights to have basic needs met, to healthy psychosocial development, and to moral development. Substantial evidence as well as common sense indicates that education can facilitate progress toward full development in these and other areas.

The importance of all these aspects of human rights and capacities and the necessity for education to support their achievement has been recognized, explicitly or implicitly, in the articles of the United Nations Convention on the Rights of the Child. The Convention is the world's statement and vision of children's rights to protection, nurturance, development and participation. The Convention was adopted without dissent by the United Nations General Assembly November 20, 1989. It is the most successful human rights treaty in history in terms of the quickness and extent to which it went into effect and has been ratified.

One of the hallmarks of the Convention is that it goes beyond a commitment to application of education toward the needs and areas of development just cited. The Convention gives clear and strong emphasis to achieving the highest levels of human capacity and fulfilment – to realizing the quintessential characteristics of humans. Hodgkin and Newell (1998) brought this into focus when they indicated that the Convention sets forth the perspective that the basic aims of learning are 'to develop children's full potential, to prepare children for "responsible lives in a free society" and to enshrine the values of respect for all others and for the natural environment' (p. 391).

Children's rights experts and advocates have increasingly recognized the significance of relationships between human rights and education. This recognition led to the convening of the first International Conference on Children's Rights in Education, which was held at the Royal Danish School of Educational Studies in Copenhagen, 26–30 April 1998. This conference provided the major impetus for the development of this book. The major purpose of the conference was to advance respect and support for children's rights and the full development of children through education. The conference provided a structured exchange among international and national experts on theory, research, policy and practices relating children's rights to education. The United Nations Convention on the Rights of the Child, particularly education articles 28 and 29, and article 23 on children with disabilities, provided the fundamental framework for the exchange. The

Danish Ministry of Education was the primary organizer and sponsor of the conference. In presenting the conference, the Ministry had the co-operative involvement of the International Bureau of Education, Education International, the NGO Group for the Convention on the Rights of the Child, the International School Psychology Association, and the Office for the Study of the Psychological Rights of the Child (School of Education of Indiana University-Purdue University Indianapolis), as well as numerous Danish national organizations. Approximately 200 participants registered for the conference, including individuals from 49 countries spanning all major regions of the world and representing ministries of education, professional educators, educational psychologists, child advocates, parents and children.

The conference program was organized into three major themes:

1. progress made so far to achieve children's rights in education
2. rights of children with special needs
3. directions for advancing children's rights through education.

Each theme was introduced by a keynote plenary presentation and followed by four simultaneously run presentation and working group sessions, each dealing with a major dimension of the overall theme. Twelve internationally respected experts from ten countries presented and facilitated presentation/working groups on the following topics: cultural issues; models for reporting on progress; possibilities for agreement between legislation, political decisions and practices; home and school cooperation; children's experiences of their rights; inclusion and integration in education for students with special needs; rights of students and parents when receiving special needs support; financial considerations for special needs education; curricular guides and practices fostering rights and full development; education toward democracy; ways for students to express their views and achieve influence; and expectations and demands for teachers and parents. Selected youths from four countries participated throughout the conference, and presented their views in a final plenary session and in an eight-page newspaper they produced for the conference. Approximately two thirds of one day of the conference was devoted to visits to Danish schools to observe school programs and to interact with and interview students, faculty, administrators and school-community representatives.

The conference was a genuine success. It achieved its major purposes – to advance respect and support for children's rights and the full development of children through education. Participants considered a substantial amount of information about targeted issues. This led to the formation of a wide variety of formal and informal alliances between participants for the purpose of pursuing joint educational projects. An edition of *Prospects* (Vol. SSIS, no. 2, June 1999), the journal of the International Bureau of Education, presented an 'open file' theme issue on the convention and its topics.

The chapters of this book extend and expand the themes of the International Conference on Children's Rights in Education. The majority of the chapters are written by experts who were faculty members for the conference. The first four chapters describe the context of relationships between children's rights and education, the Convention on the Rights of the Child and other related treaties, and the history and projected future for implementing associated international standards. The first chapter, by Sandra Prunella Mason (Chairperson, UN Committee on the Rights of the Child, 1996–1998) and Cynthia Price Cohen (Director, ChildRights International Research Institute), includes an overview of the Convention and describes the manner in which the Committee on the Rights of the Child works with national governments to encourage the Convention's full implementation. Chapter 2, by Gerison Lansdown (freelance children's rights consultant, previously Director of the Child Rights Unit, United Kingdom), describes the nature of progress made in implementing the Convention and issues and opportunities which must be recognized and dealt with if the full spirit of the Convention is to be realized through implementation. Chapter 3, by Ulf Fredriksson (Education Officer for Education International), describes the discrepancies between what international standards require and existing conditions, reasons for those discrepancies, and some of the ways to achieve better agreement between legislation, political decisions and everyday practice. The fourth chapter, by Lukas Scherer (Chairperson, Education and Media SubGroup, NGO Group for the Convention on the Rights of the Child), and Stuart N. Hart (Chairperson, Children's Rights Committee of the International School Psychology Association and Director, Office for the Study of the Psychological Rights of the Child), presents the results of analyses of initial and periodic reports to the Committee on the Rights of the Child from nations on the status of achieving the Convention's education standards, identifies significant omissions and inadequacies in reporting, and proposes an alternative structure and procedure for reporting to overcome identified deficiencies.

The next three chapters deal with major human rights themes in educating children – democracy, inclusion and participation. Chapter 5, by F. Clark Power (Professor of Liberal Arts, Notre Dame University, and past-president of the International Moral Education Association), explains the meanings and significance of democracy and democratic practices, and describes the manner in which young people can learn democracy through their school experiences. Lena Saleh (formerly Chief of UNESCO's Special Needs Education in its Division of Basic Education) in Chapter 6, identifies the obligations and responsibilities for educating children with special vulnerabilities or special needs, making it clear that education should apply the full Convention to all children and ensure participation, empowerment and full inclusion. In Chapter 7, Mary John (Professor Emeritus, Education, University of Exeter, UK), discusses the importance of children's views, their participation rights, being respected in education and the roles that children and adults can and should take to achieve this.

Chapters 8 and 9 concentrate on the roles of adults, in formal and informal positions of power, that can further children's rights in education. Målfrid Flekkøy (the world's first national ombudsman for children, Norway 1981–1989) explains what a national ombudsman is, why it is important to have an ombudsman for children, their relevance for children's rights and education, and the kinds of cases they consider. In his chapter, Eugeen Verhellen (Professor of Juvenile Justice and Juvenile Criminology and Director of the Children's Rights Centre of the University of Gent, Belgium) suggests that we build on a new child image, one of subject rather than object – bearer rather than recipient of rights – to operationalize rights through full inclusion, legal protection, intentional and systematic children's rights education policy, and education of parents and teachers.

The last two chapters conclude the book in two ways. Chapter 10, by John Bennett (formerly director of Early Childhood and Family Education at UNESCO and presently senior consultant to the Organization for Economic Cooperation and Development, Paris) and Stuart N. Hart provide the history, supports, and a project to develop learning environments – school communities – in which human rights are respected, lived and learned, giving attention to many of the themes of earlier chapters. In the final chapter, Martha Farrell Erickson (Director of the Children, Youth and Family Consortium of the University of Minnesota and Minneapolis, USA) provides concluding perspectives through identifying major themes that fall within and cut across the chapters of this book and the implications of these themes for advancing children's rights in education.

Note: The full text of the UN Convention on the Rights of the Child is available at http://www.unhchr.ch

References

Barrow, J. D. and Tipler, F. J. (1998) *The Anthropic Cosmological Principle.* Oxford: Oxford University Press.

Hart, S. (1991) 'From property to person status: Historical perspective on children's rights.' *American Psychologist, 46*, 1, 53–59.

Hodgkin, R. and Newell, P. (1998) *Implementation Handbook for the Convention on the Rights of the Child.* New York and Geneva: UNICEF.

Nash, M. 'Fertile minds – Special report.' *Time Magazine*, 3 Feb 1997, pp.48–56.

Ryan, R. M. and Deci, E. L. (2000) 'Self-determination theory and the facilitation of intrinsic motivation, social development, and well-being.' *American Psychologist, 55*, 1, 68–78.

CHAPTER 1

Children's Rights in Education

Sandra Prunella Mason and Cynthia Price Cohen

Introduction

Traditionally, children have not been perceived as the subjects of rights, but rather as the objects of legal protection. Adoption of the Convention on the Rights of the Child by the United Nations General Assembly in 1989[1] effectively and appropriately removed the child, and the concept of his/her rights, from the periphery of national and international thinking to centre stage – resulting in a change of attitude and perception of who a child really is. The Convention is considered innovative. It envisages the rights of the child not as being in conflict with the rights of the adult, nor as an alternative to or an abrogation of the rights of parents, but as an integral part of human rights. It recognizes the child as an individual with needs that evolve with age and maturity. Accordingly, it goes beyond existing treaties by seeking to balance the rights of the child with the duties of parents and others responsible for the child's survival, development and protection, by giving the child the right to participate in decisions affecting the child's life.

The Convention on the Rights of the Child is not, and was not meant to be, a mere grouping of articles embodying divergent or independent principles. In fact, the Convention's strength lies in the concept of the indivisibility and interdependence of all the rights enshrined therein, rights which are inherent to the human dignity of the child and are necessary for the full and harmonious development of the child's personality, including the child's civil and political rights and cultural, social and economic rights. In other words, by ratifying the Convention, States have committed to providing a better life for all children under their jurisdiction by taking the necessary measures (legislative, administrative and other measures) for its implementation.

Historical perspective of education as a right

The principle of education as a fundamental right of children did not have its inception with the Convention on the Rights of the Child. By its resolution 217A (III) of 10 December 1948, the General Assembly of the United Nations adopted the Universal Declaration of Human Rights.[2] This document was conceived as a 'common standard of achievement for all peoples and all nations' and thus became the gauge by which to measure the degree of respect for and compliance with international human rights standards. The Universal Declaration proclaimed education as a fundamental right in its article 26, which states:

1. Everyone has the right to education. Education shall be free, at least in the elementary and fundamental stages. Elementary education shall be compulsory.

   Technical and professional education shall be made generally available and higher education shall be equally accessible to all on the basis of merit.

2. Education shall be directed to the full development of the human personality and to the strengthening of respect for human rights and fundamental freedoms. It shall promote understanding, tolerance and friendship among all nations, racial or religious groups, and shall further the activities of the United Nations for the maintenance of peace.

3. Parents have a prior right to choose the kind of education that shall be given to their children.

Since then, various international human rights instruments have reiterated and reinforced this principle.[3] For example, the International Covenant on Economic, Social and Cultural Rights,[4] one of two treaties that were drafted to make the Universal Declaration's principles legally binding, recognized the right of everyone to education. The text of its article 13, which calls for different levels of education, also defines the purpose of education and the role of parents in the education process in paragraph 3:

> The States Parties to the present Covenant undertake to have respect for the liberty of parents and, when applicable legal guardians to choose for their children schools other than those established by the public authorities, which conform to such minimum educational standards as may be laid down or approved by the State and to ensure the religious and moral education of their children in conformity with their own convictions.[5]

Article 13 provided the foundation for articles 28 and 29 of the Convention on the Rights of the Child.[6] Article 28 of the Convention sets the basic standards for education and roughly replicates paragraph 2 of article 13, but with the addition of measures 'to encourage regular attendance at school and the reduction of school dropout rates.'[7] It also includes standards for the administration of school discipline[8] and provisions for international cooperation if required by a country to fulfil the article 28 requirements.[9] Article 29 of the Convention, which outlines the purpose of education, is based on paragraph 3 of article 13.

Background of the Convention on the Rights of the Child

The Convention on the Rights of the Child is the primary outcome of the 1979 International Year of the Child (IYC),[10] which was proclaimed to celebrate the twentieth anniversary of the 1959 Declaration of the Rights of the Child.[11] As a celebratory initiative, the Polish government proposed that the rights originally enshrined in the 1959 Declaration be put into legally binding form. The Commission on Human Rights responded by setting up an Open-Ended Working Group to draft a Convention on the Rights of the Child (Working Group).[12] The process was begun in 1979, using as a model a draft Convention that had been submitted by the Polish government. An earlier draft, that was basically a replication of the Declaration with the addition of a very weak implementation, was rejected by the Commission.[13] The draft used by the Working Group was a revised version that, while still emphasizing the child's right to care and protection, also recognized the child's right to express his or her views in matters affecting the child.[14]

The proposal to draft the Convention, while ultimately approved by the Commission on Human Rights was not without its detractors. Many people – government delegations and legal scholars – argued that there was no need for a special treaty to protect children's human rights. In their view children's rights were already adequately covered by other existing human rights treaties. For example, article 24 of the International Covenant on Civil and Political Rights especially addresses the child's right to a name and a nationality.[15] However, once the Convention's drafting process was begun, it became obvious that children indeed had special rights that needed protecting and that the drafting process was not to be just an exercise in translating existing human rights treaties into child-related language. In fact, the final draft of the Convention went far beyond what had been envisioned by its original proponents. Instead of just protecting the child's health, education and welfare, as had been done in the 1959 Declaration, the Convention on the Rights of the Child demands full respect for the child's human dignity.

At first, many governments were somewhat reluctant to take part in the Working Group. However, as the years passed, interest in the Convention grew, so that by the second reading of the Convention, when the text was finalized, participation by both governmental and non-governmental bodies had more than doubled – a startling contrast to the original worldwide apathy about children's rights.[16] In fact, to everyone's surprise, on the day that it was opened for signature, more governments signed the Convention on the Rights of the Child than had ever before participated in a human rights treaty signing ceremony. This wave of enthusiasm for the Convention did not end there. Countries began to ratify it immediately and by 2 September 1990, it had already gone into force, having quickly obtained the required 20 ratifications.[17]

On 30 September of that year, world leaders met at United Nations Headquarters in New York to hold a World Summit for Children that had been organized to ensure that the rights of the child would not slip from the international agenda.[18] The World Declaration on the Survival, Protection and Development of Children, which was agreed to at the Summit, recognized that the provision of basic education and literacy for all are among the most important contributions that can be made to the development of the world's children. The accompanying Plan of Action for implementing World Summit Declaration posited, *inter alia*:

> Besides its intrinsic value for human development and improving the quality of life, progress in education and literacy can contribute significantly to improvement in maternal and child health, to protection of the environment in sustainable develop-

> ment. As such, investment in basic education must be accorded a high priority in national action as well as international co-operation.[19]

It is ironic, therefore, that approximately 50 years after the initial acceptance of education as a fundamental right, it still should be reported that:

- more that 100 million children, including 60 million girls, have no access to primary schooling;
- more than 960 million adults, two thirds of whom are women, are illiterate, and functional illiteracy is a significant problem in all countries, industrialized and developing;
- more than one third of the world's adults have no access to the printed knowledge, new skills and technologies that could improve the quality of their lives and help them shape, and adapt to social and cultural change; and
- more than 100 million children and countless adults fail to complete basic education programs and millions more satisfy the attendance requirements but do not acquire essential knowledge and skills.[20]

Definition of education

Childhood education is usually viewed as the imparting of academic instruction within some sort of formal school system. The Convention on the Rights of the Child, while not proffering an exact definition, does appear to infer a more all-encompassing connotation. Article 28 makes mention of primary education,[21] secondary education including vocational education[22], higher education,[23] attendance at school and reduction of drop-out rates.[24] Article 29 speaks of the kind of education which would prepare the child for an active adult life in a free society and foster respect for the child's parents, his or her own cultural identity, language and values, and for the cultural background and values of others and involves the:

- development of the child's personality, talents and mental and physical abilities; – development of respect for human rights and fundamental freedoms;

- inculcation of the spirit of understanding, peace, tolerance, equality of the sexes, and friendship among all peoples; and
- development of respect for the material environment.[25]

Education thus involves a complete system and as UNESCO puts it:

> The word 'education' implies the entire process of social life by means of which individuals and social groups learn to develop consciously within, and for the benefit of, the national and international communities, the whole of their personal capacities, attitudes, aptitudes and knowledge. This process is not limited to any specific activities.[26]

This therefore is the standard to which each State should aspire on behalf of its children in order to fulfil the Convention's obligations regarding the right of the child to education.

Interrelatedness of the Convention

Some people have voiced concern that, by giving children rights for the State to protect, the Convention thrusts itself too deeply into family relationships. This is a mistaken impression. In fact, article 18 and numerous other articles of the Convention on the Rights of the Child recognize the primacy of parents in the upbringing and development of the child.[27] The State, however, does have the obligation to render appropriate assistance to parents in the performance of their child-raising responsibilities and to ensure the development of institutions, facilities and services for the care and development of children. The State can therefore be seen as *supporting* the parental role rather than conflicting with it. The responsibility of the State is further underscored by article 4, which indicates that with regard to economic, social and cultural rights, the State must undertake measures for their implementation 'to the maximum extent of available resources and where needed within the framework of international co-operation.'[28]

Implementation of these rights therefore usually requires financial investments, and the State's obligation to use available resources to the 'maximum extent possible' in certain cases requires budgetary reallocations. Thus, while not interfering with the family's right to supervise the child's education, responsibility for the financial component of that education does not rest solely with the family – it is incumbent upon the State to ensure its provision.

The child's education rights are not confined to articles 28 and 29 of the Convention on the Rights of the Child. The Convention does not function in a vacuum. In fact, its interrelatedness can be expressed in ten distinct clusters – each of which touches upon education, educational opportunity and on the quality of education. Underpinning and permeating all the interrelated rights of the Convention are its four basic principles: non-discrimination (art. 2); the best interests of the child (art. 3); the right to survival and development (art. 6); and the right of the child to express his or her views (art. 12).

The *first* cluster of articles illustrates how these primary principles are related to education. As pointed out above, the State has an obligation to ensure the child's education to the maximum extent of its available resources (art. 4); to ensure the survival and development of the child (art. 6) – who is a person under the age of 18 years of age (art. 1) – without discrimination (art. 2) and with the best interests of the child as a primary consideration (art. 3); while affording the child the opportunity to express his or her views in all matters affecting the child (art. 12).

The *second* cluster demands that the State must guarantee: freedom of expression (art. 13); freedom of thought, conscience and religion (art. 14); and freedom of association (art. 15); as well as protection of privacy (art. 16); while also ensuring accessibility to information and materials from diverse sources (art. 17).

The *third* calls on the State to take all appropriate measures to: protect the child from all forms of physical and mental violence (art. 19); prohibit the child's illicit use of narcotic drugs and the child's participation in drug trafficking (art. 33); eradicate child sexual exploitation and sexual abuse (art. 34); prevent the abduction of, the sale of or traffic in children (art. 35) and all other forms of exploitation (art. 36).

Fourth, the State must recognize the special needs of the disabled child and ensure access to education and the services and to a full and decent life and special care and promote self-reliance and facilitate the child's active participation in the community (art. 23).

Fifth, the State must ensure the right of the child to protection from economic exploitation and from performing work that is likely to be hazardous to or interfere with the child's education and to be harmful to the child's health or physical, mental, spiritual, normal or social development (art. 32).

Sixth, the State must respect the right of the child to rest and leisure, play and recreational activities, and to participate in cultural life (art.

31). The State must also ensure that a child belonging to a minority or indigenous group is not denied the right to enjoy and practice his or her culture, religion or language (art. 30).

Seventh, the State must recognize the right of the child to an adequate standard of living; material assistance, nutrition, clothing and housing must be guaranteed by the State (art. 27), as well as the rights to the highest attainable standard of health (art. 24), including health education.

Eighth, the State must provide special protection for a child deprived of the family environment and to assure that appropriate alternative family care or institutional placement is available in such cases (art. 20). The State is also obliged to ensure that a refugee child, or a child seeking refugee status, receives appropriate protection and humanitarian assistance (art. 22). For those children placed in care for their protection and treatment, the State must periodically review and evaluate such placement (art. 25).

Ninth, the State must ensure that no child is subjected to torture or other cruel inhuman or degrading treatment or punishment and that neither capital punishment nor life imprisonment without possibility of release is meted out to a child (art. 37). In the case of a child in conflict with the law, the State must ensure that the rules of natural justice apply (art. 40).

Finally, *tenth*, the State must recognize the right of the child to education on the basis of equal opportunity, provide compulsory and free primary education to all, and access to different forms of secondary education, to educational and vocational information and guidance and to higher education according to capacity, take measures to promote regular school attendance and reduction of drop-out rates and to ensure school discipline that is consistent with human dignity (art. 28). Significantly, the education provided must promote personality development, respect for human rights, fundamental freedoms, cultural identity and national values and prepare the child for responsible life in a free society, as well as allow the development of respect for the environment (art. 29).

In addition to all of the above obligations, the State that ratifies the Convention on the Rights of the Child must agree that the principles and provisions of the Convention are to be disseminated as widely as possible by appropriate means to adults and children alike (art. 42).

Implementing the child's right to education

The implementation process for the Convention on the Rights of the Child is laid out in articles 43–45. Article 43 calls for the establishment of a Committee on the Rights of the Child to evaluate the extent to which the countries that ratify the Convention – known as States Parties – have lived up to their treaty obligations. The Committee is to be made up of ten members[29] of 'high moral standing and recognized competence' in the field covered by the Convention.[30] Committee members are elected by States Parties from among their nationals and serve in their personal capacities for terms of four years.[31]

In accordance with article 44 of the Convention, States Parties must report regularly (initially two years after the Convention comes into force in the country and thereafter every five years) to the Committee on the Rights of the Child, detailing the measures adopted to give effect to the rights enshrined in the Convention and on the progress made in the enjoyment of these rights. Included in these reports, which are to be made 'widely available' to the public in the country concerned,[32] must be an indication of any factors and difficulties affecting the fulfilment of the State's obligations.[33]

When a State Party submits its report, the document is first translated into the Committee's three languages (English, French and Spanish) and given an official document number. It is then assigned a date and time for oral examination in the Committee's future session schedule. In an effort to deal with the enormous number of reports submitted, the General Assembly granted the Committee three four-week sessions each year. During the first three weeks of each session, the Committee holds a series of public dialogues with representatives of the States Parties whose reports are being examined at that session. The fourth week is devoted to consideration of the reports of States Parties that are to be considered at the Committee's following session and preparations for the examination of those reports.

The process of reporting by States to the Committee on the Rights of the Child, and the examination of reports, signals the only external accountability which States encounter for the way they treat their children.[34] The Committee is committed to making that process one which has a lasting impact on the quality of children's lives. Crucial to that process is the issue of practical implementation with regard to the obligations enshrined in the Convention.

To assist States in the preparation of reports, guidelines for the submission of both initial and periodic reports have been drawn up by the Committee.[35] The guidelines place the articles of the Convention in clusters that are interrelated.[36] When reporting on education, States are first of all required to indicate the measures adopted, including those of a legislative, administrative and budgetary nature, to recognize and ensure the right of the child to education and to achieve that right progressively and on the basis of equal opportunities.[37]

Before the Committee meets in public session with States Parties to formally consider and discuss their reports, it meets in private in pre-sessional meetings[38] to analyse and determine whether the reports fulfil the requirements of the reporting guidelines. Unlike the monitoring processes of some of the other United Nations human rights treaties, evaluation of a State Party's success in implementing the Convention on the Rights of the Child is not confined to information provided solely by the States Parties themselves.[39] Article 45 gives the Committee on the Rights of the Child access to information from a wide range of sources including such United Nations bodies as the United Nations Children's Fund, the International Labour Organization and the World Health Organization, as well as national and international non-governmental organizations. To make the most of the opportunities provided by article 45, the Committee uses its closed pre-sessional preparatory meetings as an opportunity to talk directly with representatives from these organizations and from non-governmental organizations based in the countries whose reports it will be examining. At this time it will also take into consideration any written material that may have been submitted in connection with the particular State Party report to be examined.

On completion of its analysis, the Committee draws up a list of issues which, for example, need to be clarified, or in which rights might have been omitted from the report. The Committee on the Rights of the Child constantly reminds States Parties of the principle of the 'first call for children' promoted at the World Summit for Children and of the Convention's article 4, both of which emphasize that general lack of financial resources cannot be used as a justification for neglecting to establish social programs to protect the most vulnerable groups of children.[40] Accordingly, the Committee suggests in some cases that a review should be undertaken to determine the consistency of the economic and social policies being developed in line with the State

Party's obligations under the Convention and any improvement of social protection (i.e., social security programs, etc.).[41]

Based on the over 80 initial reports that had already been considered by the Committee at the time of this writing, it is safe to say that the sections on Education, Leisure and Cultural Activities (as well as the section on Basic Health and Welfare) are usually better documented than those on other topics.[42] In spite of the depth of information provided, some issues, which the country has not considered, do surface. For example, in the case of New Zealand, the Committee needed to ask: 'Has any evaluation process of the system of education, including the decision-making powers of schools, sought the views of the students?'[43] Similar additional education questions were put to Uruguay, Panama, the Syrian Arab Republic, Ethiopia and Colombia, among others.[44]

In keeping with the overarching nature of the general principles of the Convention – namely the best interests of the child, the right of the child to life, survival and development, respect for the views of the child, and non-discrimination – States Parties' reports must contain an analytical application of these general principles to the right of the child in education. In other words, reports must reflect:

1. the proportion of the overall budget (at the central, regional and local, and where appropriate at the federal and provincial levels) devoted to children and allocated to the various divisions of education
2. the consideration given to the real cost to the family of the child's education and the appropriate support provided
3. the measures adopted to ensure that children may be taught in local, indigenous or minority languages
4. mechanisms developed to ensure access by all children, including girls, children with special needs and children in especially difficult circumstances, to quality education adapted to the child's age and maturity
5. the steps taken to ensure that there are sufficient teachers in the school system, to enhance their competence, and to ensure and assess the quality of teaching
6. the measures adopted to provide educational facilities that are accessible to all children

7. the rate of illiteracy under and over 18 years, and the rate of enrolment in literacy classes, including organization by age, gender, region, rural/urban area, and social and ethnic origin
8. any system of non-formal education
9. any system or extensive initiatives by the State to provide early development and education services for young children, especially for young children from disadvantaged social groups
10. the changes that have occurred in the education system (including with regard to legislation, policies, facilities, budgetary allocation, quality of education, enrolment, drop-out and literacy)
11. any monitoring mechanism developed, factors and difficulties encountered and targets identified for the future; and
12. other relevant disaggregated data on the children concerned, including education outcomes *inter alia* by gender, age, region, rural/urban area, and national, ethnic and social origin.

Reports should indicate the particular measures adopted including: the activities and programs developed, both at the bilateral and regional levels; the target groups identified, including by age, gender and national, social and ethnic origin; the financial assistance provided and/or received and the priorities established; and the consideration given to the aims of education as identified by article 29 of the Convention, including any evaluation made of the progress achieved and of the difficulties encountered. Mention also should be made, whenever appropriate, of the involvement of UN organs and specialized agencies and non-governmental organizations in the State's education process.

Concluding observations of the Committee

Formal discussion of each State Party's report is carried out during three half-day meetings and consists of a series of questions based on the list of issues that the Committee submitted to the State Party, its replies (if any) and information from non-governmental organizations (who are known as NGOs) and various UN bodies. For the formal discussions, the States Parties typically send a delegation of several people from different branches of government in order to be adequately prepared for any issue that the Committee might raise. Particular topics are chosen and questions are asked by various Committee members. The purpose of these discussions is not to pressure or criticize the State Party, but rather to establish a constructive dialogue in order to assist the State Party in achieving full compliance with the Convention's standards.

At the end of the formal discussions with the States Parties, the Committee draws up its Concluding Observations detailing the 'positive indicators', the 'factors and difficulties impeding the implementation of the Convention', the 'concerns' of the Committee regarding the status of implementation and proffering suggestions and recommendations for remediation, including in the area of international cooperation.

This document, which therefore represents an assessment of the State's performance and compliance with the Convention, tends to have a catalytic effect in that it informs the next steps to be taken by the State in the performance of its obligations in ensuring/guaranteeing the rights of the child. It is assumed also that the 'concerns' expressed by the Committee in its Concluding Observations will be addressed by the State Party in its next report. One persisting 'concern' regarding the requirements of article 28 is that education is to be implemented on the basis of equal opportunity and non-discrimination and that special measures are to be adopted regarding special categories of children such as: those in rural or remote areas; children from minority groups; disabled children; children in detention or under special health or mental care; and children involved in unusual conflicts. Also regularly included in the Committee's Concluding Observations are comments about a number of matters that impinge upon the child's education, such as: status of the girl child and general discrimination on the basis of gender (early marriage, teenager pregnancy, domestic labour, school drop-out, boy child preference); children in rural or remote areas (lack of specific allocation of human, economic and organization resources); the importance of specific training for teachers and adaptation of the school curriculum to cater to their specific requirements, especially in case of time schedules; children from minority groups who need bilingual educational services (e.g. special training for teachers; need for an awareness-raising campaign on diversity).

Role of non-governmental organizations

It should be noted that successful implementation of the Convention cannot be and is not expected to be carried out be governments alone. Articles 42, 44 and 45 require respectively that:

1. the public be informed about the Convention
2. the State Party's reports and the Committee's Concluding Observations be widely available to the public
3. information from 'other competent bodies' – in addition to UNICEF and other UN bodies – be available to the Committee.

This language in article 45 was intended to give NGOs a role in the Convention's implementation process, clearly emphasizing the part played by civil society in protecting the rights of the child.[45]

Of all human rights treaties, the Convention on the Rights of the Child is undoubtedly the one that has felt the most continuing influence of non-govermental organizations (NGOs). From 1983, throughout the remainder of the drafting process until the Convention was adopted by the General Assembly, a group of NGOs in Geneva banded together to collaborate and pool their expertise to influence and improve the final text of the Convention.[46] It was due to their highly professional and credible work that the Working Group saw fit to include the words 'other competent bodies' in article 45. Once the Convention went into force, NGOs – national and international – from every corner of the globe began to organize to ensure that the Convention's standards would be recognized and upheld at the local level.[47]

This continuing surveillance by local citizens is especially important to protecting the rights of the child. Eleanor Roosevelt has been quoted as saying:

> Where, after all, do universal human rights begin? In the smallest places close to home – so small that they cannot be seen on any maps of the world. Until these rights have meaning there, they have little meaning anywhere.[48]

This is even more true when it comes to protecting the rights of the child. In fact, one might paraphrase Mrs Roosevelt by saying that human rights must not only be found in the 'smallest places' but also guaranteed to the 'smallest persons'. The Convention on the Rights of the Child has given children the right to human dignity. Considering that the Preambles of both the Declaration of Geneva and the 1959 Declaration of the Rights of the Child assert that 'Mankind owes to the child the best that it has to give',[49] it behoves all of civil society to unite in making all of the rights of the child a reality.

Conclusion

The key to the development of any nation is through the educating of its people. No civilized, humane or progressive society can ignore that right to schooling and education of its citizens, particularly its children. Therefore, to implement the right of the child to a development-oriented education is a fundamental condition for improving the child's quality of life, including spiritual and moral dimensions, and his/her ability to function fully as a constructive member of society. The child needs supportive conditions, not only to survive, but also to develop into a responsible human adult. Education must make the present and future well-being of the young generation as its ultimate goal, of which one of the most important conditions is to ensure the full realization of its rights as stipulated by the Convention on the Rights of the Child, for education in the broadest sense continues beyond school and throughout life in myriad social contexts.

Endnotes

1 The Convention on the Rights of the Child was adopted by the United Nations General Assembly on November 20 1989. *Convention on the Rights of the Child, adopted* Nov. 20 1989, 18 I.L.M. 1448 (1989), *corrected at* 29 I.L.M. 1340 (1990) (entered into force Sept. 2, 1990) [hereinafter *Convention*].

2 *Universal Declaration of Human Rights*, G.A. Res. 217A (III) U.N. Doc. A/810 (1948) [hereinafter *Universal Declaration*]. The Universal Declaration was drafted to clarify the meaning of the words 'human rights' in the United Nations Charter. (See, e.g., preamble and article 62 of the Charter.)

3 *Declaration of the Rights of the Child*, G.A. Res. 1386, U.N. GAOR, 14th Sess., Supp. No. 16, at 19, U.N. Doc. A/4354 (1959) [hereinafter *1959 Declaration*] reprinted in The United Nations Convention on the Rights of the child: A Guide to the 'Travaux Préparatoires' App. (Sharon Detrick ed., 1992) [hereinafter *Detrick*]. Principle 7 of the United Nations Declaration of the Rights of the Child of 1959 (below) stipulates that every child is entitled to receive education:

Principle 7

The child is entitled to receive education, which shall be free and compulsory, at least in the elementary stages. He shall be given an education which will promote his general culture and enable him, on a basis of equal opportunity, to develop his abilities, his individual judgement, and his sense of moral and social responsibility, and to become a useful member of society.

The best interests of the child shall be the guiding principle of those responsible for his education and guidance; that responsibility lies in the first place with his parents.

The child shall have full opportunity for play and recreation, which should be directed to the same purposes as education; society and the public authorities shall endeavor to promote the enjoyment of this right.

4 The International Covenant on Economic, Social and Cultural Rights is the companion of the International Covenant on Civil and Political Rights. These two treaties were adopted by the United Nations in order make the Universal Declarations principles legally binding. *See* International Covenant on Economic, Social and Cultural Rights, *adopted* Dec. 16, 1966, 993 U.N.T.S. 3 (entered into force Jan. 3, 1976) [hereinafter *ICESCR*] and International Covenant on Civil and Political Rights, *adopted* Dec. 16, 1966, 999 U.N.T.S. 171 (entered into force Mar. 23, 1976) [hereinafter *ICCPR*].

5 Article 13 of the International Covenant on Economic, Social and Cultural Rights reads:

1. The States Parties to the present Covenant recognize the right of education to everyone. They agree that education shall be directed to the full development of the human personality and the sense of its dignity, and shall strengthen the respect for human rights and fundamental freedoms. They further agree that education shall enable all persons to participate effectively in a free society, promote understanding, tolerance and friendship among all nations and all racial, ethnic or religious groups, and further the activities of the United Nations for the maintenance of peace.

2. The States Parties to the present covenant recognize that, with a view to achieving the full realization of this right:

(a) Primary education shall be compulsory and available free to all;

(b) Secondary education in its different forms, including technical and vocational secondary education, shall be made generally available and accessible to all by every appropriate means, and in particular by the progressive introduction of free education;

(c) Higher education shall be made equally accessible to all, on the basis of capacity, by every appropriate means, and in particular by the progressive introduction of free education;

(d) Fundamental education shall be encouraged or intensified as far as possible for those persons who have not received or completed the whole period of their primary education;

(e) The development of a system of schools at all levels shall be actively pursued, an adequate fellowship system shall be established, and the material conditions of teaching staff shall be continuously improved.

3. The States Parties to the present Covenant undertake to have respect for the liberty of parents and, when applicable, legal guardians to choose for their children schools other than those established by the public authorities, which conform to such minimum educational standards as may be laid down or approved by the State and to ensure the religious and moral education of their children in conformity with their own convictions.

No part of this article shall be construed so as to interfere with the liberty of individuals and bodies to establish and direct educational institutions, subject always to the observance of the principles set forth in paragraph 1 of this article and to the requirement that the education given in such institutions shall conform to such minimum standards as may be laid down by the State.

6 Articles 28 and 29 of the Convention on the Rights of the Child (see *Convention supra* note 1) reads as follows:

Article 28:

1. States Parties recognize the right of the child to education, and with a view to achieving this right progressively and on the basis of equal opportunity, they shall, in particular:

(a) Make primary education compulsory and available free to all;

(b) Encourage the development of different forms of secondary education, including general and vocational education, make them available and accessible to every child, and take appropriate measures such as the introduction of free education and offering financial assistance in case of need;

(c) Make higher education accessible to all on the basis of capacity by every appropriate means;

(d) Make educational and vocational information and guidance available and accessible to all children;

(e) Take measures to encourage regular attendance at schools and the reduction of dropout rates.

2. States Parties shall take all appropriate measures to ensure that school discipline is administered in a manner consistent with the child's human dignity and in conformity with the present Convention.

3. States Parties shall promote and encourage international co-operation in matters relating to education, in particular with a view to contributing to the elimination of ignorance and illiteracy throughout the world and facilitating access to scientific and technical knowledge and modern teaching methods. In this regard, particular account shall be taken of the needs of developing countries:

Article 29:

1. States Parties agree that the education of the child shall be directed to:

(a) The development of the child's personality, talents and mental and physical abilities to their fullest potential;

(b) The development of respect for human rights and fundamental freedoms, and for the principles enshrined in the Charter of the United Nations;

(c) The development of respect for the child's parents, his or her own cultural identity, language and values, for the national values of the country from which he or she may originate, and for civilizations different from his or her own;

(d) The preparation of the child for responsible life in a free society, in the spirit of understanding, peace, tolerance, equality of sexes, and friendship among all peoples, ethnic, national and religious groups and persons of indigenous origin;

(e) The development of respect for the natural environment.

2. No part of the present article or article 28 shall be construed so as to interfere with the liberty of individuals and bodies to establish and direct educational institutions, subject always to the observance of the principles set forth in paragraph 1 of the present article and to the requirements that the education given in such institutions shall conform to such minimum standards as may be laid down by the State.

7 *Id.* at art. 28 para. 1 (e).

8 *Id.* at art. 28 para. 2.

9 *Id.* at art. 28 para. 3.

10 For a general background overview, see Cynthia Price Cohen (1993), 'The Developing Jurisprudence of the Rights of the Child.' *6 St. Thomas Law Review 1.*

11 See *1959 Declaration supra* note 3.

12 See Cynthia Price Cohen (1996), 'Drafting of the United Nations Convention on the Rights of the Child: Challenge and Achievements.' In Eugeen Verhellen (ed) *Understanding Children's Rights.* Gent, Belgium: Children's Rights Centre. [hereinafter *Verhellen*]

13 See *Question of a Convention on the Rights of the Child.* UN ESCOR 34th Sess., 1438th mtg., Supp. No. 4 at 75, UN Doc. E/CN.4/1292 (1978). First Polish draft.

14 See *Question of a Convention on the Rights of the Child: Note to the Division of Human Rights by the Polish People's Republic.* UN Commission on Human Rights, 36th Sess., Agenda Item 13, at 2, UN Doc. E/CN.4/1349 (1979) at article 7.

15 Article 24 states:

1. Every child shall have, without any discrimination as to race, colour, sex, language, religion, national or social origin, property or birth, the right to such measures of protection as are required by his status as a minor, on the part of his family, society and the State.

2. Every child shall be registered immediately after birth and shall have a name.

3. Every child has the right to acquire a nationality

16 See *Verhellen supra* note 12.

17 See *Convention supra* note 1 at art. 49 (below).

Article 49

1. The present Convention shall enter into force on the thirtieth day following the date of deposit with the Secretary-General of the United Nations of the twentieth instrument of ratification or accession.

2. For each State ratifying or acceding to the Convention after the deposit of the twentieth instrument of ratification or accession, the Convention shall enter into force on the thirtieth day after the deposit by such State of its instrument of ratification or accession.

18 No one involved in drafting the Convention, including Adam Lopatka, chairman of the Working Group, would have predicted that the Convention would already be in force at the time of the 1990 World Summit for Children.

19 See 'World Declaration on the Survival, Protection and Development of Children' (1990) [hereinafter *World Summit Declaration*] as printed in UNICEF, *First Call for Children.*

20 Preamble, *World Declaration on Education for All* (1990).

21 See *Convention supra* note 1 at article 28 para. 1 (a).

22 *Id.* at art. 28 para. 1 (b).

23 *Id.* at art. 28 para. 1 (c).

24 *Id.* at art. 28 para. 1 (e).

25 See *Convention supra* note 1 at art. 29 para. 1 (a), (b), (c), (d), (e).

26 Recommendation Concerning Education for International Understanding, Co-operation and Peace and Education Relating to Human Rights and Fundamental Freedoms (1974)

27 In addition to the Preamble, the following articles in the Convention on the Rights of the Child make reference to the parent–child relationship: 2, 3, 5, 7, 8, 9,10,11,14,16,18, 20, 21, 22, 23, 24, 27, 37 and 40.

28 See *Convention supra* note 1 at art. 4, which reads:

States Parties shall undertake all appropriate legislative, administrative, and other measures for the implementation of the rights recognized in the present Convention. With regard to economic social and cultural rights, States Parties shall undertake such measures to the maximum extent of their available resources and, where needed, within the framework of international co-operation.

29 See *Convention supra* note 1 at art. 43 (2). Although the text of the Convention calls for the Committee to be made up of ten members, the government of Costa Rica initiated a resolution calling for an amendment to the Convention that would enlarge the Committee's membership to 18. It is expected that a sufficient number of States Parties will approve this proposal so that the enlargement will take place in the year 2001.

30 *Id.*

31 The first members elected to the Committee included: *Mrs Hoda Badran, Egypt; Mgr Luis A. Bambaren Gastelumendi, Peru; Ms Akila Belembaogo, Burkina Faso; *Ms Marie de Fatima Borges de Omena, Brazil; *Ms Flora Euphemio, Philippines; Mr Thomas Hammarberg, Sweden; Mr Youri Kolosov, Russian Federation (former USSR); Mrs Sandra Prunella Mason, Barbados; *Mr Swithun Mombeshora, Zimbabwe; and *Mrs Marta Santos Pais, Portugal. An asterisk denotes a two-year term. These two-year delegates were reelected in 1993 to new four-year terms that expired in 1997, while those members who originally drew four-year terms were up for reelection in 1995. See UN Doc A/47/41 (1992). For a list of current members of the Committee on the Rights of the Child see the website of the UN High Commissioner for Human Rights: www.unhchr.ch.

32 See *Convention supra* note 1 at art. 44 (6).

33 *Id.* at para. 2.

34 Unlike the American Convention on Human Rights or the European Convention on Human Rights and Fundamental Freedoms, which review claims of human rights violations in court proceedings and can award money judgments, UN human rights treaties have no method of 'enforcement'. States Parties which violate children's rights are not required to pay damages or to make restitution to the injured child or even force a country to change its laws. The only implementation tool is moral suasion which is obtained through publication of the Concluding Observations of the Committee on the Rights of the Child and which usually influences a country to make appropriate changes.

35 See *Committee on the Rights of the Child: General Guidelines Regarding the Form and Content of Initial Reports to be Submitted by States Parties Under Article 44, Paragraph (a) of the Convention,* UN Doc. CRC/C.5 (30 Oct. 1991) [hereinafter *Guidelines*]; UN Doc. A/47/41 (1992) at Annex III. Also see Cynthia Price Cohen and Susan Kilbourne (1998), 'Jurisprudence of the Committee on the Rights of the Child: A Guide for Research and Analysis', 19 Mich.J. Int'l L. 633 [hereinafter *Jurisprudence*].

36 *Id.* Cluster VII is entitled 'Education, Leisure and Cultural Activities'. Included in this cluster are articles: 28 (right to education); 29 (aims of education) and 31 (leisure, recreation and cultural activities). See *infra* note 42 for an overview of the topics covered by the Guidelines' other clusters.

37 *Id.* For full text of article 28 see *supra* note 6.

38 The Committee on the Rights of the Child meets at the Palais des Nations in Geneva for four weeks, three times a year. The first three weeks of each session are devoted to examination of State Party reports. The final week, known as the 'pre-sessional week', is devoted to preparation for the next session's review of States Parties' reports.

39 The Convention on the Rights of the Child is the only UN human rights treaty explicitly to make provisions for submission of information by NGOs to the treaty's monitoring body. (See *infra* note 45) This does not mean, however, that NGOs are barred from submitting relevant information to other treaty-monitoring bodies. In the case of the Human Rights Committee – which monitors the International

Covenant on Civil and Political Rights – NGOs pass their information to Committee members informally. Other monitoring bodies, such as the Committee on Economic, Social and Cultural Rights and the Torture Committee have allowed for NGO information submission in their *Rules of Procedure.*

40 See *supra* note 28.

41 See the Committee's *Concluding Observations* on the report of Nigeria. (UN Doc. CRC/C/15/Add.51).

42 Sections I and II of the *Guidelines* ask comprehensive questions about the country (demographics, etc.), the measures that been taken to implement the Convention and how the State Party defines the word 'child'. The remaining sections cover: III. General Principles; IV. Civil Rights and Freedoms; V. Family Environment and Alternative Care; VI. Basic Health and Welfare; VII. Education, Leisure and Cultural Activities; and VIII. Special Protection Measures.

43 Unpublished notes of Sandra Prunella Mason, Chairperson of the Committee on the Rights of the Child.

44 For the complete text of the Committee's oral examinations of the reports of these and other States Parties, see the website of the United Nations High Commissioner for Human Rights at www.unhchr.ch. **Also see** *Jurisprudence supra* note 35.

45 See *Convention supra* note 1 at art. 45:

Article 45:

In order to foster the effective implementation of the Convention and to encourage international co-operation in the field covered by the Convention:

(a) The specialized agencies, the United Nations Children's Fund, and other United Nations organs shall be entitled to be represented at the consideration of the implementation of such provisions of the present Convention as fall within the scope of their mandate. The Committee may invite the specialized agencies, the United Nations Children's Fund and other competent bodies as it may consider appropriate to provide expert advice on the implementation of the Convention in areas falling within the scope of their respective mandates. The Committee may invite the specialized agencies, the United Nations Children's Fund, and other United Nations organs to submit reports on the implementation of the Convention in areas falling within the scope of their activities;

(b) The Committee shall transmit, as it may consider appropriate, to the specialized agencies, the United Nations Children's Fund and other competent bodies, any reports from States Parties that contain a request, or indicate a need, for technical advice or assistance, along with the Committee's observations and suggestions, if any, on these requests or indications;

(c) The Committee may recommend to the General Assembly to request the Secretary-General to undertake on its behalf studies on specific issues relating to the rights of the child;

(d) The Committee may make suggestions and general recommendations based on information received pursuant to articles 44 and 45 of the present

Convention. Such suggestions and general recommendations shall be transmitted to any State Party concerned and reported to the General Assembly, together with comments, if any, from States Parties.

46 In 1983 a group of non-governmental organizations met in Geneva to establish the NGO Ad Hoc Group on the Drafting of the Convention on the Rights of the Child (NGO Group). They met twice yearly to discuss the proposed articles and to collaborate in making recommendations regarding the text of the Convention. For more detail see *Verhellen supra* note 12.

47 After the Convention was adopted by the UN General Assembly, the original NGO Group reorganized under the name NGO Group for the Convention on the Rights of the Child. This has been a highly successful and continuing collaboration. The NGO Group not only interacts with the Committee on the Rights of the Child, providing information about States Parties whose reports are scheduled for examination, but also works to assist national NGOs to present their information to the Committee.

48 Eleanor Roosevelt, as quoted in: 'You and Human Rights' March 27, 1958 (UN pamphlet).

49 The Preamble of the Declaration of Geneva, the first international child rights instrument – adopted by the League of Nations in March 1924 reads:

By the present Declaration of the Rights of the Child, commonly known as the Declaration of Geneva, men and women of all nations, recognising that mankind owes to the child the best that it has to give, declare and accept it as their duty...

while the 1959 UN Declaration of the Rights of the Child simply uses the following phrase as its fifth preambular paragraph:

Whereas mankind owes to the child the best that it has to give...

CHAPTER 2

Progress in Implementing the Rights in the Convention

Factors helping and hindering the process

Gerison Lansdown

Education is a universal human right, indispensible as a means of realizing other rights.[1] This principle has long been recognized in the international arena. The right to education for all was included in the 1948 Universal Declaration of Human Rights. It was extended in the International Covenant on Social, Cultural and Economic Rights, and reasserted as a specific right for all children in the UN Convention on the Rights of the Child. However, education rights extend beyond the basic provision of education. The Convention on the Rights of the Child (CRC) places three key obligations on governments with regard to education:

- to recognize education as a human right for all children
- to respect the human rights of children within the education system
- to provide education for human rights.

There are significant political, economic and cultural barriers to be overcome before those rights begin to be respected for all children. Behind the rights rhetoric, there are many competing agendas in the provision of education systems. Education is both a right of individuals and a necessity for society. For governments, there are two major goals in funding education – to develop the economic workforce and potential wealth of the future and to promote social cohesion and integration. Education is crucial to both. It is the route through which economically and socially marginalized adults and children can escape poverty and participate fully in their communities. It plays a vital role in safeguarding children from exploitative and hazardous labour and sexual exploitation, promoting human rights and democracy, protecting the environment and controlling population growth. Further, education is acknowledged to be one of the best financial investments.[2] The development of mass education in the twentieth century has played an important role in promoting national integration and uniformity in both industrialized countries and the developing world (Graham Brown 1994). For parents, too, there are two demands on the education system. Most parents want to see their children achieve an education which will equip them for a successful future life. They also look to schools to transmit their values, culture, language – in other words, they seek in the education system the reinforcement and promotion of their own beliefs. There is recognition in international law of the right of parents to educate their children according to their beliefs.[3] It reflects the need to introduce boundaries on the exercise of power by a state to impose its political and religious agenda on children.

The UN Convention on the Rights of the Child introduces an additional perspective. It imposes boundaries not only on the state but also on parents. It insists that children's best interests must be a primary consideration in all matters affecting them (art. 3), that their views must be given serious consideration (art. 12) and that respect must be given to the child's evolving capacities (art. 5). In other words, the Convention diminishes the parental prerogative – parental rights to determine their children's education are never absolute and are seen to recede as children grow older (Hodgson 1996).

There are then significant and often competing demands on the education system – from governments who are providing the legal and administrative framework and funding, from parents responsible for their children's upbringing and children themselves as the recipients of education. In analysing how far we have progressed in meeting the obligations undertaken by governments in respect of education rights, it is important to bear in mind these political and social realities and the inevitable tensions that they produce.

Education as a human right

Article 28 of the CRC sets out the basic principle of entitlement to education, stressing the need for states to make primary education compulsory and available free to all children on the basis of equality of opportunity, and to encourage the development of secondary education for all children. In promoting the realization of the right to education, governments must make it *available* to all children through adequate provision, *accessible* without discrimination to all children, *acceptable* in providing quality education appropriate to the cultural needs of all children, and *adaptable* to the changing and different needs of children.[4]

A total of 191 governments have ratified the Convention on the Rights of the Child – a record unparalleled by any other human rights treaty. The commitment undertaken by governments in so doing represents a unique and important opportunity to raise awareness of the education rights of children on the national and international political agenda. At the 1990 World Summit for Children, a goal of access to basic education and achievement of primary education for 80 per cent of primary school age children was established. The Summit declared that 'The provision of basic education and literacy for all are among the most important contributions that can be made to the development of the world's children'.[5] In the same year, the Jomtien World Conference on Education for All brought together representatives from 155 governments, with NGOs, multilateral agencies and donors to discuss the world crisis in education. It established a goal of education for all by the year 2000 with time-bound targets. In 1995 at the Social Development Summit, the international community committed itself to achieving universal primary education by the year 2015. But despite these international commitments, progress has been profoundly disapppointing. The World Education Forum held in Dakar in 2000, whilst acknowledging some progress, highlighted the continuing scale of the challenge ahead.

The reality is that that too many promises made on the world stage by governments have failed to materialize. These promises are not merely a matter of good will. They are underpinned by clear human rights obligations on the part of governments. Too many governments in the developing world have failed to 'undertake measures to the maximum extent of their available resources' (art. 4) to ensure the right to education is realized for all children. Furthermore, the right to education is a shared responsibility, and too many of the richer nations are in breach of their obligations to promote international cooperation in education 'with a view to contributing to the elimination of ignorance and illiteracy throughout the world and facilitating access to scientific and technical knowledge and modern teaching methods' (art. 28.3).

An analysis undertaken by Stuart N. Hart and Scherer of the first 49 reports submitted to the Committee on the Rights of the Child indicates that 88 per cent of the reports claimed that their countries provided compulsory, free primary school education of around six years duration whilst 78 per cent claimed to meet the requirement to provide secondary education (See Chapter 4). However, the realities behind these statistics reveal a very different, and much bleaker picture. The grim facts remain that more than 130 million children of school age still have no access to any kind of basic education and 855 million people are functionally illiterate (UNICEF 1998a). Some 150 million children enter the education system but fail to complete the basic programmes they start (UNICEF 1998b). Millions more are experiencing substandard provision where little learning takes place. And behind the statistics lies the corrosive impact of the failure to provide education: higher mortality rates (a ten per cent increase in girls' primary enrolment can decrease infant mortality rates by over four deaths per thousand (UNICEF 1999)), restricted employability, limited capacity to promote healthy living, impeded progress towards democracy.

Obviously many of the poorest countries in the world experience profound difficulties in finding the resources to provide adequately for children's education. Crippling debt and the imposition of structural adjustment policies have forced governments to divert resources away from education. In Tanzania, for example, debt servicing represents four times the spending on primary education. In Zambia, whereas 2.5 per cent of annual spending was on education, 10 per cent was spent on debt-servicing (Oxfam 2000). Yet accumulated evidence demonstrates that increased investment in education is of critical importance in the struggle for sustainable development (Dall 1995). Countries cannot afford *not* to invest in education. However, it is not just a question of resources, but also a matter of political commitment. Remarkable progress has been made by many developing countries in providing access to basic education. For example, amongst countries with per capita GNPs below $300, Bangladesh, Kenya, Malawi, and Vietnam have rates of enrolment of over 80 per cent, about 20 percentage points above what could be expected at their income level. In a similar income range, Haiti, Ethiopia, Mali and Niger enrol less than 30 per cent of children. Zimbabwe, with a per capita GNP of $540, achieves a rate of 90 per cent compared with Guinea which has the same GNP but enrols less than 30 per cent (UNICEF 1997). The Southern Indian state of Kerala has achieved universal literacy (UNESCO 1995). In other words, it is possible to make significant progress towards the realization of the right to basic education even in the poorest of countries where the political will exists.

Equality of access

The problem of access to education, however, is not merely one of national availability of resources. It also reflects how those resources are distributed. The requirement in article 28 to provide education on the basis of equality of opportunity needs to be read alongside article 2, which insists that all rights in the Convention apply to all children without discrimination on any grounds. The only discrimination permitted would be positive discrimination to ensure greater educational opportunities to groups of children traditionally denied access. But there are many groups of children who remain excluded from education – girls, rural children, disabled children, children from many minority or indigenous groups or children caught in armed conflicts. This paper will consider four such groups:

- children in poverty
- girls
- disabled children
- minority groups.

Children in poverty

Child poverty represents one of the most formidable barriers inhibiting access to education. For individual families there are often costs associated with education, rendering it beyond their reach: school fees that are still often imposed despite the obligation under article 28 to make free primary education available to all, costs of uniforms, requirement to provide educational materials, books, or transport costs. Even where the education is provided completely free, the loss of the child's potential earnings whilst they are in school might render it uneconomic for the child to attend. Schools often fail to make education and work compatible for children.

The impact of poverty extends beyond mere access to formal schooling. It also determines the quality of environment in which children grow up, often with devastating impact on their early development and subsequent potential for physical, intellectual and emotional growth (Dall 1995). A Harvard University study has concluded that poverty may be the most significant factor determining children's development (UNICEF 1992b). However, what is not known is whether the damage inflicted by poor socio-environmental conditions in early years can be reversed. If not, children may be unable to benefit from any subsequent investment in their education. In other words, the right to education cannot be guaranteed by its provision alone. Poverty and deprivation must also be tackled if children are to acquire real educational opportunities. The right to an adequate standard of living for their proper development, the right to the best possible health and access to health care, the right to play are all fundamental entitlements embodied in the CRC, which impact directly on a child's capacity to take advantage of education. Unless and until these macro issues of poverty and economic injustice are tackled, the right to education for very poor children will be denied.

Girls

In Hart and Scherer's survey, 65 per cent of governments claimed to provide education on the basis of equality of opportunity. But, in reality, the principle of equal rights of access to education for boys and girls remains as yet a distant goal. All world indicators expose the continuing disparity. Girls represent two thirds of the 130 million children without access to either primary or secondary education (UNICEF 1998a). These disparities are particularly high in Africa, South Asia and the Middle East (UNICEF 1992a). In literacy terms, the evidence is even more damning. Of the nearly 900 million people who are illiterate, 700 million are women. The seriousness with which the problem is now being recognized led to the convening of the Pan-African Conference on the Education of Girls in Ougadougou in Burkina Faso in 1993. This conference acknowledged that whilst the education of girls was probably the single most important vehicle toward development and economic progress, gender gaps continue to be high at all levels of the education system.

The causes are multiple. The Committee on the Rights of the Child has identified a number of contributory factors:

- customary attitudes which fail to recognize the importance of education for girls
- expectations of girls undertaking a level of household tasks which are incompatible with the demands of full time education
- shortage of women teachers which can inhibit the enrolment of girls
- resistance to allowing girls to be educated with boys.

Other contributory factors emerging from recent research indicate that persistent poverty requires the contribution of daughters to household survival, exacerbated by a lack of flexibility in schedules enabling girls to combine school and household tasks. The distance between school and home, particularly in rural areas, raises fears of exposure to molestation or abuse. School is too often a negative experience for girls. The teachers are frequently male, the culture of school aggressive and male-dominated, and lessons and text books filled with messages of the superiority of boys (UNICEF 1991).

Whilst the challenge ahead is considerable, enhanced understanding of the causes does provide opportunities for intervening to break the cycle of discrimination and exclusion. A commitment to developing strategies and mobilise resources to achieve those objectives was made at the Ougadougou conference in 1993 (Hammerberg 1997). They included the need to:

- locate schools nearer to communities
- make schools safer learning environments
- make more efforts to develop culturally appropriate facilities
- develop rural water, roads and electricity to ease the workloads of women and therefore girls
- provide more training for teachers to become gender-sensitive and recruit more women as teachers

- increase community participation in the management and improvement of local schools
- design systems to support the needs of female students such as installation of water and sanitation facilities, flexible schedules, gender-based monitoring and a curriculum of interest to girls and their aspirations.

Disabled children

Article 23 stresses that disabled children have the right to education in a manner conducive to the achievement of the fullest possible social integration and individual development. This obligation must be considered alongside articles 28 and 2 which affirm that education for disabled children must be provided without discrimination.

The Committee on the Rights of the Child has expressed concern about the low proportion of disabled children enrolled in schools worldwide. For example, in Egypt only one per cent of disabled children are in school. Indeed, in most developing countries, it is estimated that only two per cent have such access. The Committee has further stressed the importance of developing measures to promote inclusion of disabled children in mainstream schools (Hodgkin and Newell 1998, art. 23). In 1996, in a survey on educational provision for disabled people, the Special Rapporteur for Disabled People found that of 80 countries providing information, 10 gave no guarantees in law to education for disabled children and that, although many developing countries have recognized the right to education, it has in many cases not been applied to disabled children.[6] These shocking findings are confirmed by UNECSO in a review of 65 countries, where only 44 reported that general legislation applied to children with special educational needs. Thirty-four countries reported that children with severe disabilities were excluded from education, and further, that in 18 of those 34, disabled children were actually precluded by law from the public educational system. The Special Rapporteur has concluded that disabled children are predominantly still provided for in segregated institutions and that the rates of enrolment are very low in far too many countries.

The World Conference on Special Needs Education in 1994 produced the Salamanca Statement, signed up to by 92 countries, which stressed that children with special educational needs must have access to regular schools. It urged all governments to give the highest policy and budgetary priority to improve their education system to include all children regardless of individual difficulties.[7] In 1997, the Committee on the Rights of the Child devoted its General Discussion day to the rights of disabled children, focusing on the child's right to inclusion and participation, with a particular emphasis on education. A number of factors impeding access of disabled children to inclusive education were identified:

- deep-seated prejudice and fear of disability which is often viewed as a curse, stigma, or punishment. The isolation of disabled children serves to perpetuate such myths
- a lack of understanding about the potential of *all* children to develop if provided with a responsive environment
- the prevalence of discriminatory laws which fail to provide equal rights of access to disabled children
- persistence of the medical model of disability in which the disabled person is defined as the problem. This contrasts with the social model, where a child is perceived as having an impairment, but is disabled by attitudes and the environment
- the failure to recognize the potential economic and social benefits of inclusive education for society as a whole.[8]

These obstacles represent a formidable challenge. However, there are glimmers of hope for change. The Special Rapporteur for Disabled People has made a commitment to pursuing the principle of inclusion in all forms of development cooperation, and in so doing is collaborating with UNESCO, ILO, UNICEF and the WHO (Lindquist 1997). UNESCO, in collaboration with OECD and the European Commission have carried out a joint study on disability to develop a special instrument for collecting data on education which would help define indicators, and could serve as a resource for the Committee on the Rights of the Child (Saleh 1997). The Committee at its General Discussion day proposed 14 recommendations designed to enhance the rights of disabled children and a working party has been established to further those recommendations. At national level, initiatives are being developed in many countries to promote inclusive education and can be disseminated as models of good practice.

But it is not enough. Unless and until the barriers of prejudice and ignorance surrounding disability are broken, little will change. There is a need in most countries throughout the world for:

- legal reform to enshrine rights in law
- public education to challenge attitudes
- reallocation of resources to promote inclusion
- support for families to encourage them to see the importance of education for disabled children
- training of teachers to enable them to work with disabled children
- a commitment to policies for de-institutionalizing children and finding alternatives within local communities.

Minority groups

Article 30 places obligations on governments to respect the rights of minority and indigenous groups to enjoy their own language, culture and religion. Most societies in the world include such communities – Australian aborigines, the Catholics in Northern Ireland, the Palestinians in Israel, the Mayas of Guatemala, Hutus in Rwanda. They usually have a separate language and culture which isolates them from the mainstream education system. This poses three profound challenges to governments in implementing the Convention. How are their rights to education to be secured? How will governments ensure that in providing that education, their right to respect for language, culture and religion is protected? And finally, in protecting those rights, how will they ensure that children's access to the mainstream culture is secured in order that they are not excluded from opportunities to participate in employment, training and higher education?

Access to education

The Convention places an unequivocal demand on governments that they take active measures to ensure that education is accessible without discrimination to all children. The Committee has criticized a number of governments for failing to take sufficient action to protect these rights for minority children (Hodgkin and Newell 1998, art. 28). For example, in Vietnam and China, those areas with the highest ethnic minority communities have the lowest enrolment and school completion rates. In India, certain tribal groups in the Gujerat have enrolment rates eight per cent below the average for the area, and four out of every five children drop out of school by Grade 5 compared with an overall completion rate in the Gujerat of fifty per cent.

Segregated or integrated education

Efforts to protect the rights of minorities to education whilst preserving their cultural rights, have prompted considerable debate over the alternatives of segregated or integrated provision. In respect of segregated education, it can be argued that it provides opportunities for children to be educated in their own language, and in accordance with their parents' own philosophical beliefs. For example, in Northern Ireland, almost all schools remain segregated on religious grounds. In the concluding observations of the Committee on the Rights of the Child (February 1995), it was recommended that the UK Government provide greater support to promote integrated schools. Little progress has been made to date and this reflects, in part, the resistance on behalf of much of the population to integrated education policies, where there is mistrust that it would serve to undermine the integrity of the separate communities. However, segregation can also serve the cause of inequality and perpetuation of prejudice and stereotypes. The segregated schools of minority groups are too often characterized by poorer teaching and fewer resources. In South Africa, the separate education systems sustained and perpetuated the apartheid system. In Israel, where there have been two educational strategies – integration for all Jews of whatever ethnic origin, and separate education for Arabs – one outcome has been significant inequality for the Arab community. Its education is chronically underfunded, children have become disadvantaged with regard to jobs and higher education because of their weak command of Hebrew, and Arab teachers are often inadequately trained (Graham Brown 1994).

On the other hand, integration brings its own problems. It often serves as a strategy by the dominant culture to impose its values on children, as a weapon in cultural repression. By forcing children to learn in the national language and adopt its political and social values, it can erode, either deliberately or by default, the culture of minority communities. Children in many countries are required to learn in schools which disregard their history, language, religion and culture. In Kosovo, for example, education in the Albanian language was not allocated any state funds, teaching aids in Albanian were not published and the curriculum and approach of teachers in the mainstream Serbian schools was highly politicized in favour of the dominant culture (UNICEF [forthcoming]). Similarly in Turkey, Kurds are punished for using their language in schools and teachers dismissed for permitting it to be spoken (UNICEF [forthcoming]). In the UK, state schools are required by law to hold religious assemblies which must be wholly or mainly of a Christian character.[9] The religious syllabus, too, must reflect the fact that religious traditions are mainly of a Christian nature, despite the fact that in some schools, as many as 95 per cent of the children might come from Muslim families.

However, in recent years there has been a growing recognition that policies of assimilation that seek to impose a presumption of the desirability of cultural homogeneity are neither morally acceptable nor ultimately effective. In some countries – for example, Italy, France and India – there has been an insistence on secular education in which priority is given to no individual set of beliefs. Others have sought to introduce multi-cultural education, although this is often met with criticism both from the establishment – suspicious that it is being used to water down the dominant culture – and minority groups themselves, who often perceive it as a top-down initiative simply focusing on minority culture as an object of study.

Protecting the rights of minorities to education is a complex and challenging task. There are 5000 languages in the world, posing logistical problems with enormous resource implications if the right of all minorities to be taught in their own language were to be respected. Greater emphasis is needed to promote pluralist policies which allow for the preservation of distinct cultures whilst seeking to create equal opportunities for education for all children. International human rights law provides us with a framework for addressing these issues, but offers no easy solutions. It requires that governments evolve education systems which seek to promote social integration whilst respecting diversity of culture. It requires that children are recognized as being themselves subjects of rights and that their wishes and feelings with regard to education must be given consideration. To date, many governments throughout the world have had difficulty in recognizing the importance and value of respecting the education rights of minority groups as defined by parents. Little if any debate has, as yet, taken place to address the added dimension of acknowledging that children's preferences might differ from those of their parents. There are no simple solutions, but some of the changes that could be explored to promote appropriate education for minority children include:

- curriculum adaptation to make it more meaningful for minority children
- bilingual teaching
- after school or weekend classes to help minority children keep pace with peers
- improvements in teacher training to reduce prejudice towards minority cultures
- recruitment and training of minority and indigenous teachers
- decentralization of education structures to allow more local say over management and educational content
- involvement and participation of minority parents and children in the decision-making in schools.

Children in Western countries

The right to education is, in principle, fulfilled to a much greater degree in developed countries where statutory entitlement to full-time education exists at both primary and secondary levels. However, these countries cannot afford to be complacent. Growing problems of truancy and exclusion from school are emerging in many European countries. In England, for example, there has been a significant increase in the numbers of children permanently excluded from school during the 1990s, from around 2000 a year at the beginning of the decade to 13,000 towards the end (Parsons 1996). Many children, once excluded, fail to re-enter the education system with the consequent loss of qualifications, and increased risk of unemployment, involvement in criminal activity, poverty and poorer health. Furthermore, the patterns of exclusion indicate discrimination against some groups of children in its use as a sanction. Afro-Caribbean boys in England, for example, are up to four times more likely to be excluded than their white counterparts, and children in the care of the local authority and those with special educational needs are also significantly over-represented amongst those excluded.

To date, then, the right to education is far from being fulfilled for all children. The four essential elements – accessibility, availability, acceptability and adaptability – remain for too many an unattainable dream. Implementation of rights to education requires more than a legal framework of entitlement. It requires policies for translating the law into practice on the ground, diversion of resources to implement the legislation, and clear strategies for ensuring that vulnerable children, whether through poverty, gender, ethnicity or disability or any other status, achieve equal access. It also requires global action and practical commitment from the governments of the developed world, the international finance institutions and the relevant UN agencies. Then, and only then, can the right to education for all become an achievable goal.

Respect for human rights in the educational system

The Convention formulates a philosophy which promotes respect for children as individuals and recognizes each child as unique in characteristics, interests and needs. This philosophy needs to be reflected in the organization, structure and ethos of educational provision. It is implicit in a number of principles in the Convention: the right of children to express their views and have them taken seriously; the right to freedom of expression, thought, conscience and religion; the right to information; the obligation to administer school discipline in a manner consistent with children's dignity, to promote the child's best interests and to aim to fulfil the child's potential. The spirit of the Convention suggests the creation of schools which are child-friendly and in which children are encouraged to be curious, to argue, to challenge, to be creative, to explore and find out, to be listened to and respected. The Committee on the Rights of the Child has consistently recommended that governments take further steps to encourage greater participation by children in schools (Hodgkin and Newell 1998, art. 12). The Convention also stresses that as children begin to develop the ability to take decisions for themselves, they should be encouraged and enabled to do so. It recognizes the important role that parents and others with responsibility for children have in providing them with direction and guidance, but expects them to do so in ways which respect that as children grow older, they become more capable of taking responsibility for themselves. In other words, children should be given every opportunity to be involved in matters of concern to them, and as they acquire the understanding and maturity necessary to take decisions for themselves, they should be encouraged to do so.

But this philosophy is significantly at odds with the cultural traditions of education in most countries throughout the world, where schools are characterized by authoritarianism with the child constructed as the passive recipient of adult wisdom and expertise. It is still the case that in too many schools children sit in rows, learning by rote, and are punished by beating or other forms of humiliation for minor misdemeanours or difficulties in learning.

These challenging demands of the Convention on educational orthodoxy bring most sharply into relief the tensions described earlier between the goals of governments, parents and children in the provision of education. If governments are concerned to promote social cohesion, then isn't the traditional approach to education more likely to be effective in suppressing conflict and challenges to the status quo? If parents want children to acquire greater understanding of and respect for their cultural traditions, then surely legitimating the right to question those values may threaten that process?

Nevertheless, there are both principled and pragmatic arguments in favour of developing a more child-centred approach. It is clearly right that children are treated with respect in schools and that governments fulfil the obligations they have voluntarily undertaken in ratifying the Convention. But ultimately its implementation in schools will be of practical benefit not only to the individual but to the wider society as a whole.

Enhancing the skills necessary for the world of work

It is through learning to question and to express views, and having opinions taken seriously, that children will acquire the skills and competence to develop their thinking and to exercise judgement in the myriad of issues that will confront them as they approach adulthood. And respecting these rights of individual children is entirely consistent with the broader agenda of governments to produce an economically viable workforce. In a world where the skills needed at work are increasingly those of communication, conflict-resolution and negotiation, schools must provide children with the opportunities to develop those competencies. The ethos and environment of the school needs to create opportunities for active involvement of pupils. The world of business increasingly recognizes the benefits of creating more democratic workplace environments. But it is a lesson not yet fully learned either by politicians or the teaching profession.

Promoting democracy

In both well established and newly formed democracies, the education system must play a part in helping children understand the principles and practice of democratic decision making. And as so many countries face heightened internal tensions which threaten democracy, such awareness takes on an even greater significance. Children need to learn through experience what their rights and duties are, and how their freedom is limited by the rights and freedoms of others. They need opportunities to participate in democratic decision-making processes within school, and learn to abide by subsequent decisions that are made. Only by experiencing respect for their views, will they acquire the capacity and willingness to listen to others and so begin to understand the processes and value of democracy.

Creating effective schools

There is a significant body of evidence which indicates that schools which do involve children and introduce more democratic structures are likely to be more harmonious, have better staff–pupil relationships and a more effective learning environment (see, for example, Lansdown 1995). Children who feel valued, feel that there are systems for dealing with injustices and children who are consulted over the development of school policies are far more likely to respect the school environment. If the devastating drop-out rate of pupils in so many countries in the world is to be stemmed, schools must become places where children want to be, where they experience respect and engagement with their concerns. If they are to experience some ownership of the school, and develop a sense of commitment and responsibility towards it, then they need opportunities to be involved in the decisions, policies and structures of the school that affect them on a daily basis.

Despite these compelling arguments in favour of a commitment to a more participative model of education, many countries have not yet begun to address the changes necessary for compliance with the philosophy of the Convention. This is not surprising. Children generally are not viewed as individuals with rights to express themselves and be taken seriously. Prevailing cultural attitudes towards children throughout the world persist in constructing them as the property of the adults with responsibility for them. Children are discouraged from asking questions and expressing curiosity. Education is seen as a one-way process of passively receiving information and knowledge, rather than an interactive process. And in non-democratic countries and those with governments reluctant to face criticism, there are difficulties in making the case for respecting children's participation when the price will inevitably be a more challenging and articulate young generation.

There are exciting and imaginative initiatives being developed throughout the world – school councils that give children a genuine say in the running of the school; peer counselling where children are trained as mediators to help other children resolve problems; teaching styles rooted in respect for children and their abilities (see, for example, Davies and Kirkpatrick 2000 and UNICEF 1999). However, they are far from widespread or mainstream. The process of ratification of the Convention has begun to open up debate internationally on these issues. It is increasingly recognized that it is not sufficient to discuss the *scope* and *uptake* of educational provision but that governments must also address the *nature* of that provision. There is an urgent need not only to disseminate examples of working more collaboratively with children, but to undertake evaluation of such approaches in order to accumulate the evidence of their potential benefits.

Of equal importance in promoting respect for the human rights of children in schools is the need to challenge the use of corporal punishment and other forms of humiliating treatment. The Convention demands not only that children are protected from all forms of violence, but also that school discipline is administered in a manner consistent with the child's dignity (arts. 19, 28). The Committee on the Rights of the Child has consistently challenged the use of violence as a form of discipline in schools (Hodgkin and Newell 1998, art. 28). Yet corporal punishment continues to be condoned in schools throughout many countries in the world and too few governments have taken measures against its use. Teachers throughout the world also continue to humiliate and bully children. However, change is accelerating in the context of the Convention and the Committee's recommendations. All European countries have now banned corporal punishment in schools. In the UK, it was, until recently, still lawful to beat children in private schools, a fact that was strongly criticized by the Committee on the Rights of the Child when the UK Government appeared before it in 1995.[10] However, legislation passed in 1998 has finally outlawed this practice.[11] Other countries such as Namibia, South Africa, Ethiopia, and Korea are also addressing these issues seriously by banning all use of corporal punishment and seeking to construct a more positive approach to discipline in schools.

Physical discipline by teachers against pupils is not the only expression of violence that arises in schools. Much violence is perpetrated by children against children, behaviour which it is equally important to challenge. Bullying is widespread in schools throughout Europe. In the UK, for example, research in 1994 revealed that of over 700 children interviewed, 43 per cent of secondary pupils reported having been bullied, 33 per cent were upset by the experience, and 29 per cent commented that it had made them less able to concentrate at school (Sharp and Smith 1994). Even more worrying is the evidence that as many as 50 per cent do not report the bullying, believing that school staff will fail to take any action. Schools must make active commitments to non-violent conflict resolution through whole school policies in which everyone takes responsibility for prevention (Forum for children and violence 1998). Such policies might include circle time, peer counselling, clear sanctions, increased playground supervision and redesigning playgrounds which have all proved effective in tackling bullying. Additionally, an explicit message from teachers, communicated through their own behaviour and attitudes towards non-violence, is crucial.

Explicit recognition of the human rights of children within school has added significance in view of the compulsory nature of education. Children do not have the freedom to opt out if their rights are violated. It is therefore imperative that their rights are explicitly recognized, embodied in legislation and clearly promoted and enforced within the school.

Education to promote human rights

Respect for children's rights in schools is clearly closely linked with the obligation to provide human rights education. Article 29 asserts the need for education rooted in a commitment to the development of the child's potential, promotion of respect for fundamental human rights, respect for parents, one's own and other cultures, for diversity and equality of sexes. The importance of imparting these values could not be greater. In a world facing growing evidence of ethnic conflict and violence, there is an overwhelming imperative to educate children in tolerance, respect for others and for peace and democracy. But responses to date to the Committee on the Rights of the Child expose a failure on the part of too many governments to recognize that imperative.

In Scherer and Hart's review, there was significantly less attention paid to the obligations in article 29 than was the case for article 28. Less than half indicated that their educational systems are dedicated to the fulfilment of children to their optimum potential, and similar figures are reflected in the commitment to teaching respect for human rights. Only one third gave positive answers indicating support for the aim of preparing children for a responsible life of peace, tolerance and freedom. Even less attention was given in these reports to difficulties experienced in the implementation of article 29. Only two reports mentioned problems in meeting the standards it demands. This lack of response is unlikely to reflect an adequate and comprehensive commitment to the aims delineated in article 29.

The Committee consistently presses governments to incorporate human rights education in the school curriculum. Yet the failure to do so is evident in reading its concluding observations – Belgium, Columbia, Finland, Guatemala, Iceland, Italy, Nicaragua, Lebanon, Norway, Portugal, Ukraine and the UK are amongst those that have been criticized for failing to teach human rights (Hodgkin and Newell 1998, art. 29). But its introduction into the curriculum cannot happen in a vacuum. At present, there are a number of barriers impeding progress which need to be addressed before human rights education becomes a reality:

- Promoting respect for human rights is not a matter simply or even primarily of the curriculum. Democracy cannot be taught in an undemocratic environment. The principles must also permeate the ethos of the school. Children need to be included as participants in school decision-making processes – for example, curriculum, behaviour codes, teaching methods, school policies.
- Human rights need to be incorporated throughout the curriculum. It is not a discrete subject, but can be addressed, for

example, in geography to explore the issue of unequal access to resources, in biology to consider issues relating to genetic testing and the right to life of disabled babies, in chemistry, to examine the impact of environmental pollution and the right to health. There is a need for the development of materials and tools to help teachers in this work.

- Teachers need training on human rights and help in learning how to teach about rights. This will also involve learning to understand that their behaviour must be consistent with respect for the rights being taught. Abusive and violent attitudes towards children cannot be accepted in a school seeking to promote tolerance, understanding and respect for others.

These changes involve a profound reconsideration of the way education is provided in most countries in the world. But if we are committed to promoting democracy, respect and tolerance of all peoples, as well as the fulfilment of children's potential, they are changes which must be made to happen.

Conclusion

Near universal ratification of the UN Convention on the Rights of the Child constitutes a huge leap forward for children. The commitments made at the World Summit for Children, the 1990 World Conference for Education for All and at the World Education Forum in 2000 by international institutions and individual governments to respecting the education rights of children are important. But paper commitments are not enough. This brief overview of the current state of children's education rights highlights how far we have to go. The Convention provides us with a tool, a philosophy and a framework of standards against which to monitor progress. The challenge is to use it to develop concrete plans of action to implement its principles on the ground for all children. Right now, many schools fall far below its standards. Too often, teachers are poorly paid, badly educated and inadequately trained. The curriculum is irrelevant, boring or inappropriate. The material conditions of both buildings and equipment is poor. The authoritarian ethos is inimical to respect for human rights. Violence is endemic. Parents and local communities are excluded from the life of the school. Huge numbers of children are excluded altogether from the education system.

Clearly poverty and inequality in many countries serves as a brake on the potential for progress. But the goal of universal access to education is not a pipedream. The cost of putting every child in school by the year 2000 was estimated at $60 billion dollars. Compare that with the $800 billion dollars spent annually on weapons, or indeed the $100 billion spent on the Gulf War (Dall 1995). What is needed is a massive shift in political priorities at national and international level. But those priorities should not be directed solely at raising enrolment and reducing drop-out. They must also address the equally fundamental principles embodied in the Convention demanding respect for the dignity of children. So doing will be ultimately beneficial not only to individual children but also to the needs of the wider society. Children will become less disaffected if the curriculum is relevant to their needs. They will learn more effectively if they are valued as individuals. They will become socially responsible if they learn respect for human rights through their own treatment in school. The traditional 19th-century model of education is no longer either appropriate or desirable if we are to meet the needs of our children in the 21st century. Indeed, the whole approach to school needs to be rethought in the light of social, economic and technological change. School is not synonymous with education. There is a great deal to change; it will take time and will require more resources. But the outcome is win-win. There can be no excuse for failing to make an active commitment to the fullest possible implementation of the Convention. We owe it to the world's children.

Endnotes

1. General Comment No. 13, 21st Session, 1999, Committee on Economic, Social and Cultural Rights.
2. See note 1.
3. e.g. Article 26(3) of the Universal Declaration of Human Rights, article 18(4) of the International Covenant on Civil and Political Rights, and article 2 of Protocol No. 1 to the European Convention on Human Rights.
4. Report to the Commission on Human Rights by the Special Rapporteur on the Right to Education (E/CN.4/1999/49, para. 50).
5. World Declaration on the Survival, Protection and Development of Children and Plan of Action for its implementation, World Summit for Children, UN New York, September 1990.

6 Commission for Social Development, 'Report of the Special Rapporteur on monitoring the implementation of the Standard Rules on Equalisation of Opportunities for Persons with Disabilities', A/52/56, 23 December 1996.

7 The Salamanca Statement and Framework for Action on Special Needs Education, UNESCO, ED–94/WS/18, 1994.

8 General Discussion on the Rights of Children with Disabilities, CRC/C/SR.418 and 419, October 1997.

9 Section 386(2) Education Act 1996.

10 UK Initial report concluding observations, Add 34, para. 16, and Summary record, 206, para. 5.

11 School Standards and Framework Act 1998.

References

Commission for Racial Equality (1996) *Exclusion from school: the public cost.* Commission for Racial Equality: London.

Dall, F. (1995) 'Children's Right to Education: reaching the unreached.' In James Himes (ed) *Implementing the UN Convention on the Rights of the Child: resource mobilization in low-income countries.* Florence: UNICEF.

Davies, L. and Kirkpatrick, G. (2000) *The Euridem Project: A review of pupil democracy in Europe.* London: Children's Rights Alliance for England.

Forum for children and violence (1998) *Checkpoints for promoting non-violent schools.* London: Forum for Children and Violence.

Graham Brown, S. (1994) 'The Role of the Curriculum.' In *Education Rights and Minorities.* Florence: UNICEF/Minority Rights Group.

Hammarberg, T. (1997) *Inclusive education: a framework for change.* Bristol: Centre for Studies in Inclusive Education.

Hammarberg, T. (1997) *A School for Children with Rights.* Florence: UNICEF International Development Centre.

Hodgkin and Newell (1998) *Implementation Handbook.* UN Convention on the Rights of the Child. New York and Geneva: UNICEF.

Hodgson, D. (1996) 'The international human right to education and education concerning human rights.' *The International Journal of Children's Rights,* 4, 237–262.

Lansdown, G. (1995) *Taking Part: Children's participation in decision-making.* London: IPPR.

Lindquist, B. (1997) 'Child Convention and Standard Rules.' Paper given at the General Discussion day (6 October 1997) of the UN Committee on the Rights of the Child.

Oxfam International (2000) *Education Now: Break the Cycle of Poverty.* London: Oxfam.

Parsons (1996) 'Permanent exclusions from schools in England in the 1990s: Trends: causes and responses'. *Children and Society*, 10.3.

Saleh, L. (1997) Paper on Inclusive Education given at the General Discussion day (6 October 1997) of the UN Committee on the Rights of the Child.

Sharp, S. and Smith, P. (1994) 'Bullying in UK Schools: the DES Bullying Project.' In *Early Childhood Development and Care*, vol. 77, 47–55 and paper delivered to British Psychological Society, July 13 1994.

UNESCO (1995) *The education of girls and women: Towards a universal framework for action.* UNESCO.

UNICEF (1991) *Challenges for children and women in the 1990s.* Regional Eastern and Southern Africa Office, Kenya. UNICEF.

UNICEF (1992a) *Educating Girls and Women.* Florence: UNICEF.

UNICEF (1992b) *Policy Guidelines for the Implementation of Early Childhood Development Programmes.* Report presented at the meeting on Early Childhood Pre-school Education. New York: UNICEF.

UNICEF (1997) *Progress of Nations.* New York: UNICEF.

UNICEF (1998a) *Facts and Figures.* New York: UNICEF.

UNICEF (1998b) *The State of the World's Children 1998.* UNICEF/Oxford University Press.

UNICEF (1999) *The State of the World's Children 1999.* UNICEF/Oxford University Press.

UNICEF (forthcoming) 'Educational policies and ethnic divisions'. Draft paper, Innocenti Research Centre/UNICEF.

CHAPTER 3

What Can Be Done to Implement International Standards Concerning Children's Right to Education Worldwide?

Ulf Fredriksson

Introduction

The most important provision made by governments worldwide for children is to provide schooling. A majority of children in the world spend at least some years in primary education, but it also has to be recognized that large numbers of children do not get any education. From this perspective, it is important to examine how the right to education can be further emphasized in order to achieve education for all and how the right of the child is met in educational institutions. This article examines which international recommendations and conventions are of relevance for these issues, their implementation and the related problems that can be found in implementating them and finally what can be done to further better agreement between international recommendations and conventions, legislation, political decisions and everyday practice.

International recommendations and conventions

Several international recommendations and conventions deal with children's rights to and in education.

The Universal Declaration on Human Rights

The most important international recommendations mentioning children's right to education are found in article 26 of the Universal Declaration on Human Rights adopted by the General Assembly of the United Nations on 10 December 1948 (United Nations 1988). In principle it can be said that this declaration, as the basis for the United Nations, has been accepted by almost all governments in the world.

In order to make it possible for governments to incorporate the principles expressed in the declaration, two conventions based on the declaration have been developed within the UN system: the International Covenant on Economic, Social and Cultural Rights and the International Covenant on Civil and Political Rights. In the International Covenant on Economic, Social and Cultural Rights, article 13 deals with the right to education. This Covenant recognizes that primary education should be compulsory and available free for all (United Nations 1988). It has been ratified by 133 countries (United Nations 1995).

The Convention of the Rights of the Child

Another important document is the Declaration on the Rights of the Child. This declaration has also been developed into a convention – The Convention on the Rights of the Child. (For more information on the Convention on the Rights of the Child, see other chapters in this book.)

The Recommendation on the Status of Teachers

In 1966 UNESCO and ILO (International Labour Office) jointly adopted the Recommendation on the Status of Teachers. Even if this document does not deal specifically with the rights of the child, there are certain principles in this document that are of importance for this discussion:

> 10...:
>
> (a) it is the fundamental right of every child to be provided with the fullest possible educational opportunities; due attention should be paid to children requiring special educational treatment...
>
> (c) since education is a service of fundamental importance in the general public interest, it should be recognised as a responsibil-

> ity of the State, which should provide an adequate network of schools, free education in these schools and material assistance to needy pupils...
>
> (g) as an educational objective, no State should be satisfied with mere quantity, but should seek also to improve quality...
>
> (k) there should be close co-operation between the competent authorities, organisations of teachers, of employers and workers, and of parents as well as cultural organisations and institutions of learning and research, for the purpose of defining educational policy and its precise objectives...
>
> (International Labour Office 1990)

EFA – Education for all

The EFA (Education for All) initiative was conceived in 1990 when UNDP, UNESCO, UNICEF and the World Bank convened the World Education Forum in Jomtien, Thailand. The right to education for all as a principle was confirmed in 1990 by the Jomtien Conference.

> Every person – child, youth and adult – shall be able to benefit from educational opportunities designed to meet their basic learning needs. These needs comprise both essential learning tools (such as literacy, oral expression, numeracy, and problem solving) and the basic learning content (such as knowledge, skills, values, and attitudes) required by human beings to be able to survive, to develop their full capacities, to live and work in dignity, to participate fully in development, to improve the quality of their lives, to make informed decisions, and to continue learning. The scope of basic learning needs and how they should be met varies with individual countries and cultures, and inevitably changes with the passage of time.
>
> (Article 1, paragraph 1, World Declaration on Education for All)

In the Framework for Action to Meet Basic Learning Needs, it was even suggested that countries could set the target 'Universal access to, and completion of, primary education (or whatever higher level of education is considered as "basic") by year 2000' (World Conference on Education for All, 1990, Framework for Action to Meet Basic Learning Needs, paragraph 8, section 2).

Ten years after the Jomtien Conference, a new World Education Forum was convened in Dakar, Senegal, on 26–28 April 2000. It synthesized the results of a two-year Education for All Assessment, which was conducted in 181 countries. The World Education Forum emphasized that there had been progress in many countries, but that large numbers of children still did not have access to primary education and that the number of adults who are illiterate was unacceptably high.

The delegates representing 181 countries adopted a new Framework for Action committing their governments to achieve quality basic education for all, with a particular emphasis on girls' education and a pledge from donor countries and institutions that 'no country seriously committed to basic education will be thwarted in the achievement of this goal by lack of resources'.

The participating governments committed themselves to achieve the following goals:

1. Expand and improve comprehensive early childhood care and education, especially for the most vulnerable and disadvantaged children.
2. Ensure that by 2015 all children, especially girls, children in difficult circumstances and from ethnic minorities, have access to and complete free and compulsory primary education of good quality.
3. Ensure that the learning needs of all young people are met through equitable access to appropriate learning and life skills programmes.
4. Achieve a 50 per cent improvement in levels of adult literacy by 2015, especially for women, as well as equitable access to basic and continuing education for adults.
5. Eliminate gender disparities in primary and secondary education by 2005 and achieve gender equality by 2015 – with a special focus on ensuring full and equal access for girls to basic education of good quality.
6. Improve all aspects of the quality of education to achieve recognized and measurable learning outcomes for all, especially in literacy, numeracy and essential life skills.

Countries are requested to prepare a comprehensive, national Education for All (EFA) Plan by 2002 at the latest, including consultation with national civil society. The plan will specify reforms, include mid-term performance indicators and establish budget priorities for achieving the goals no later than 2015.

International Labour Office

Since its creation in 1919, ILO has dealt with the question of how to reduce and abolish child labour. In 1973 old conventions were consolidated into a single convention (No. 138). It provides that States that ratify the convention undertake to pursue a national policy designed to ensure the effective abolition of child labour and to raise progressively the minimum age for admission to employment or work at a level consistent with the fullest physical and mental development of young persons. Ratifying States should specify a minimum age for admission to employment, which should not be less than the age of completion of compulsory schooling and, in any case, should not be less than 15 years – or 14 as an initial step for developing countries. A higher age, 18 years, is laid down for any type of employment or work which might jeopardize the health, safety or morals of young persons (Valticos 1979).

A growing international consensus emerged during the 1990s stressing the need to proceed immediately with the abolition of 'the most intolerable forms of child labour', namely the employment of children in slave-like and bonded conditions and in dangerous and hazardous work, the exploitation of very young children, and the commercial sexual exploitation of children. These children cannot wait for longer-term developmental issues to be resolved before they are freed from their intolerable situations. This has prompted the development of new ILO standards.

On 17 June 1999, delegates at the International Labour Conference unanimously adopted a historic convention prohibiting the worst forms of child labour. The event marks the first time in ILO history that a convention or treaty has been adopted with the unanimous support of all members.

Officially entitled 'Convention concerning the Prohibition and Immediate Action for the Elimination of the Worst Forms of Child Labour

(Convention 182)', it calls for States to take swift and effective measures to prevent the most damaging child exploitation practices.

The Convention also contains some important references to education. States are required to take 'into account the importance of education in eliminating child labour' (article 7: 2) and to take effective and time-bound measures to 'ensure access to free basic education' (article 7: 2C). According to the latest available information from ILO (ILO 2000) Convention 138 has been ratified by 83 countries and Convention 182 by 73 countries.

The value of international recommendations and conventions

It is important to make a distinction between conventions on the one hand and recommendations, declarations etc. on the other hand. When conventions are ratified by a country, the country makes a commitment to incorporate the content of the convention into national legislation. By ratifying an international convention a country often also commits itself to various types of monitoring procedures, such as providing international bodies with reports about the implementation of the convention and, in some cases, the rights for individuals and organizations to submit complaints to international bodies concerning the fulfilment of the convention. Recommendations could be regarded as more general commitments, but from a moral point of view they could be considered as equally binding.

The value and the content of international recommendations and conventions can of course be questioned, but basically, what we can identify as international legislation and a political will expressed by the international community stands on a sound basis.

Implementation

The next question of course is to what extent international recommendations and conventions are followed by national governments.

The right to education

According to the latest available statistics, the gross enrolment in primary education in 1998 was 97 per cent. Even if the figures at world level do not look particularly bad, there are large groups of children in some countries that are not enrolled in school. In Sub-Saharan Africa, the gross enrolment ratio in primary education is 75 per cent. There are still at least 12 countries in the world where more than 50 per cent of the children are not enrolled. In total there are about 113 million out-of-school children in the world (International Consultative Forum on Education for All 2000).

Even though a large majority of children in the world today start primary education, there are many who only attend school for a few years. During the years 1990–95, 77 per cent of all children starting in primary education reached grade 5. There are big differences between regions. In the industrialized countries, this figure is 99 per cent, while in the least developed countries it is 58 per cent (UNICEF 1998).

Quality education

The right to education is not only a right to attend lessons in a school, but also to receive quality education. A report on education in Bangladesh, based on simple tests of children's life skills and knowledge, reading skills, writing skills and numeracy skills, concludes that only 29.6 per cent of the children interviewed successfully reached the minimum level of basic education (Campaign for Popular Education 1999). A World Bank report on primary education in India provides an overview of recent research and notes that children who have reached the final year of lower primary education have often mastered less than half the curriculum taught the year before (World Bank 1997).

The Southern Africa Consortium for Measuring Educational Quality (SACMEQ) analysed the reading levels for pupils in Grade 6 in Southern Africa. The study found that pupils were generally performing poorly when judged by the standards of mastery set down by the respective ministries' own reading experts. In only two of the five countries, Mauritius and Zimbabwe, did at least half of the pupils attain the minimum level of reading fluency (SACMEQ 1998).

In Ghana in 1991 the Ministry of Education constructed tests in Mathematics and English for grade 6 in primary school. The first tests were administered in 1992 and repeated in 1993, 1994, 1995 and 1996. Each sample corresponded to about 5 per cent of all students in grade 6 in primary school. The mastery level in English was to solve 60 per cent of the test items and in Mathematics 55 per cent of the test items. A very small number of students reached mastery level in the two subjects. In 1992, 2 per cent reached this level in English and in 1996

5.5 per cent. In Mathematics the percentage that reached mastery level in 1992 was 1.1 per cent and in 1996 1.8 per cent (Quansah 1997).

There are also problems regarding the quality of education in industrialized countries. The level of basic skills such as reading comprehension is not sufficiently good among large groups of the population in several industrialized countries. In a recent report from OECD, it is claimed that more than 20 per cent of adults in some of the richest countries in the world are unable to read or write except at the most elementary level (OECD/Human Resource Development Canada 1997).

Equal rights to education

All children have the right to receive education without any discrimination and all children should be given the same opportunity to learn and develop in school, but there are differences between different groups of children.

The net enrolment ratio for girls in primary education is 80 per cent and for boys 87 per cent. In Sub-Saharan Africa, the corresponding figures are 54 per cent and 66 per cent (International Consultative Forum on Education for All 2000).

It is difficult to get figures from many countries showing the access to education for different minorities, but those figures that are available clearly show that ethnic minorities, nomads, indigenous people and migrants are groups who have less access to education than other groups in societies. In the industrialized countries, children from migrant families continue to academic routes in secondary education and to tertiary education to a lesser extent than children from the majority population (Fredriksson 2001).

Schools

The state of many school buildings is far from acceptable. On behalf of UNESCO and UNICEF, a group of researchers examined primary schools in some of the least developed countries in the world (Schleicher, Siniscalco and Postlethwaite 1995). The schools rarely had even basic equipment such as a blackboard, a world map, cupboards, teacher chair, teacher desk, desks for the students and chairs for the students. For example in Ethiopia, 72 per cent of the students in schools covered by the study received their education in schools that needed basic repairs or even to be totally rebuilt.

In India, the PROBE survey found that 31 per cent of the schools visited did not have any acceptable classrooms. Many schools were badly maintained. The survey found that only 16 per cent of the schools visited were not in need of any repair (The PROBE team 1998). In a recent study of the situation in two districts in Uttar Pradesh, it was found that 17 per cent of the school buildings were unusable or even dangerous and 56 per cent were in a state of decay (Nornvall 1999).

The democratic school

It is generally agreed and stated in several international recommendations and conventions that education should prepare young people for life as citizens in a democratic society. This has implications for everyday life in schools.

The right of the child to express an opinion can be seen as an obligation of the school to organize the work in such a way that the child has the opportunity to express his or her opinion. Without training, children are not always able to express their views, especially in more formal situations. From this perspective, schools have an important task to teach children how to express an opinion, both orally and in writing, and how to participate in a discussion.

It is critical that the child not only learns to read and write, but also that the child learns to examine information critically. Important objectives for education therefore are to develop the skills necessary to compile and work with information, to make judgements and to express opinions.

The child should not be forced to think and believe in a certain way. This applies to political opinions as well as religious and philosophical beliefs. If the child has a certain belief, this should be respected. This does not always mean that the teacher has to accept the beliefs of the child. On occasion the teacher can discuss and argue with the child, but this must always take place with appropriate respect for the child's right to have her or his own beliefs.

Children should have the right to form their own student organizations. This right should be applicable independent of the age of the children, but in an appropriate way taking age differences into consideration.

In countries where the rights to express an opinion, freedom of thought and freedom of association are not given, or are only partly given, to adults it is obviously difficult to see how they can be realized for children. Some governments do not like to operate in a democratic environment where their actions are scrutinized by the public. If children are supposed to be given these rights in a limited context and even to be encouraged to express their opinions, such actions may start to change the whole political climate. Governments ruling in an authoritarian style are not enthusiastic about implementing these parts of the international recommendations and conventions.

Child labour

According to a recent ILO estimate, the number of working children worldwide aged between 5 and 14 years is around 250 million, of which at least 120 million are working full-time and are involved in work that is hazardous and exploitative (ILO 1999).

There has been an explosion of child workers in the informal, unregulated sector of the economy, as a result of increasing migration, urbanization and industrialization. Many children are 'bonded' or forced to work under slave-like conditions. A large part of the world's child workers are in the textile industry, especially in the production of carpets.

One of the most efficient ways of preventing children from being used as child workers is education. When society organizes and monitors compulsory primary education for children, there are fewer possibilities for the children to work and it is more difficult for the parents to force them into the workplace. Children's presence in school allows supervision that ensures that legislation is implemented. This is particularly important in ensuring that girls receive education and are not forced into domestic service. A good example of this can be found in India. In the state of Kerala, the work participation rate of children is much lower than in India as a whole and the enrolment rate for primary education, as well as the literacy rate, is higher than the average in India. The Kerala government has made no special effort to end child labour. It is the expansion of the school system that has reduced child labour (Weiner 1991).

Conclusion

It can be concluded that many of the principles covered in international recommendations and conventions are not met in national education systems.

- There are still large groups of young people who do not get any education or only some years of primary education.
- There are many children who, in spite of some years of schooling, have not learned basic literacy and numeracy skills.
- Girls receive education to a lesser extent than boys and there are substantial differences in the enrolment ratios between boys and girls in some countries.
- Children from ethnic minorities, nomads, indigenous populations, migrants and other minorities get education to a lesser extent than children from the majority groups in societies.
- Many school buildings are in bad repair and lack basic equipment.
- Many children do not receive an education where they learn about basic democratic rights and get the opportunity to practice these rights.
- Many children are never given a chance to get basic education and are instead forced to work as child workers.

There is unfortunately still a long way to go to meet the objectives expressed in the international recommendations and conventions.

Where to find the problems?

Almost all countries in the world recognize the right for children to receive education. Primary education is compulsory in a large majority of countries in the world according to legislation. The fundamental problems are not found in national legislation or policy.

Implementation

The real problem is the lack of implementation of legislation and policy. In some cases, it is doubtful if the intention ever was to implement the policy. Policy statement can fill purposes other than indicating a real intention. Often, such statements are made for political effect, sometimes to convince international donors that the intentions are good. Certain statements can be made in order to be elected or to receive some popularity, at least in the short term. In many cases lip service is paid to objectives such as education for all. In some cases, the lack of implementation can be explained by political ignorance. There might be a lack of understanding of the need for implementation in some political circles. It is believed that the difficult part of the process is to take the right decision. Policy makers and planners might believe that policies, once in place, are automatically implemented.

Another possible reason for the lack of implementation could be that the objectives were unclear from the very beginning or even contradictory. The intention could have been too vague or even unrealistic. In some cases policies are not implemented properly because they were not based on sufficient information. Reliable information about numbers and costs could have been missing. The implementation of policies can also fail because of an incompetent bureaucracy that does not have the skills to implement, or the will to implement.

Yet another possible explanation for the lack of implementation is that policy makers and planners did not consult those who were supposed to implement the policies, usually teachers and head teachers (see section on 'The teachers' on p.76). Other important stakeholders such as parents and students could also have been forgotten. The policies have been formulated and decided by a small group of politicians and/or administrators without sufficient contacts with the reality in which the reform is supposed to be implemented.

Lack of funding

One of the main problems behind poor fulfilment of the principles of education for all is lack of funding. This is probably especially valid in discussions about policies aimed at increasing enrolment, further expansion of the education system or improvement of the system's quality (Psacharopoulos 1990).

Many of the least developed countries in the world allocate 20 per cent or more of their national budgets to education without being able to enrol all children and young people in school. Due to the population growth governments are forced to increase continuously the resources allocated to education to maintain the same ratio of children enrolled in school. To be able to increase the enrolment, it would be necessary to further increase the allocation to education. In national budgets that are already under heavy pressure, this might be difficult. Due to structural adjustment policies, government expenditure in many countries is at a level where every reallocation of items within the budget might have severe effects on other essential services to the citizens.

Debt service and re-payment of loans to international financial institutions take a considerable part of the national budget for many of the least developed countries, in some cases 20 per cent or more of the national budget. These large sums are effectively blocking increased investment in other areas. If in Sub-Saharan Africa just 20 per cent of the $10 billion to $13 billion annual cost of servicing the foreign debt of over $200 billion could be used for educational investment it would mean that, for example, every child could be provided with a place in a classroom (Sawyerr 1997).

It is impossible to give a universal estimate of what the costs per student should be for quality schooling. Obviously these costs shift between countries and even within countries. In spite of this it is obvious that the resources spent on a child's education are inadequate in many countries. In the developed countries, the average public expenditure per student in 1995 was $4979 and among the least developed countries $33 was expended. The more developed regions, basically the industrialized countries (in total 26 countries in the UNESCO statistics), spent $1109.9 billion on education, which is 79 per cent of all the public expenditure on education in the world. The least developed countries in the world (in total 48 countries in the UNESCO statistics) were spending $5.3 billion on public education, which is 0.4 per cent of all the public expenditure on education in the world (UNESCO 1998).

Lack of political will

In some countries the lack of investment in education is due to financial constraints, while in others there is a lack of political will. The resources are available, but used for other purposes.

The International Commission on Education for the Twenty-first Century (the so called Delors Commission) suggested that every country should allocate at least 6 per cent of its Gross National Product (GNP) to education ('...not less than 6 per cent of GNP should be devoted to education... '(1996, p.165)). Out of the 130 countries for which figures on expenditure on education, expressed as a percentage of GNP, were given in UNESCO's education statistics published in 1998, 96 had spent less than 6 per cent on education. Twenty-six per cent of the countries for which statistics were available spent more than 6 per cent on education and 16 per cent of the countries spent less than 3 per cent.

Some countries still invest heavily in military expenditure, while education is given considerably less in the national budget. If just $3 billion to $6 billion of the estimated $680 billion devoted worldwide to military expenditure per year could be diverted to education, many experts believe that every child would have a place in a decent school (Sawyerr 1997).

In this context, corruption also has to be mentioned. It is impossible to estimate how much money is wasted in the world because it is used to support unfair privileges, buying things not needed, put in the pockets of politicians and/or administrators etc. If only some of these resources could be traced and used for appropriate causes, it would probably add considerably to educational budgets.

The lack of will is not only related to the policies of developing countries, but also to the policies of the rich countries. Most rich countries are still allocating much less to development cooperation than the 0.7 per cent of GNP recommended by the United Nations and reaffirmed by the UN General Assembly Special Session in June 1997. The international aid given in 1997 was at the lowest level ever. The OECD countries were allocating 0.22 per cent of GNP to development aid (Eurostep/ICVA/Norwegian Peoples Aid 1998).

The portion of international aid dedicated to education declined steadily from 17 per cent in 1975 to 9.8 per cent in 1990. Perhaps some hope can be seen in the fact that there has been a slight increase since 1990 and the figure in 1994 climbed to 10.7 per cent (UNICEF 1997). On the other hand, the total aid for education in real terms has been falling compared with 1990, due the sharp overall decline in international aid. A depressing fact is that, according to the independent review of international aid, just 1.4 per cent of the total aid was allocated to basic education (Eurostep/ICVA/Norwegian Peoples Aid 1998). If international aid could increase and if a quarter of development aid could be devoted to the funding of education, as suggested by the International Commission on Education for the Twenty-first

Century (1996), it would mean that new resources should be given to education.

Economic theory

In political discussions today there is a tendency to allow economic considerations to be of the greatest importance. Obviously, to some extent this is unavoidable. Without financial resources, it is not possible to achieve anything and financial resources are limited, even in the richest countries in the world. Priorities and choices have to be based on a sound theory and reasonable assumptions as to how limited resources can be best used. This is basically what economists are supposed to do. The question is the extent to which economic theory takes into consideration the long-term needs of societies and, from that perspective, how economic theory deals with education and the needs and rights of children.

During recent years, international markets have been playing a growing role in governments' decision-making. Many current economic operations on international markets are based on short-term advantage and quick gains. Governments, especially in small countries and countries depending on foreign investors, are forced to play along with these market forces. Governments basically want to attract investors and try to adapt their policies to demands they assume the investors make. It is assumed that investors like to pay low taxes and favour policies of tax reduction and public sector cuts. Such policies will certainly have a price. The problem is that the price might not be seen immediately. If public-sector cuts lead to policies that work against children, the full costs might not be seen until 10 or 20 years after.

Economists have started to realize that the environment has a price and that destruction of environmental values has to be taken into consideration when gains and losses of economic transactions are calculated. It has been understood, at least partially, that it is cheaper to minimize environmental damage before it takes place than to try to cure irreparable destruction afterwards. In the same way, it is necessary to start to realize the need for long-term investment and the support of children and their education (de Vylder 1997).

The teachers

It has to be recognized that any school authority, government or intergovernmental organisation that seriously wishes to improve education has to acknowledge the key role teachers play in the education process.

There are many examples of reforms and innovations in the education systems that have simply not been implemented because the reformers forgot about the teachers (Villegas-Reimers and Reimers 1996). In a questionnaire to member organizations of Education International in some of the most populated countries in the world, the most striking conclusion from the answers given was the reporting of insufficient, or in some cases absence of, consultations between governments and education unions (Education International 1996). The same observation has been made in other reports to Education International from several member organizations (Education International 1997). ILO (1996) has also observed that teachers' formal bargaining power and their consultative participation at the site level have been under attack or ignored as part of structural adjustment policies.

A study of the educational conditions in some of the least developed countries revealed that in some of these countries 60 per cent of the teachers had only primary school education and in many countries 20–30 per cent of the teachers had no teacher education (Schleicher, Siniscalco and Postlethwaite 1995).

Many countries are facing problems in recruiting students to teacher education. Education International has received reports from several countries about difficulties in recruiting students to the teacher training colleges (Education International 1995). There are reports from several Latin American countries indicating that the shortage of teachers causes training institutions to accept those who apply, even if their academic background is deficient (Villegas-Reimers and Reimers 1996).

During recent years, there has been an increased emphasis on in-service training. Many governments have reduced the pre-service training of teachers with the declared intention of reallocating resources from pre-service training to in-service training. In many cases the result has been a reduction of pre-service training without any improvements in in-service training (ILO 1996).

What to do?

Based on the discussions above, several actions can be proposed to further better agreement between the legislation, political decisions and everyday practice.

International recommendations and conventions have to be defended. They play an important role in setting acceptable standards concerning education and children's rights. International recommendations and conventions have to be revised and improved on a continuous basis.

The problems with educational policies in many cases are not found in the legislation or official policies, but in the implementation. One important reason behind the lack of implementation is insufficient resources. It is crucial to *increase investment in education.* In some cases countries have to change priorities and reallocate resources to education from other sectors in society. In other cases it is important that the international community contributes. Most rich countries are still allocating much less to development cooperation than the 0.7 per cent of GNP recommended by the UN. The international aid given in 1997 was at the lowest level ever.

There is an urgent need to develop and elaborate the knowledge about economic policy and its impact on children. The long-term effects that different measures have on children should be further studied and specifically what the effects are of investment in education in the long term.

The concept 'the democratic school' has to be further developed, meaning developing methods for students to learn about democracy and to practice democracy. The democratic school is a school where the rights of students, teachers and parents to be part of decision-making processes are recognized.

The need to consult the teachers about educational policies has to be recognized. In each country there should be machinery for consultation between school authorities/governments and teachers, represented through their organizations. Information should be provided on a continuous basis. In the case of changes in teachers' working conditions, negotiations should take place.

Teacher education has to be reformed. It has to be realized that there is a need to organize teacher education as a process of life-long learning for teachers. There is a need to find a new concept with a high quality pre-service education giving the future teachers a good foundation in theory and practice. There is a need to have continuous in-service training that will allow professional development of the teachers and provide them with knowledge and skills to meet new challenges.

References

Campaign for Popular Education (1999) *The Education Watch Report 1999. Hopes not Complacence. Efficiency in Primary Education.* Dhaka: Campaign for Popular Education.

de Vylder, S. (1997) *Barn och ekonomisk politik. För en alternativ statsbudget.* Stockholm: Rädda Barnen.

Education International (1995) *Quality of Education.* Discussion Papers on Education No. 1, May 1995, Brussels: Education International.

Education International (1996) *Education for all – mid-decade review – the teachers' perspective.* Brussels: Education International.

Education International (1997) *Report to the Special Session of the Joint ILO/UNESCO Committee of Experts on the Application of the Recommendation Concerning the Status of Teachers, UNESCO, Paris, 15–19 September 1997.* Brussels: Education International.

Eurostep/ICVA/Norwegian Peoples Aid (1998) *The Reality of Aid. An Independent Review of Poverty Reduction and Development Assistance 1998/1999.* London: Earthscan.

Fredriksson, U. (2001) *Interkulturell undervisning, språk och läsning.* Institute of International Education, Stockholm University (in press).

The International Commission on Education for the Twenty-first Century (1996) *Learning: The Treasure Within. Report to UNESCO of the International Commission on Education for the Twenty-first Century.* Paris: UNESCO Publishing.

International Consultative Forum on Education for All (2000) *Education for All 2000 Assessment. Statistical Document.* Paris: UNESCO Publishing.

International Labour Office (1990) *Teachers and international labour standards: A handbook.* Geneva: ILO.

International Labour Office (1996) *Impact of structural adjustment on the employment and training of teachers.* Geneva: ILO.

ILO (1999) Website http://www.ilo.org

ILO (2001) Website http://www.ilo.org

International Labour Office (2000) *Ratifications by Convention and by country as of 31 December 1999.* Geneva: ILO.

Nornvall, F. (1999) *Foregoing the Future. Educational Deprivation, Social Capital and the State in Uttar Pradesh.* Uppsala University, Department of Government. Master thesis, spring 1999.

OECD/Human Resources Development Canada (1997) *Literacy Skills For The Knowledge Society. Further Results from the International Adult Literacy Survey.* Paris: OECD (Organisation for Economic Co-operation and Development), Human Resources Development Canada.

The PROBE team (1998) *Public Report on Basic Education in India.* New Delhi: Oxford University Press.

Psacharopoulos, G. (1990) *Why Educational Policies Can Fail. An Overview of Selected African Experiences.* No 83 World Bank Discussion Papers, African Technical Department Series. Washington D.C.: The World Bank.

Quansah, K. B. (1997) *Monitoring Standards in Basic Education Using Criterion-Referenced Tests.* Institute for Economic Affairs Round Table Discussion Paper, 18 July 1997, Ghana Education Service Accra.

SACMEQ Policy Research (1998) Reports No 1–5. IIEP. UNESCO.

Sawyerr, H. (1997) *Quality education: One answer to many questions.* In *The Progress of Nations 1997.* New York: UNICEF.

Schleicher, A., Siniscalco, M. T. and Postlethwaite, N. (1995) *The Conditions of Primary Schools in the Least Developed Countries. A Report to UNESCO and UNICEF.* Paris: UNESCO Publishing.

UNESCO (1998) *World Education Report 1998.* Paris: UNESCO Publishing.

UNICEF (1997) *The Progress of the Nations 1997.* New York: UNICEF.

UNICEF (1998) *The State of the World's Children 1998.* UNICEF/Oxford University Press.

United Nations (1988) *Human Rights. A Compilation of International Instruments.* New York: United Nations.

United Nations (1995) *Basic Facts About the United Nations.* New York: United Nations.

Valticos, N. (1979) *International Labour Laws.* Deventer: Kluwer.

Villegas-Reimers, E. and Reimers, F. (1996) 'Where are the 60 million teachers? The missing voice in educational reform around the world'. *Prospect XXVI,* 3 September 1996, 469–492.

Weiner, M. (1991) *The Child and the State in India.* Princeton University Press.

World Bank (1997) *Development in Practice. Primary Education in India.* Washington D.C.: The World Bank.

World Conference on Education for All (1990) *World Declaration on Education for All and Framework for Action to Meet Basic Learning Needs.* World Conference on Education for All. 5–9 March 1990, Jomtien, Thailand. UNESCO/EFA Forum Secretariat.

CHAPTER 4

Reporting on the Status of Education to the UN Committee on the Rights of the Child

Lukas P. Scherer and Stuart N. Hart

Introduction

Any discussion of the lives and futures of children requires giving special attention to their education. From the long history of recorded philosophy through all the centuries to this 21st century, the goals and impact of education on human society and the well-being of children have been emphasized. The early Greek philosophers recognized the importance of education, but the humanist view on the bringing up of children in general, and the perspectives of others concerned with the human condition have agreed that education is one of the most important foundations for a free society.

The education articles of the Convention on the Rights of the Child, articles 28 and 29, incorporate ideas that have been espoused and championed by a wide variety of thinkers from the distant past to the present (see Scherer 1999). These articles embody the central spirit of the Convention. They set expectations for the full development of the child and for a free, democratic society. They cover fully the major positive possibilities and qualities of human beings included in the other articles of the Convention. The World Education Forum in Dakar (April 26–28 2000) confirmed the significance of the themes and standards of the education articles and prescribed plans of action for the UN Decade of Education for All.

The significance of good reports on the status of implementing the education articles

Through information lies the opportunity for power. Good and accurate information about the conditions and significant issues of quality of life in the possession of influential and well-intentioned people can provide immense power to do good and to provide the help most needed to accomplish the requirements of the education articles.

The administrative and procedural articles of the Convention establish a system encouraging progressive movement toward fulfilment of the Convention's standards. They set expectations for: (a) accurate reporting of relevant conditions of societal status and trends; (b) availability of relevant information to all interested and affected parties; and (c) application of moral persuasion by States Parties and an informed public. At the core of this system is the requirement that States Parties report the status of implementation of the Convention to the Committee on the Rights of the Child two years following ratification of the Convention by a State Party and every five years thereafter. These reports are to be made public to the national population of the State Party, as well as to the broader international community. This allows the Committee and others, including the non-governmental community of the State Party, to critique the report, seek clarification as needed, develop alternatives targeting critical and disputed issues, and make recommendations for further progress.

The argument has been made that the Convention's education articles are particularly important in that they express the spirit of the Convention in terms of child development goals and because specific identifiable societal institutions have the responsibility for achieving these goals. Therefore, it seems reasonable to set high expectations for good monitoring and reporting of progress States Parties make toward meeting the standards of the education articles.

This present research was conducted to examine the degree to which the expectation of full and accurate reporting to the UN Committee on the Rights of the Child is a reality. As a follow-up of the results, an experimental reporting system was constructed to explore the possibilities for State Parties as well as non-governmental organizations to achieve more effective and efficient reporting.

Results of the analyses of the first 49 Initial State Party reports

Analyses of the initial reports of the first 49 States Parties that reported to the Committee on the Rights of the Child were undertaken, giving attention to each thematic standard of articles 28 and 29. Emerging and developed countries and diverse cultures from all continents of the world were represented in this set of 49 States Parties.[1]

Some common tendencies as well as substantial differences across countries were revealed. See Tables 4.1 and 4.2, which present findings in a manner supporting comments to be made in this section. The tables are divided into three categories: fulfilled responses, problems indicated, and no comments provided for each thematic standard of articles 28 and 29. All State Party reports gave some information about situations relevant to their education systems. Very few countries indicated problems in regard to any of the major issues or questions about educational conditions. The reports of some countries indicated most of the standards of the Convention had been met, whereas others provided indications of fulfilment for none or only one standard. Some States Parties provided just a few sentences on education, while others included some 200 pages giving extensive details about the educational system, financial matters and acts related to education.

As expected, big differences were found between the answers or statements for aspects of article 28 compared to article 29. The percentage of positive responses to article 28 standards was much higher than that for article 29.

Findings for standards of article 28 (see Table 4.1)

Nearly all States Parties that referred to the education articles indicated that primary school exists, which is about six years of duration, compulsory and free of charges (88% of all replies). A smaller number but still high percentage (78%) answered that they met the requirement of providing a variety of forms of secondary schools. Fewer States Parties wrote that there is access to higher education (49%), related to the abilities of the youngsters; while 78 per cent of all reports indicate the provision of vocational information and guidance to their children. Equal opportunity for access to the educational system is stated to be assured by 65 per cent of the States Parties. Respect of the child's dignity in disci-

Table 4.1 Results for Article 28

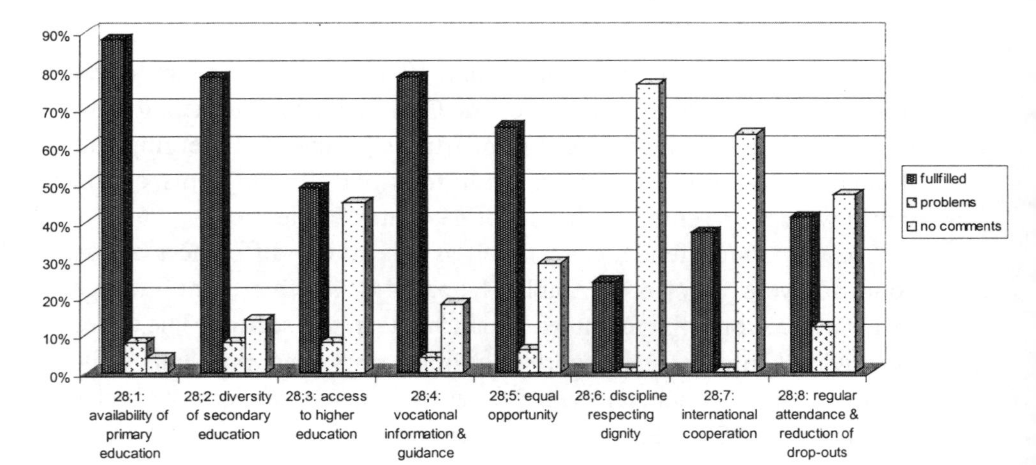

pline is indicated to be in place by 24 per cent of the countries, while 37 per cent mention that international cooperation is supported in education. Programmes to strengthen regular school attendance and to reduce drop-out rates were indicated to exist in 41 per cent of all States Parties reporting.

As previously noted, very few States Parties make any statements about problems. Only 4 out of the 49, or 8 per cent, indicated difficulties in meeting the standards of article 28. Problems were expressed only in reports of a small number of States Parties from Africa and the Caribbean, and the problems were defined as lack of money.

Findings for standards of article 29 (see Table 4.2)

Article 29 standards were less frequently indicated as met in comparison to article 28 standards; in the case of each and all standards, less than 50 per cent of the 49 States Parties gave a positive response. The first paragraph standard – development of the child to its fullest potential – received the most frequent positive responses, with 23 reports out of 49 indicating that this item is fulfilled (47% of all answers). In 43 per cent of all reports it was indicated that the educational systems teach respect for human rights. Only 19 reports, or 39 per cent, indicated fulfilment of the item requiring development of respect for the child's parents. This means less than two out of five countries declared that this standard

Table 4.2 Results for Article 29

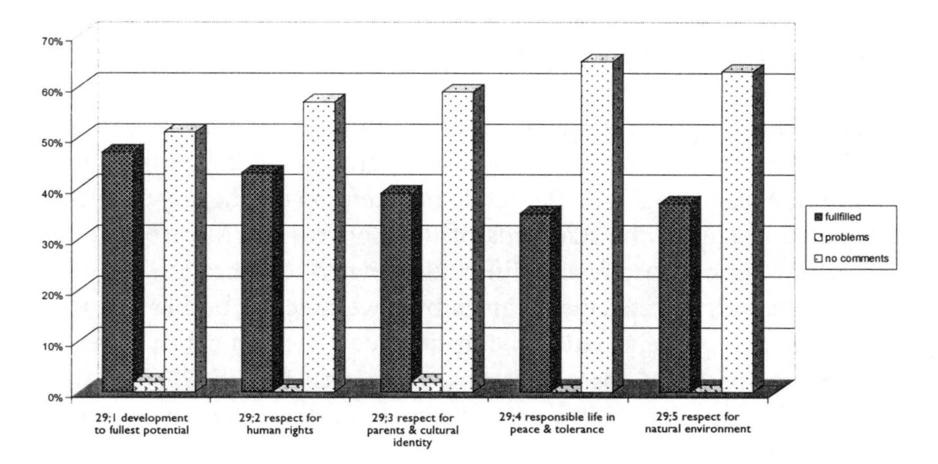

is satisfied. In 35 per cent of all reports there were positive answers indicating support of the educational aim to prepare a child for a responsible life of peace, freedom and tolerance. Respect for natural environment was indicated as supported in 37 per cent of the reports.

As was the case for article 28, there were very few indications of problems concerning fulfilment of article 29's aims of education. In fact, this occurred even less than it did for article 28. For article 29, only 2 (!) State Party reports out of 49 mentioned problems associated with meeting these very important standards. However, in comparison with the positive answers for items, not a single comment was made in 51 per cent of all reports for the paragraph one standard, supporting development to the child's fullest potential. For the paragraph two standard, teaching respect for human rights in education, 57 per cent of all reports said nothing! In 59 per cent of all analysed reports nothing is found about the respect for parents of children and their cultural identity. In 65 per cent of the reports, nothing was found that referred to the aim to prepare the child for a responsible life in a free society in peace and tolerance. In 63 per cent of the reports there was not a single phrase about respect for natural environment.

Implications of findings

One of the main findings of this research is that the majority of the first 49 countries to provide initial reports indicate that children have the opportunity to go to primary school and that it is compulsory and free of charge. In bold contrast, it has been found that most countries do not specify their support, if any, for teaching respect for tolerance, peace and human rights. This is worthy of concern, as is the fact that, with very few exceptions, States Parties do not mention having any problems in fulfilling any of the standards of the Convention. Most of the 49 countries did not specify any difficulties related to education.

The majority of statements given by governmental bodies describe their status positively while giving little or no commentary directly related to the standards paragraphs of articles 28 and 29. In other words, although reports indicate that some of the Convention articles concerning education are fulfilled, many of the paragraphs of the governmental reports about education do not say anything of substance specific to the Convention's standards. Therefore, an important finding is that the standards of the Convention are to a large part not mentioned in the reports. Additionally, it has been noted that the standards of article 28, versus those of article 29, seem to be more directly dealt with in reports.

Multiple possibilities exist for explaining the reporting patterns noted. They are worthy of mention but must be recognized to be speculative in nature and not determinant.

The inadequacy of information provided specific to the education articles of the Convention may be due to: (a) the information not being available, having not been requested or recorded previously; (b) tendencies to report only positive information which reflects well on the State Party and, therefore, to leave out negative findings; (c) an inability or unwillingness to devote the necessary resources to the reporting process; (d) lack of clarity and demand quality in the reporting requirements; and/or (e) the first 49 States Parties reporting responded in unusual ways, not representative of the larger body of States Parties. To investigate the last possibility, a review was conducted of 5 randomly selected State Party reports from among the additional 44 that had reported by the time this chapter was being completed (which also means that 98 State Parties had not yet provided initial reports). The reporting patterns were quite similar to the ones cited here.

Combinations of the other factors may be applicable within any State Party. For example, the finding that States Parties generally indicate no problems relative to meeting education standards may be due to lack of availability of relevant information as well as a general preference to place one's country or governmental office in a good light. The tendency to provide more positive information about the standards of article 28 versus article 29 may be due both to the fact that most of the article 28 standards express somewhat concrete and unambiguous provisions, and that relevant information has traditionally been gathered and recorded in state offices, while these factors apply less well to article 29's standards. The requirements of article 29, which give form and direction to the purposes, effects, and products of education, are much more complex and demanding. What the country's aims of education are, evidence of resources specifically applied to them, and progress toward them may not be clearly set forth or monitored within some countries.

Among these plausible explanations for the response patterns found, the nature of the reporting system itself may limit or frustrate reporting compliance. The authors chose to explore this possibility further. A review of the guidelines for initial reports (Committee on the Rights of the Child 1996) as they deal with education found coverage to be very brief, less than one page, and to be quite general, with no direct encouragement to report on the thematic standards within articles 28 and 29. It is possible and seems probable that a reporting system that does not require specifically that each important standard be dealt with in terms of formal commitment, resource application, supportive practices, and outcomes, will result in reporting in a less than comprehensive and systematic fashion by busy people in government offices. The issue of the nature of reporting systems is further explored in the next section.

Initial and periodic reports of 11 states parties – a comparison

As mentioned earlier in this chapter, States Parties have to report to the Committee on the Rights of the Child two years after ratification of the Convention (initial report) and every five years thereafter (periodic report). Analyses of 11 States Parties periodic reports were more recently conducted. These eleven States Parties reports were randomly chosen and analysed. The reports were formulated by the States Parties using the more detailed guidelines (54 pages) provided by the Committee for the development of periodic reports (Committee on the Rights of the Child, 1996). Periodical reports in additional to these 11 will be analysed in the future.

The results were better but displayed characteristics similar to those found for initial reports. More of the thematic standards were given attention, with positive responses (see Table 4.3), but there were major standards for which no comments were made (see Table 4.4). As with the findings for the initial reports, the weakest results found were those relating to problems noted in the reports (see Table 4.5). Across this set of 11 States Parties, in each case just one to two standards of article 29 were reported as having been fulfilled, only one standard was stated to have been associated with problems in fulfilment, and three to four standards in each case were not mentioned in the reports. The periodic reports tend to be more complete and to indicated a higher frequency of fulfilment of standards but are still weak in giving clear detail on fulfilment and in recognizing the problems of implementing the Convention on the Rights of the Child. Table 4.6 presents the results for these eleven States Parties.

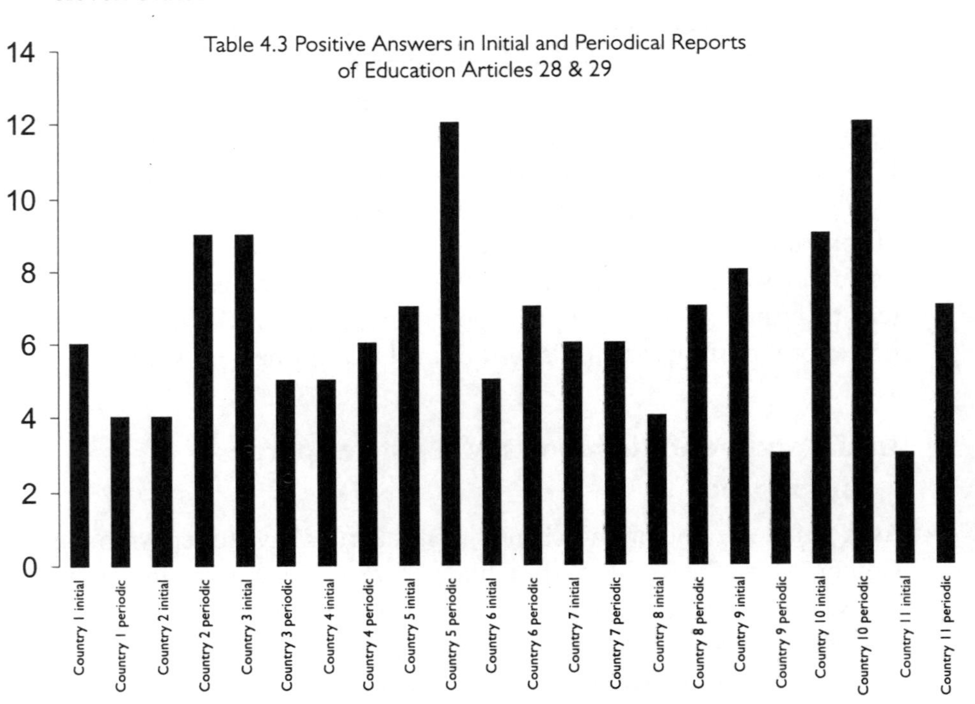

Table 4.4 Comments in Initial and Periodical Reports of Ecuation Articles 28 & 29

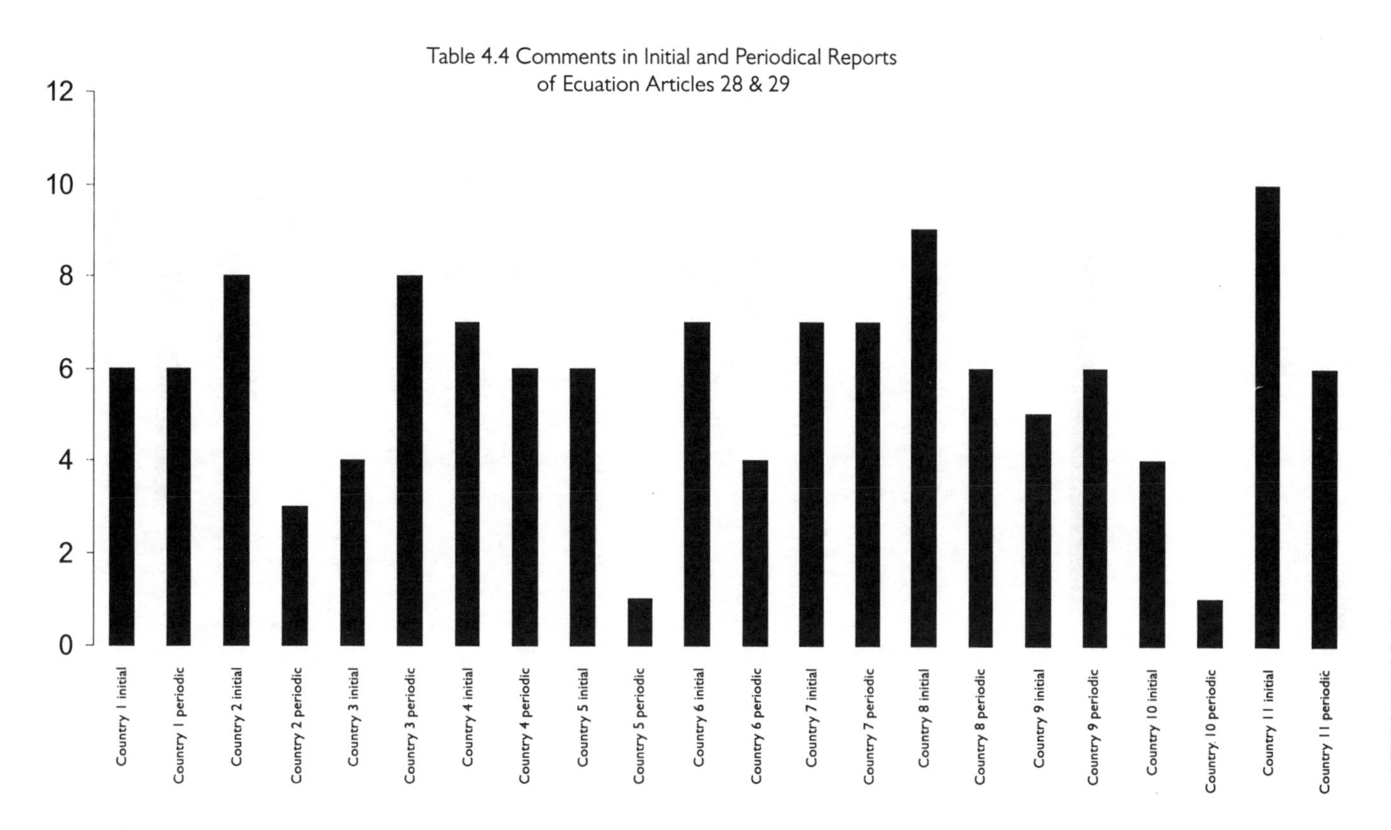

Table 4.5 Problems Noted in Initial and Periodic Report on Education Articles 28 & 29

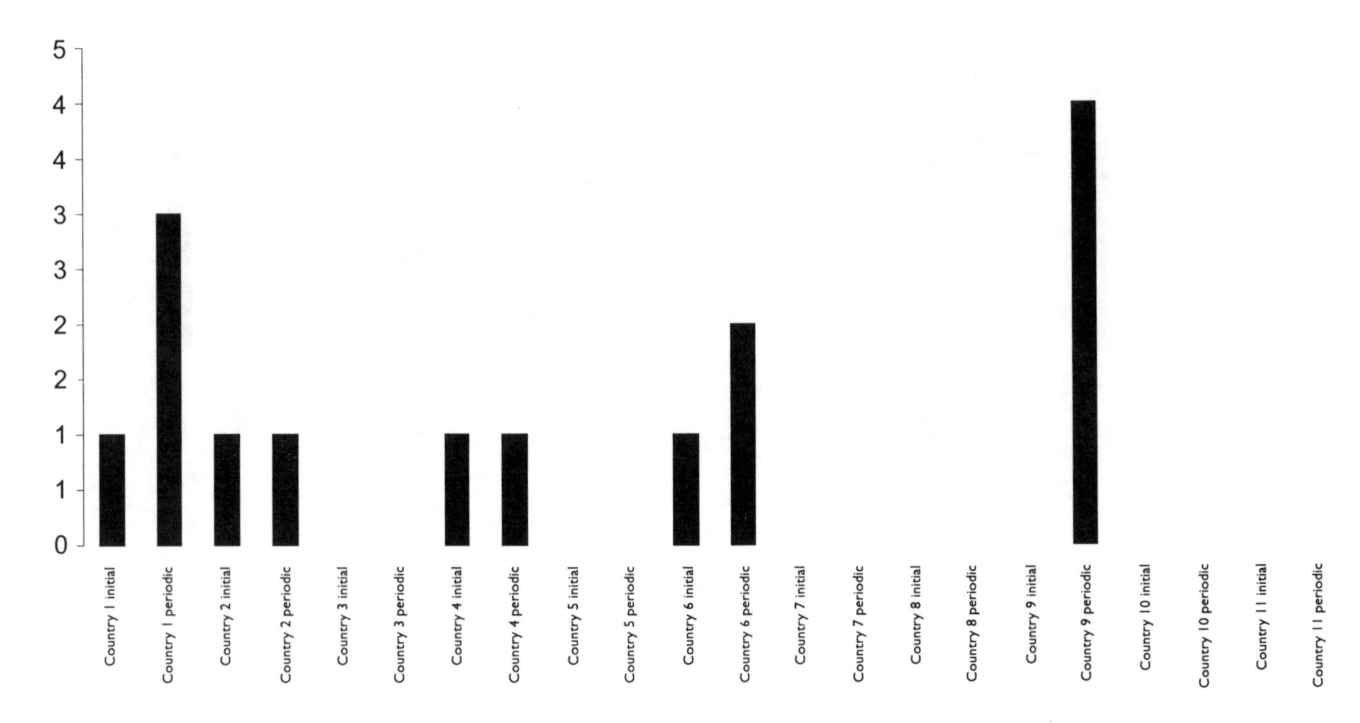

Table 4.6 Initial and periodic report comparisons for 11 States Parties

	28;1	28;2	28;3	28;4	28;5	28;6	28;7	28;8	29;1	29;2	29;3	29;4	29;5	"+"	"-"	"0"
Country 1 initial	1	1	1	1	1	0	0	-1	1	0	0	0	0	6	1	6
Country 1 periodic	1	-1	-1	0	1	1	1	-1	0	0	0	0	0	4	3	6
Country 2 initial	1	1	0	1	1	0	0	-1	0	0	0	0	0	4	1	8
Country 2 periodic	1	1	0	1	1	0	0	-1	1	1	1	1	1	9	1	3
Country 3 initial	1	1	0	1	1	0	1	1	1	1	1	0	0	9	0	4
Country 3 periodic	1	1	1	0	1	0	0	1	0	0	0	0	0	5	0	8
Country 4 initial	1	1	0	1	1	0	0	-1	1	0	0	0	0	5	1	7
Country 4 periodic	1	1	0	1	1	0	0	-1	0	1	0	0	1	6	1	6
Country 5 initial	1	1	0	0	1	0	1	0	0	1	1	0	1	7	0	6
Country 5 periodic	1	1	0	1	1	1	1	1	1	1	1	1	1	12	0	1
Country 6 initial	1	1	-1	1	1	0	0	0	0	1	0	0	0	5	1	7
Country 6 periodic	1	1	-1	0	0	1	1	1	0	1	1	-1	0	7	2	4
Country 7 initial	1	1	0	1	1	0	0	0	1	0	1	0	0	6	0	7
Country 7 periodic	1	1	0	1	0	0	0	1	0	1	0	1	0	6	0	7
Country 8 initial	1	1	0	0	1	0	0	0	0	1	0	0	0	4	0	9
Country 8 periodic	1	0	1	1	1	0	0	1	0	1	1	0	0	7	0	6
Country 9 initial	1	1	0	0	0	1	0	1	1	1	1	0	1	8	0	5
Country 9 periodic	1	-1	-1	-1	1	0	0	-1	0	0	0	0	1	3	4	6
Country 10 initial	1	1	1	1	1	1	1	0	0	0	0	1	1	9	0	4
Country 10 periodic	1	1	1	1	1	0	1	1	1	1	1	1	1	12	0	1
Country 11 initial	1	1	0	0	0	0	0	1	0	0	0	0	0	3	0	10
Country 11 periodic	1	1	0	1	1	0	1	1	0	0	0	1	0	7	0	6
Total initial														66	4	73
Total periodic														78	11	54

Explanations: First Row 28;1 – 29;5: Paragraphs of the Education Articles 28 and 29; 1 indicates a positive answer was found in the State Party Report; -1 indicates that some information was found of Problems fulfilling the paragraph; 0 says that no information could be found in the State Part Report on this paragraph.

Proposal for an Experimental Reporting System

The inadequacies of States Parties reports regarding the education articles of the Convention were judged to be at least partially due to the need to provide more guidance and structure for the development of reports. Working under this assumption, the authors undertook the construction and testing of an alternative instrument for the development of reports.

The first aims for the experimental system were to simplify the writing of reports and to increase the likelihood reports would produce well-focused, accurate and meaningful results. The primary focus of this project was on the education articles, 28 and 29, of the Convention on the Rights of the Child. The system envisioned would ask directly for answers related specifically to the themes in each paragraph of the education articles. This led to a kind of questionnaire in which expectations were established that data would be provided for all the major standards of the Convention.

Additional aims were set for the new reporting system. It should provide a comprehensive and dependable structure that could be used by different organizations monitoring and reporting on accountability.

This objective would allow comparisons of reports from both governmental as well as non-governmental organizations within the same country. It was also desired that the new reporting system should explore the possibilities of including the data requirements of more than one international agency.

The importance of efficiency, not only in producing a report but also in comprehending a report, must be underlined. In this research it was found that to peruse a State Party Report in order to find information for just one standard took as much as 30–45 minutes, even when using the support of an electronic search engine. Under these conditions a thorough and meaningful review of just the education standards of the Convention would be an extremely inefficient and arduous undertaking. Clearly it will be very difficult to realize the spirit of the Convention unless changes are made. States Parties, national non-governmental organizations, and the Committee on the Rights of the Child will find it hard to be responsible in their monitoring and reporting roles unless improvements are made in the reporting system.

Development and field testing of the experimental reporting system

Numerous steps were taken in developing and testing an experimental reporting system. Second detailed analyses were undertaken for the Convention's education articles (i.e. 28 and 29) and for the education guidelines of International Bureau of Education. All meanings of relevant paragraphs were identified and included in the reporting system. For each resulting item, where appropriate, indications are to be made of the percentage achieving a standard and the type of evidence available to verify this judgment. This procedure allows a simple comparison, statistical analyses, and use by both governmental and non-governmental organizations.

Selections from the Experimental Reporting System are provided in Exhibits 4.1, 4.2, and 4.3. Exhibit 4.1 indicates the type of information required to describe the portion of the child population for whom the report is relevant. Exhibits 4.2 and 4.3 are from the 'Data Summary' section of the Experimental Reporting System and provide indications of the System's manner of dealing with information about the themes of articles 28 and 29. The 'Documentation of Evidence for Data Summary and Commentary' section of the System, not shown here, sets expectations and provides guidance for efficiently documenting supportive law, formal commitments, practices, and measures of achievement and for presenting clarifying comments. The full Experimental Reporting System can be acquired from the authors or accessed through the website of Child Rights Education-International (www.childrightseducation.org).

Throughout the development of the Experimental Reporting System, the International Bureau of Education provided supportive consultation and access to its archives of national reports on education. Two officers of the Danish Ministry of Education cooperated with the first author to test the Experimental Reporting System. They applied the System to organize Danish data on education so that they could give guidance to the System's refinement. The supportive involvement of the Danish Ministry was extremely valuable to this project.

Please indicate the child population for which you are completing this form. It is requested that each State Party to the Convention complete this form for the general child population; and that, in addition, separate reports should be completed for any specific child population for which significant or important differences in conditions exist.

Number of children (6 years – 18 years): ____________

Number of children (6 years – 11 years): ____________

Number of children (12 years – 16 years): ____________

Number of children (17 years to 18 years): ____________

Filled out for: ☐ general population

☐ minority group: ☐ special need children: ____________ (identify)

☐ gender group: ____________ (identify)

☐ minority group: ____________ (identify)

☐ or: ____________ (identify)

Exhibit 4.1: Experimental Reporting System form for indicating relevant population demographics

Article 28, §1 (a): Make primary education compulsory and available free to all.

	Degree to which this goal is achieved for child population (mark one)				Evidence types (mark all relevant)			
Primary education is:	<10%	11–49%	50–90%	91–100%	Law	Commitment	Practices	Measurements of achievement
• compulsory for all								
• available to all								
• free for all								

Article 28, §1 (b): Encourage the development of different forms of secondary education, including general and vocational education, make them available and accessible to every child, and take appropriate measures such as the introduction of free education and offering financial assistance in case of need.

	Degree to which this goal is achieved for school population (mark one)				Evidence types (mark all relevant)			
Development is encouraged to establish:	<10%	11–49%	50–90%	91–100%	Law	Commitment	Practices	Measurements of achievement
• different forms of secondary education								
• secondary education available and accessible to every child								
• financial assistance offered in case of need								

Exhibit 4.2: Examples of Experimental Reporting System's inclusion of standards for article 28

Article 29, §1, (d): The preparation of the child for responsible life in a free society, in the spirit of understanding, peace, tolerance, equality of sexes, and friendship among all peoples, ethnic, national and religious groups and persons of indigenous origin.

	Degree to which this goal is achieved for child population (mark one)				Evidence types (mark all relevant)			
Preparation of the child:	<10%	11–49%	50–90%	91–100%	Law	Commitment	Practices	Measurements of achievement
• for a responsible life in a free society								
• in the spirit of understanding								
• for peace								
• for tolerance								
• for friendship among all peoples, ethnic, national and religious groups and persons of indigenous origin								

Exhibit 4.3: Example of Experimental Reporting System's inclusion of standards of article 29

Results and findings from field testing

The results of the first field test in applying the Experimental Reporting System by the Danish Ministry of Education were quite encouraging. The Ministry official who undertook the task emphasized that the report made it quite simple to give accurate and valid information. Ministry officers are generally working under strong time pressures. They were particularly pleased with the fact that this report required only 40 minutes to complete in total, including identifying the evidence for indicated results.

A comparison between information provided in the initial Danish report to the Committee on the Rights of the Child and the information provided through the use of the Experimental Reporting System found many differences. Although the initial State Party Report of Denmark was better than most of the reports of other States Parties, more specific answers are found in the completed Experimental Reporting System. Statistical information provided by the Ministry in the report makes it simple to calculate the percentage of students attending school and the degree to which teachers and authorities deal with them according to the Convention (dignity, development to the fullest potential, respect for parents). In particular, the detailed reporting structure for article 29 produced more information on each of the themes in its sub-paragraphs.

The Danish application of the Experimental Reporting System shows that even in one of the most developed educational systems the Convention is not fulfilled for all students. The Experimental Reporting System allows the simple indication of the percentage of students for whom requirements are fulfilled, which reveals the percentage for which they are not fulfilled. The full initial Danish report to the Committee on the Rights of the Child may show very similar results but it would have to be read and reread painstakingly to find essential information. Using the Experimental Reporting System, a clearer picture is more quickly available regarding each specific standard and quantitative values are provided which indicate the degree to which the standard is met.

The inclusion of the IBE standards was successful in that the information seems to be easily incorporated by officials. It also should be noted that the Experimental Reporting System could be improved. Through this research with the Danish Ministry it has become apparent that some of the items as presently stated are not likely to produce answers which are sufficiently meaningful. For example, there is an item which requests the responding agency to identify hindering factors for fulfilling the Convention's standards and which provides minority inequality as an option. This item must be better focused through additional detail to be very useful. Further suggestions and strategies for improving questions or items such as this will need to be developed.

Analyses of additional reports written on the basis of the new guidelines of the Committee on the Rights of the Child showed a certain increase of the results but nevertheless many of the same weaknesses as the initial reports. Article 29 in particular was not reported on adequately; again, information on most of the standards was not provided and only one States Party indicated that problems were experienced in fulfilling the standards.

At the first International Conference on Children's Rights in Education (Copenhagen, April 1998), the reporting system was presented to several international experts including the Chair of the Committee on the Rights of the Child. The reactions to this proposed system were very encouraging. From all sides a continuation of this project was supported. As a result of learning about this research and project, the Chairperson of the Committee on the Rights of the Child (at that time, Sandra Mason) formally encouraged collaboration efforts to achieve further advances.

Concluding comments

Good information on the status of education can be used by responsible parties to improve the educational opportunities and the development of young people. A single system for reporting on the national status of education that would incorporate all the standards of importance to international and national interests is possible and practical. The systems which have been used for initial and periodic State Party reports to the UN Committee on the Rights of the Child have been found insufficient for these purposes, but they do have the potential to be integrated and modified to create the envisioned system. The project described herein has attempted to produce such a system and its early results show promise.

Endnote

1 The first 49 countries reporting to the Committee on the Rights of the Child were (in alphabetical order, not order of reporting): Argentina, Belarus, Boliva, Burkina Faso, Canada, Chile, Columbia, Costa Rica, Croatia, Cyprus, Denmark, Egypt, El Salvador, Finland, France, Germany, Holy See, Honderas, Indonesia, Italy, Jamaica, Jordan, Madagascar, Mexico, Mongolia, Nambia, Nicaragua, Norway, Paraquay, Peru, Phillipines, Poland, Portugal, Republic of Korea, Romania, Russian Federation, Rwanda, Senegal, Slovenia, Spain, Sri Lanka, Sudan, Sweden, Tanzania, Tunisia, United Kingdom and Northern Ireland, Ukraine, Viet Nam, Yemen.

References

Committee on the Rights of the Child (1991) *Guidelines regarding reporting for initial State Party Reports and United Nations.* Geneva: United Nations Human Rights Center.

Scherer, L. (1998) *State Party reports on the status of education to the United Nations Committee on the Rights of the Child and the International Bureau of Education: Analyses, comparisons, and a proposition for an experimental reporting system.* Thesis presented to the Faculty of Arts of the University of Zurich. Zurich: University of Zurich.

Scherer, L. and Hart, S. N. (1999) 'Reporting to the UN Committee on the Rights of the Child – analyses of the first 49 State Party Reports on the education articles of the Convention on the Rights of the Child and a proposition for an experimental reporting system for education.' *International Journal of Children's Rights, 7,* 349–363.

UNICEF (1998) *The Convention on the Rights of the Child.* Text and Unofficial Summary. Web page: . 8.9.1998.

United Nations (1991) Convention on the Rights of the Child, Committee on the Rights of the Child: General Guidelines Regarding the Form and Content of Initial Reports to be submitted by States Parties under article 44, Paragraph 1 (a) of the Convention, CRC/C/5, adopted on 15 October 1991.

United Nations (1996) Convention on the Rights of the Child, Committee on the Rights of the Child: General Guidelines regarding the Form and contents of Periodic Reports to be submitted by States Parties under article 44, Paragraph 1 (b) of the Convention, CRC/C/58, adopted on 20 November 1996.

CHAPTER 5

Democratic Education and Children's Rights

F. Clark Power, Ann Marie R. Power, Brenda Light Bredemeir and David Light Shields

The United Nations Convention of the Rights of the Child challenges all of those responsible for the education of children to think in new ways about how to prepare them for democratic citizenship. Article 29 of the United Nations states that education should prepare the child 'for responsible life in a free society'. Other articles note that children have a right to express their views on matters that affect them (article 12) and that children have a right to assemble, raise questions and voice opinions (articles 13 and 15). These articles suggest that educational, political and other societal institutions need to provide opportunities not only for children to express their views but also for them to develop as responsible citizens in a democratic society. Such opportunities are not typically available to children, even in countries that have long histories of democratic government, and will require significant institutional change if they are to be implemented responsibly. Institutional change will also entail careful rethinking of how we understand and care for children.

The development of autonomy in children

Those who are responsible for children's welfare are keenly aware that children lack the competence to make many unilateral decisions that will influence their own welfare or the welfare of others. Children depend upon adults for protection and guidance. For example, adults cannot give children complete freedom about what to eat, where to play, or when to go to school because children lack sufficient knowledge and will to act in their own best interests. The fact that adults must exercise what has traditionally been called a paternalistic role over children does not imply that adults are free to ignore children's preferences and views. If children have inherent rights as persons, then adults who make decisions on children's behalf have an obligation to limit their decision-making to those areas in which children lack competence. Moreover, in deciding what is best for a child, those exercising paternalistic authority must try to take into account what the child would decide if the child were a fully competent adult. As John Rawls (1971) puts it, 'Paternalistic intervention must be justified by the evident failure or absence of reason and will; and it must be guided by principles of justice and what is known about the subject's more permanent aims and preferences...' (p. 250). In his treatment of paternalism, Rawls does not distinguish children from adults who are, for example, experiencing a serious mental illness that renders them incompetent. Adults generally have permanent aims and preferences, children, on the other hand, are in the process of developing enduring aims and preferences. Paternalism towards children must, therefore, take into account that children are developing as autonomous persons.

One way of respecting children's autonomy is to protect them from making decisions social structures that would be harmful to them in the future or that would unnecessarily close off promising options and thereby compromise their autonomy in the future. A concern for autonomy, for example, would seem to dictate that parents sometimes override children's preferences for sweets over vegetables or for playing instead of doing their homework. A concern for autonomy also has implications for the social structures that we provide for children. Schools, for example, can best respect children's autonomy, particularly in the early grades, by avoiding early specialization and providing a basic and balanced curriculum. Children's future possibilities will be greatly enhanced if we cultivate their tastes and aptitudes across the arts and the sciences. A concern for autonomy should make us wary of rigidly 'streaming' or 'tracking' students into career-oriented curricula before they are mature enough to make free and informed decisions about their life paths.

How far should parents and educators go in keeping children's futures open? Should parents, for example, avoid raising children within a particular religious community in order to maximize children's freedom to choose as adults? In the selection of children's educational experiences, should we consistently favour diversity over depth? These questions raise a more fundamental question about the way in which children acquire enduring aims and preferences. The notion that we can decide upon our aims and preferences the same way in which we decide upon merchandise displayed in a mail-order catalogue is a by-product of a consumer-oriented society. We cannot simply pick and choose among possible goods from some value-neutral standpoint. From the very beginning, children are influenced by their culture and by significant others. It is out of the crucible of culturally situated social experience that they form their values and notions of the good life. Before they can choose their values, they have to acquire a 'taste' or an appreciation for what is good. In order to know what is good, children, we believe, need to participate as fully as possible in particular political, religious and social institutions. Adults thus have a responsibility for initiating children into communities that will help children to develop meaningful aims and preferences.

Initiation should not be confused with indoctrination. Indoctrination implies that children will be taught in a way that discourages questioning and criticism. Indoctrination violates children's autonomy because it subverts their freedom and rationality. The challenge of education is to present one's most cherished beliefs and values in a way that is both compelling yet open to reflection and self-appropriation in the future. Education must give children the opportunity and support for self-determination and exploration. Autonomy must be nourished by environments that respect and support children's initiative and self-regulation (Ryan and Deci 2000).

Perhaps the greatest threat to the development of autonomy is the indoctrination into the consumerism and materialism that pervades the cultures of wealthy nations and is encroaching upon the cultures of developing nations. Advertisements bombard children as well as adults with a message that equates happiness and personal fulfilment with the possession of material goods. When the acquisition of material goods becomes one's aim, one's preferences are reduced to choices among material goods or brand names of the same good. Choosing among material goods creates an illusion of autonomy; but individual freedom is confined to the marketplace and to the fulfilment of largely artificial needs and wants. The techniques of persuasion that advertisers employ are largely subliminal, playing on irrational desires and insecurities and undermining reflection and rationally based free choice.

Educating for autonomy requires, we believe, the cultivation of a critical cultural consciousness that will inoculate children to the indoctrination of consumerism. Fostering children's autonomy cannot be attempted through a culturally neutral standpoint because no such standpoint exists. Children are going to develop within particular cultural contexts and all of those contexts are likely to be infected by influences, such as consumerism, that can, if they go unnoticed and unchecked, undermine autonomy and democratic citizenship.

There has been some confusion in psychological literature about the meaning of the term 'autonomy'. For example, Santrock (1998), in his text *Adolescence*, discusses autonomy in the context of the adolescent–parent relationship. While noting that autonomy is a 'complex' and 'elusive' concept, he links autonomy closely to independence. This notion of autonomy is different from its philological meaning – to give oneself the law or in Kantian terms to legislate for one's self (Kant 1785/1964). Independence, of course, presupposes that one is mature enough to make sound decisions for one's self, but autonomy implies much more than this. The notion of autonomy as a legislating activity implies that the individual will make decisions as a free and rational person living in a society of free and rational persons (Rawls 1971). Autonomy can thus be understood as based on moral principles. Some psychologists, however, tend to reduce autonomy to separation from parents or accepting responsibility for one's self, but these notions are too individualistic, insufficiently cognitive, and subject to wide cultural variation.

Although the dynamics of separation undoubtedly play a role in the achievement of autonomy, the dynamics of attachment seem equally relevant, as Santrock (1998), in fact, acknowledges. There is a growing body of research demonstrating that secure attachment to parents fosters adolescents' personal development, including their relationships with peers (e.g. Armsden and Greenberg 1987). Further research emphasizes the role of attachments in providing the security necessary for a sense of well-being, self-esteem, self-confidence and intrinsic motivation (Ryan and Deci 2000). From a cognitive developmental perspective, attachments also provide opportunities for the discussion and role-taking that are indispensable for social and moral development.

Democratic education thus aims to develop autonomous citizens with a sense of agency built on interdependence. Democratic education encourages individuals to think for themselves but not solely of themselves or by themselves when making decisions. Autonomy is both self-regarding and other-regarding. It is self-regarding in the sense that autonomous individuals accept responsibility for their own life goals and pursuits and other-regarding in the sense that autonomous individuals must have respect and regard for others, who are likewise autonomous agents. Autonomous individuals have confidence in their own judgments and effectiveness but recognize the importance of dialogue and relationships.

The challenge of democratic citizenship

A practical approach to democratic education must begin with an understanding of what a democracy entails of its citizens. The word 'democracy' means simply rule by the people. As Aristotle pointed out in *Politics*: 'Democracy is plural.' We can see the many manifestations of democracy throughout the world – from representative government in the USA to direct participatory democracy in Switzerland. Over the past decade, the majority of the countries in the world (61%) have become democratic compared to a minority (42%) only a decade ago. The major shift, of course, has occurred in Eastern Europe and the former Soviet Union. Although the majority of countries in the world now call themselves democratic, many, particularly in Africa and Latin America, are struggling to establish and maintain democratic institutions. Even countries with long traditions of democratic governance, such as the USA, face significant challenges from powerful interest groups and citizen apathy.

The criteria used to classify countries as democratic – free elections and majority rule – are purely descriptive. Yet democracy is more than a particular form of government – democracy represents an ideal of popular participation; we can and do speak of countries as being more or less democratic. Two key criteria for evaluating a particular democracy are (1) the extent of popular participation, and (2) the quality of popular participation. We typically assess the extent of popular participation in terms of voter turn-out, which fails to encompass the wide range of citizenship responsibilities in a democratic society. We generally fail to assess the quality of democratic participation altogether because the quality of democratic participation is difficult to categorize. The quality of democratic participation, we believe, relates to the discourse involved in democratic deliberation. Ideally, being a citizen in a democracy requires interacting with other citizens to construct policies that serve the common good, which is not reducible to the good of the majority. Being a citizen in this full sense requires a developed sense of justice, which the psychologist Kohlberg (1984) regards as the highest stage of moral judgment. Such a sense of justice requires moving beyond one's own self-interest or the interest of one's particular community or society to consider the interests of all.

Education for democracy

Having offered a rough sketch of what democracy entails, we will turn to the question of what kind of education a democracy ought to provide for its citizens. At the very least, citizens needed to be literate. Basic literacy is necessary for voting and for acquiring information. E. D. Hirsch (1987) argues that cultural literacy is also important if citizens are to make informed decisions. Language, whether it is used to preserve the status quo or to foment revolution, draws its power and persuasiveness from a cultural heritage, or more accurately from a multi-cultural heritage. This means that students not only know how to read and write, but that they have acquired a core of knowledge that helps them to understand their history, to assess their present situation, to envision future possibilities, and to communicate effectively.

In addition to literacy and cultural literacy, education should and generally does provide students with factual information about local and national democratic institutions. Such information makes up the content of the common 'civic education' course. This course teaches students about the particular structures of governance and law enforcement, and can go as far as giving students specific information about how to contact government officials and how to address issues at various levels of government.

Typically schools do little more than has been described above to prepare students for democratic citizenship. We seem to assume that if our students are literate and sufficiently informed, they will become good democratic citizens. Yet the evidence suggests otherwise. In the USA, almost half of those eligible do not even vote in Presidential elections, and voter participation among the youngest voters has been steadily declining. Voting for public officials is a minimal form of democratic participation. Yet many young people in democratic societies lack confidence in or feel estranged from the democratic institutions of their society. The term 'political' unfortunately connotes manipulation and corruption by special interests.

If we wish to educate citizens for democracy, then we must ask much more of our schools. Schools ought to inspire children to become involved in the political process and teach them how to deliberate in common. Children must have opportunities to experience in a profound sense their common dignity as free and equal persons, and they must learn how to make decisions together that reflect that dignity, freedom and equality. Democratic participation should be a 'way of life', as John Dewey (1916/1968) put it, and not reduced to formal participation in the political process. Children need to be taught to ask fundamental questions about themselves and their society and see themselves as agents and not simply consumers in their societies.

The kind of education for participation that we are proposing takes into account that children are not born with the competencies or dispositions to act as democratic citizens nor do they acquire them simply through maturation or enculturation. Children, we believe, develop as autonomous, democratic citizens by practising democracy in carefully structured educational contexts. We thus propose that schools and other organizations offer students an apprenticeship in democracy (Power 1992). This idea was first put forward by Horace Mann (1845/1957), the Father of the American Public School:

> In order that men may be prepared for self-government their apprenticeship must begin in childhood... He who has been a serf until the day before he is twenty-one years of age, cannot be an independent citizen after; and it makes no difference whether he has been a serf in Austria or America. As the fitting apprenticeship for despotism consists in being trained for despotism, so the fitting apprenticeship for democracy consists in being trained for self-government.

An apprenticeship involves learning through practice under the guidance of a master. An apprenticeship in democracy entails giving students the opportunity to learn the skills of democratic deliberation in schools and playgrounds with help from their teachers, coaches and other adult mentors.

The use of an apprenticeship approach for civic and moral education is by no means a new idea. Aristotle, building on the ideas of Socrates and Plato, critically examined the implications of the apprenticeship approach over 2000 years ago in the classic *Nicomachean Ethics.* He believed that children acquire the virtues more or less in the way they acquire the skills of craft – through habituation under the guidance of virtuous teachers and within the context of a virtuous community. According to this conception, the apprenticeship approach includes initiation into full communal membership. Children are motivated to acquire the virtues both because the virtues represent the general human excellences most desired by a particular community and because the virtues enable participation in the community. The virtues thus represent the shared expectations of the community and the capacity (or more literally the *virtu* or power) to discharge one's responsibilities as a citizen.

The apprenticeship approach presupposes consensus on the exemplars of craft and character. Although such consensus does appear to exist today on the leading practitioners of various crafts, such as who are the best pianists, basketball players and carpenters, far less consensus exists on those who are distinguished in the moral domain. One difficulty with making judgments of moral worth, as Aristotle recognized, is that such judgments must take into account a person's intentions. We can judge good artists by observing their work and good basketball players by observing their play, but we cannot judge good persons merely by observing them from the outside. The judgment of moral worth must take into account the souls of individuals. Even if we can make reasonably reliable character judgments, we may well disagree on what specific virtues constitute good character, especially in a pluralistic society.

The fact of moral pluralism does not, however, preclude the possibility of some agreement on at least the contours of a description of a good citizen. The political structures and ways of thinking that evolved during centuries of struggling with pluralistic divisions suggest the desirability of cultivating certain 'liberal' virtues, based on the moral principles that undergird the Convention on the Rights of the Child, such as tolerance and respect for freedom of speech and assembly, and democratic virtues, such as political participation. An apprenticeship for democracy would not necessarily require teachers who are paragons of every virtue, but it would require teachers who are committed to the principles of liberal democracy and who are willing to develop democratic classrooms and schools.

The notion of an apprenticeship in democracy appears paradoxical insofar as apprenticeships are hierarchical and democracies are egalitarian. Yet the paradox disappears once the sense of authority is clarified. Neither an apprenticeship nor a democracy relies on the positional authority that teachers exercise simply because they are teachers. In an apprenticeship, masters have authority because they have a demonstrated competence in some area; in a democracy, individuals have authority insofar as they are persuasive. Teachers in an apprenticeship-approach to democratic education have the authority of both expertise and persuasiveness. When democratic programs are being instituted, teachers play a major role establishing decision-making structures and procedural rules of order. They also shoulder the burden of responsibility for setting agendas and chairing the meetings. Furthermore, they are called upon to act as advocates in community meetings for proposals for norms and rules that embody the ideals of democratic community. As advocates, they model democratic behaviour by considering the perspectives of others, giving reasons for their positions, and demonstrating a concern for advancing the common good. Over time, the faculty surrender procedural control to the students, who help to set the agendas, take turns chairing the meetings, and speak for the norms and ideals of the community. With time and faculty support, students eventually demonstrate that they have faith in the democratic process by bringing significant issues to the group and by participating with openness and trust (Power, Higgins and Kohlberg 1989; Power and Power 1992).

The Just Community Approach

In our view, the just community approach, which grew out of the moral developmental theory and research of Kohlberg and his colleagues (Power, Higgins and Kohlberg 1989), exemplifies the apprenticeship model of democratic education. The just community approach involves students and teachers in making and enforcing rules and policies concerning student life and discipline. Rules and policies are established through direct participatory democracy: one person–one vote. The direct participatory democracy of the just community approach differs from the practice common in many high schools and junior high schools of having students elect representatives to a school-wide council. Representative democracy only grants a select group of students the invaluable experience of deliberating in common. Moreover, the students who win elections are often those who are committed to the school and who have relatively well-developed social skills, not the alienated students most in need of the benefits that can accrue through democratic participation.

The democracy established in the just community schools differs from the democracy established in the typical student council in one other important respect: the responsibilities given to the governing body. Student councils typically limit student responsibility to planning social events or to giving advice on selected topics. In the just community approach, students share responsibility for maintaining discipline and a sense of community.

Many teachers and school administrators commonly think of discipline as maintaining social control so that instruction can take place. The treatment of discipline as classroom management in the typical American teacher education curriculum reveals how far discipline has become divorced from the notion of education itself. The origins of most contemporary approaches to classroom management may be traced back to Bagely (1907), who popularized the factory metaphor in describing the classroom as a 'working unit of the school plant', and discipline as effective 'management', designed to 'return the largest dividend upon the material investment of time, energy, and money' (p. 2). Within this framework, he characterized children as the 'raw material' to be turned into a 'desired product' (p.4). This factory metaphor, which represents the antithesis of a democratic approach, persists in the classroom management texts prevalent in teacher training today (e.g. Emmer, Evertson, Clements and Worsham 1994).

A fundamental rethinking of our approach to discipline is needed if we are serious about respecting children's rights and education for democracy. The word 'discipline' is derived from the Latin *discipulus*, meaning disciple or learner. By reducing discipline to management, we fail to recognize that discipline should be a means to democratic education. Although not a proponent of democratic education, Emile Durkheim (1925/1973) recognized the value of discipline for moral and civic education:

> Too often, it is true, people conceive of school discipline so as to preclude endowing it with an important moral function. Some people see in it a simple way of guaranteeing superficial peace

> and order in the class. Under such conditions, one can come to view these imperative requirements as barbarous – as a tyranny of complicated rules... In reality, however, the nature and function of discipline is something altogether different... It is the morality of the classroom... (p. 148)

The just community approach is based, in part, on Durkheim's insight that discipline represents the morality of the classroom and Durkheim's method of moral education, which involves building shared norms and a shared commitment to a classroom community. Durkheim understood that children need to feel that they belong to a group that is worthy of their devotion. The democratic approach with its laborious legislative process provides a very effective way of establishing rules that children regard as their own.

The democratic approach also seems to embody the concern expressed in article 29 of the Convention, which states that 'school discipline should be administered in a manner consistent with the child's human dignity and in conformity with the present Convention'. Respecting the dignity of the child entails not only refraining from certain kinds of disciplinary practices, such as corporal punishment, but engaging in a process that fosters the development of autonomy by giving children a voice in making and enforcing school and classroom rules.

In just communities, the democratic process of deliberation and voting takes place in a weekly community meeting that involves all students and faculty. Kohlberg's (Power, Higgins and Kohlberg 1989) theory of moral development and its educational application in moral discussion classes provide a helpful framework for teachers to think about their role in community meeting deliberations. According to the just community approach, teachers should act as mentors in community meetings, modelling democratic behaviour by considering the perspectives of others, giving reasons for their positions, and demonstrating a concern for advancing the common good. The role of mentor includes that of facilitating student participation in the meetings, but, as noted previously, allows teachers to go further in arguing for proposals that promote shared norms and a sense of community.

The key to a successful just community is winning the confidence of the students, who are not accustomed to democratic deliberation or to being responsible for each other's behaviour. Students must acquire a faith in democracy by discovering in community meetings that the democratic process is a fair and effective way of governance. In the early months of all of the just community experiments, students expressed scepticism or bewilderment that they would have a meaningful voice in the decision-making process or that the process would address concerns that they considered important.

Research with just community programs suggests that through participation in the democratic process, students developed not only a confidence in the democratic process but an understanding of ideal democratic communication (Power, Higgins and Kohlberg 1989). This understanding appears to develop through a sequence of three levels:

> *Level 1*: Individuals feel free to exercise their concrete right to speak their mind and express their private interests.
>
> *Level 2*: Individuals should listen to, take the perspective of, and have respect for each other. Everyone should consider what is best for the majority.
>
> *Level 3*: Individuals should strive for an open dialogue with special concern for the perspective of minorities. Everyone should consider what is best for the community as a whole.

Underlying development and progress through these levels is a widening of perspective-taking. Students initially see the democratic process as a way of pursuing their own interests as individuals or at least as an opportunity to express their opinion (Level 1). They learn very quickly that democracy is more than a sequence of collective monologues; they need to respect and respond to others (Level 2). They also discover that in order to reach a decision, negotiation and compromise will often be necessary. As they make disciplinary rules, students typically begin to think about the community as an entity and about how they are to balance the welfare of the community against the perceived welfare of individuals. For example, students typically want the freedom to 'cut' classes as they see fit but also acknowledge the importance of having an attendance rule. Many students will also admit that not everyone skips class for a good reason and that a weak attendance rule will hurt the school.

One of the most significant achievements at Level 2 is that students accept the importance of submitting to the majority vote. At Level 1 students experience a contradiction between the freedom that comes with self-government and the constraint that comes with submitting to authority, even the authority of the majority. As students recognize that mere disagreement is not sufficient grounds for disobedience, they also recognize that the democratic process is open-ended and that decisions can be changed. As students experience the tensions between the individual and the community, the welfare of the majority and the welfare of the minority, and the power of rhetoric and importance argument, they come to a new understanding of community and the democratic process (Level 3). At Level 3, students develop notions of the community as a whole and the process of communication that lead to new criteria for judging what is best for the group and fair to individuals and to sub-groups.

Development through the three levels is not, in our experience or judgment, necessarily a spontaneous effect of democratic participation. As democratic mentors, teachers use a number of strategies to direct students to become aware of and confront the tensions at each level. The greatest challenge in democratic community meetings is to encourage discussion and to prevent precipitous voting. The most direct way to ensure discussion in the community meeting is to prepare students through preliminary meetings in small groups of 12 to 15 students. These meetings provide an opportunity for teachers to explain the issues that will come before the community and to involve all the students in a thorough discussion. Most just communities also require that before taking a vote on a motion, there must be a straw vote followed by a discussion that gives the minority an opportunity to speak first and to reply to each statement from a member of the majority. This procedure also helps students to move closer to a consensus on many issues and to take into account the perspective of the minority.

Many critics of the just community approach assume that students' and teachers' interests will be opposed and a tyranny of the student majority will result. Experiments with the just community approach have demonstrated that as students come to trust in and understand the democratic process surprisingly few differences surface between teachers and students. In fact, what teachers and students discover, usually to their surprise, is that they are more likely to disagree among themselves than with each other as opposing factions.

In spite of the success of the just community experiments, relatively few teachers and administrators have sought to employ the just community approach or other participatory approaches to discipline in their classrooms and schools. The hesitancy to apply participatory approaches seems rooted to a large extent in the fear that such approaches are far too permissive. Many teachers and administrators tend to equate democracy with laissez-faire neglect. They fail to see democracy as a way of exercising authority and maintaining high expectations. The apprenticeship model presupposes that students need to develop their competencies as democratic citizens while recognizing that practising democracy with assistance from their teacher-mentors is the best way to promote such development.

Two structural obstacles also stand in the way of the implementation of the just community approach: school size and time constraints on the curriculum. Large schools distance students and teachers from each other and make direct participatory democracy impossible. The problem of size can be addressed by establishing living/learning sub-units within large schools, as has been done in 'schools-within-schools' that group approximately 75 students and 4 or 5 teachers and provide a core curriculum. There is a growing consensus among administrators that such sub-units are necessary to combat the alienation and depersonalization brought about in large schools. The problem of time may be more difficult to address. The just community approach requires minimally two hours of meetings per week for all students and an additional two hours for teachers and students who deal with disciplinary cases as members of a judiciary committee. Teachers often complain that they do not have sufficient time to complete the required curriculum, particularly in situations in which they are expected to meet externally imposed criteria. Giving the just community approach a place within the curriculum involves the recognition that an apprenticeship in democracy is a worthwhile part of preparing students for democratic participation.

Democracy and perspective-taking

Democratic decision-making is a powerful means of civic and moral development because it stimulates moral reasoning through perspective-taking. Direct participatory democracy encourages two kinds of perspective-taking: that of other individuals and that of the institution. Individual perspective-taking, which appears to be fundamental to all social cognitive development (Selman 1980; Selman and Schultz 1990), occurs in the exchange of viewpoints that occurs in the deliberative process. Institutional perspective-taking occurs in legislative action, when individuals take responsibility for the community as a whole.

Students who experience alienation because of race, ethnicity, social class, or peer-group status are usually the ones who profit the most from participating in a democratic program. These students take particular delight in the experience of having adults in positions of authority listen to them and take their opinions seriously. Treating these students with respect leads these students to rise to the challenge of democratic citizenship (Higgins 1991).

Research (Power, Higgins and Kohlberg 1989) comparing samples of students in democratic schools with those in the conventional 'parent' high schools demonstrated the effectiveness of direct participative democracy in fostering both types of perspective-taking. Inherent in the development from the first to the second level of ideal democratic communication is an appreciation of the value of individual perspective-taking. Inherent in the development from the second to the third level of ideal democratic communication is institutional perspective-taking. Students in the democratic just community schools were far more inclined to refer to their school and its norms in the collective 'we' mode and to assume a far greater sense of responsibility for the welfare of their school than their peers in the comparison schools. How democratic participation can bring about both kinds of perspective-taking is evident in the following comment from a student member of a discipline committee, who had previously been brought before the committee for skipping classes. He describes how he can now take the perspective of the Assistant Principal, who traditionally had responsibility for enforcing rules:

> It was certainly an eye-opener for me. I was having my own problems and some of those kids would come in with the same stuff. Then I would push myself much harder. I realized what it looked like from the other side. My view of the housemaster has changed radically. He is not much of a tyrant after all... Being on the Disciplinary Committee, I started to feel a little more sorry for him... Being on this really gives you a better view of the high school. It gives you a better idea of what happens in the school. (Kenney 1983, p.277)

Democracy and moral authority

The just community exercise of democracy brings together two views of authority in moral education. One, broadly speaking, is Socratic. According to this view, only truth has authority, and truth is to be found in rational dialogue. Socratic moral education is essential in multi-cultural societies and a multi-cultural world because it is directed at what is universal. The second view of authority is broadly speaking Durkheimian. Durkheim (1925/1973) describes authority as a quality in which a being is regarded as having 'superior power (whether that power is real or imaginary)' (p.88). For Durkheim the only being with moral power is 'the collective being' or society: 'It is therefore from society that all authority emanates' (p.91). If society is the god-like source of morality, then Durkheim thought that the teacher should be the 'priest' of society: 'Just as the priest is the interpreter of God, he is the interpreter of the great moral ideas of his time and country' (p.155). In just communities, authority is mediated not through a teacher-priest but through the decisions of the democratic majority. The decisions made in democratic community meetings and the shared norms and values of the school culture are the expressions of that authority.

In order to illustrate how this Durkheimian notion of the sacredness of authority can be generated by a democratic community, consider the following statement from Arnold, a student in one of the just community experimental schools. He objected to changing a rule, not because he thought the change was unreasonable, but because he thought the practice of constantly changing the rules constituted a 'sacrilege':

> I myself am tired of the idea of having the rules bent and putting ourselves behind and also making our ethics sacrilegious to what we believe in, so I want the rules not to be bent, even if they are right or wrong... (Power, Higgins and Kohlberg 1989)

Note that Arnold proposes leaving the rules as they are, 'even if they are right or wrong'. He is understandably concerned that the authority of the community will erode if everyone tries to change the rules for his or her own purposes. If the community is to function, then its members must respect the rules they have made. The danger of such thinking is that the rules may become so sacred that no one will question them.

Arnold's statement illustrates a paradox of democratic rule. On the one hand, democracy attempts to institutionalize the kind of free and rational dialogue practiced by Socrates. On the other hand, the rules made by democratic majorities can become 'sacred' or 'social facts' beyond rational criticism. The challenge of the apprenticeship approach to educating for democracy is to teach respect for the authority of the majority will in a way that also teaches respect for the principles that regulate the democratic process.

The transition from just community school to democratic societies

The extent to which the just community programmes have promoted lasting democratic attitudes and behaviour has not yet been studied in a systematic fashion. A study of the graduates of the first just community alternative high school, Cluster School, by Grady (1994), however, sheds some light on this issue. Grady interviewed a sample of 30 alumni approximately 10 years after they had graduated from Cluster School and compared them with a matched group from the regular high school. She found that Cluster graduates were significantly more likely than those in the comparison group to report that their high school experience enhanced respect for women and minorities. The Cluster graduates were also more likely to be interested in politics and national affairs; have voted in local elections; have a concern for local government decisions; and have worked with others in a community to solve community problems. She also found that 63 per cent of Cluster graduates in contrast with 5 per cent of their peers found that their experience in school helped them to feel more self-confident, self-directive and efficacious in socio-political situations. Here are some of their comments:

> I learned about democracy, that when I feel strongly about something that I can stand up and state my opinions and not be afraid. I became more confident and had more self-esteem.
>
> I challenged myself to take control of situations in that program and that helped me in life. Cluster was a microcosm of the world I later entered, so I was prepared for real-life situations. I truly learned to become a responsible leader. (p.145)

The just community approach appears to play a significant role in empowering civic participation in adulthood and in helping students to be more sensitive to the concerns of the disenfranchised. On the other hand, there is no evidence that the just community approach in itself equips students to deal with the complexities and moral ambiguities of their government, particularly at the national level. Children need to become aware of how power and influence are wielded in their society and how the democratic process can be made accessible to all. Freire's (1973) consciousness-raising approach through literacy education exemplifies how to help students to reflect on their concrete experiences in ways that will lead to transformative political action.

Education for democracy in the extra curriculum

Although we should do all that we can to make schools more democratic, we should also be aware of the many possibilities for democratic education outside of the formal school curriculum. Perhaps the most promising, but largely unexplored, possibilities for democratic education exist within the extra curriculum of sports, clubs and activities sponsored by schools and community agencies. Extra-curricular activities typically provide students with an experience of face-to-face community. Moreover, students generally play a significant role in the organization and governance of extra-curricular activities. Teachers typically report that they deal more comfortably and effectively with students in after-school activities than in the classroom. Students confirm this, noting that their teachers are far more approachable in their roles of moderators and coaches.

Students have a value and voice in the extra curriculum that they are unlikely to have in school. The functioning of extra-curricular activities depends to a large extent on students' leadership and contributions, as is evident in activities such as the band, the newspaper, and sports teams. In contrast, the functioning of the curriculum seems to depend primarily on the teachers' initiative with students playing a more passive and largely reactive role. There are, of course, exceptions, particularly in the area of sports; but as a rule the extra curriculum is by its very nature a voluntary organization constituted to provide a high degree of child participation.

One of the most significant extra-curricular activities for promoting the development of democratic attitudes and values is community service (see Barber 1992 and Youniss 1997). Power and Khmelkov's (1999) longitudinal analysis of a representative sample of American high-school students shows that community service influences students' commitment to help others and to combat social inequality. Community service activities are a particularly effective avenue of democratic education. They stimulate cognitive socio-moral development by providing opportunities for understanding the perspectives of those who are often at the margins of society, the poor, the sick and the elderly. Such understanding entails not only getting to know individuals, but the social circumstances in which they live. As Power and Khmelkov's (1999) research shows, community service can teach students not only the value of helping at the interpersonal level but of addressing issues at the level of social structures. Community service seems to be habit forming. Once children and adolescents are introduced to community service, they usually remain involved. By serving, they feel that they can play a valued and responsible role in society. In this way, community service can have a profound influence on their identity development.

Of all of the extra-curricular activities, organized sports appear to have the least potential for fostering autonomy and democratic. All too often youth sports are dominated by authoritarian coaches, who foster a militaristic obedience among their players. Shields and Bredemeir (1995), however, suggest that the basic tenets of the just community approach are suitable for use with sport teams, as coaches can build a sense of moral community and empower athletes to assume responsibility for the discipline and shared life of the team. Much depends, of course, on the emphasis that coaches give to promoting fairness, cooperation and self-direction.

As the nations of the world become more democratic and seek to recognize the rights of children, we must pursue methods of education for democracy as vigorously as possible. We believe that the means of educating for democracy must be consistent with the end of democratic participation. Thus, we have emphasized the importance of democratic education. We have the resources at our disposal to provide our children with an apprenticeship in democracy. That apprenticeship will enable children not only to reach their full potential as individuals but to become responsible citizens in an international community of nations that is becoming increasingly more democratic.

References

Aristotle (1985) *Nicomachean ethics* (T. Irwin, Trans.). Indianapolis, IN: Hackett.

Aristotle (1988) *Politics* (C.D.C. Reeve, Trans.). Indianapolis, IN: Hackett.

Armsden, G. and Greenberg, M. T. (1987) 'The inventory of parent and peer attachment: Individual differences and their relationship to psychological well-being in adolescence.' *Journal for Youth and Adolescence, 16*, 427–454.

Bagley, W. C. (1914) *Classroom management: Its principles and technique.* New York: Macmillan.

Barber, B. R. (1992) *An aristocracy of everyone: The politics of education and the future of America.* New York: Ballantine Books.

Dewey, J. (1916/1968) *Democracy and education.* New York: The Free Press.

Durkheim, E. (1925/1973) *Moral education: A study in the theory and application of the sociology of education.* New York: Free Press.

Emmer, E. T., Evertson, C. M., Clements, B. S. and Worsham, M. E. (1994) *Classroom management for secondary teachers.* Boston: Allyn and BACON.

Freire, P. (1973) *Pedagogy of the oppressed.* New York: Seabury.

Grady, E. A. (1994) 'After Cluster School: A study of the impact in adulthood of a moral education intervention project.' Unpublished doctoral dissertation, Harvard University.

Higgins, A. (1991) 'The just community approach to moral education: Evolution of the idea and recent findings.' In William M. Kurtines and Jacob L. Gewirtz (eds) *Handbook of moral behavior and development, Volume 3: Application.* Hillsdale, New Jersey: Lawrence Earlbaum Associates.

Hirsch, E. D. (1987) *Cultural literacy: What every American needs to know.* Boston: Houghton Mifflin.

Kant, Immanuel (1785/1964) *Groundwork of the metaphysic of morals* (trans. H. J. Paton). New York: Harper and Row.

Kenney, R. (1983) 'The creation of a democratic high school: A psychological approach.' Unpublished doctoral dissertation, Boston University.

Kohlberg, L. (1984) *Essays on Moral Development, Volume II: The Psychology of Moral Development.* New York: Harper and Row.

Mann, H. (1845/1957) *The republic and the school; the education of free men.* New York, Teachers College, Columbia University.

Power, F. C. (1992) 'An apprenticeship in democracy: The just community approach to civic education.' *Curriculum,* 13(3), 188–195.

Power, A. M. R. and Khmelkov, V. T. (1999) 'The effects of social participation on high school students' social responsibility.' *Research in Sociology of education and Socialization,* 12, 185–210.

Power, F. C., Higgins, A. and Kohlberg, L. (1989) *Lawrence Kohlberg's approach to moral education.* New York: Columbia University Press.

Power, F. C. and Power, A. M. R. (1992) 'A raft of hope: Democratic education and the challenge of pluralism.' *Journal of Moral Education,* 21, 193–205.

Rawls, J. (1971) *A Theory of Justice.* Cambridge MA: Harvard University Press.

Ryan, R. M. and Deci, E. L. (2000) 'Self-determination theory and the facilitation of intrinsic motivation, social development, and well-being.' *American Psychologist,* 55 (1), 68–78.

Santrock, J. W. (1998) *Adolescence* (7th ed.). Boston: McGraw-Hill.

Selman, R.L. (1980) *The growth of interpersonal understanding.* New York: Academic Press.

Selman, R.L. and Schultz, L.H. (1990) *Making a friend in youth: Developmental theory and pair therapy.* Chicago: University of Chicago Press.

Shields, D. and Bredemeir, B. (1995) *Character development and physical activity.* Champaign, IL: Human Kinetics.

Youniss, J. (1997) *Community service and social responsibility in youth.* Chicago: University of Chicago Press.

CHAPTER 6

Rights of the Child with Special Needs

From rights to obligations and responsibilities

Lena Saleh

Introduction

The rights of the sizeable group of children with special needs of many different sorts require attention. These rights can be defined as just claims that are legally and morally binding on others. It is useful and necessary to consider upon whom each right in question poses a claim or imposes an obligation. This helps to ensure that the 'rights of the child' will not be reduced to a popular and appealing slogan, when what obviously should be done is to transform this powerful idea into a programme of action on behalf of children.

Nobody is against the rights of the child in the abstract. This was demonstrated by the record speed with which governments adopted the Convention on the Rights of the Child. However, action to ensure the enjoyment of the rights guaranteed in international conventions and covenants, especially as regards children who for whatever reason are difficult to reach or serve, usually falls short – often far short – of official rhetoric. The rights of children in education are willingly acknowledged, but the obligations that these rights impose upon governments, societies, communities, families and individuals often tend to be ignored or minimized.

In many countries, a large number of children are still excluded from school and in other countries and communities they are inadequately served by over-burdened institutions that have mastered the rhetoric of inclusion, but not its content, meaning and spirit. In this article, emphasis will be given not only to the rights of the child, but also – and particularly – to the obligations and responsibilities that such rights impose upon individuals, institutions and society as a whole. Particular reference will be given here to the situation of all children who continue to face barriers to learning, whether because they are unreached by educational provision, inadequately served, marginalized or excluded. This population is substantial and its needs indeed are diverse. The number of out-of-school children of primary-school age alone exceeds 100 million. If we include older children or those enrolled in school, but inadequately served by the institutions they attend, the number would be several times greater. Thus, the issue this article addresses is highly significant both for the children involved and for society as a whole because, if it does not take prompt corrective action, it will be denied the economic and social benefits that would derive from providing these hundreds of millions of children and youths with an adequate education.

Terminology and definitions

The terminology used in the field of special needs education tends to be problematic and subject to change. Indeed, although carefully selected to avoid misunderstandings, these tend to arise as soon as the terminology comes into general use. Furthermore, a change in terminology does not necessarily mean that meanings, concepts and practices are changing. However, the use of terminology has and continues to have an impact on educators, educational personnel and society at large. Language influences values and attitudes in both negative but also positive ways – facilitating change and bringing about new attitudes. Therefore, it is important to work towards a common understanding of the language and terminology used, especially in this age where ideas and words travel fast.

In regard to children, no one supports the idea that there are two different definable groups, 'regular' and 'special'. It can be agreed that there is infinite diversity among children and among the environments in which they live and learn. The more facilitating and accommodating the environment is to the needs of children, the fewer barriers there will be to children's development and learning. The essential message is that human differences are normal and their range extensive. Every human being is unique. This diversity imposes a need to suit education to the needs of the individual child.

Traditionally, special needs education has included – and has been largely limited to – those children with a range of physical, sensory, intellectual or emotional difficulties. Today, this has considerably widened to include all children who, for whatever reason, continue to face barriers to learning. This is evidently a sizeable population comprising, in most countries, 10–15 per cent or more of the school-age population.

The current vision is based on a recognition, supported by empirical research, that difficulties which impair and impede learning reside not only within students, but also within the environments in which they are living and endeavouring to learn. In many cases, especially in developing countries, the problems of affected children are the consequences of difficult conditions. Poverty, chronic malnutrition, child labour, homelessness, institutionalization, violence and abuse continue to affect hundreds of millions of children. For some children, other difficulties represent major obstacles to learning, such as situations where the language of the home is different than, sometimes even unrelated to, the medium of instruction used in the school or where, for a variety of reasons, the home and community environments provide little support for schooling. Often the most significant barriers to inclusive education are the negative attitudes and habits that prevail within schools and in the education system as a whole. The continuing use of ability grouping and the unfounded negative attitudes concerning inclusive policies are often pervasive and difficult to overcome.

It is critically important to recognize that this era is witnessing a profound transformation, the emergence of a knowledge society: a society in which knowledge more than capital or raw materials will become the key economic resource and a social order in which inequalities based on knowledge will play a growing role in determining social and economic inequalities. In this context, it becomes especially vital to provide all children with an appropriate education as a means for effective participation in society. Indeed, education becomes society's first line of defence against exclusion. Unless effective measures are taken to address the learning needs of all children at an early age, there is a clear danger that learning challenges will be converted into long-term social and economic disadvantages for the individuals concerned as well as for the society as a whole. This is essential for any society that wishes to become or remain democratic, participatory and inclusive.

Inclusion – a right, not a privilege

The right to an inclusive education is not set out as such in the United Nations Convention on the Rights of the Child. It is nonetheless implicit in the provisions of the Convention. While the right of the child with a disability to the 'fullest possible social integration and individual development, including his or her cultural and spiritual development' is made explicit in article 23, its purpose is to reinforce, not to replace, other provisions of the convention. The Preamble, by recognizing the right of children 'in exceptionally difficult conditions' to receive 'special consideration', emphasizes that article 23 is intended to provide additional protection, above and beyond the rights ensured to all children, and does not stand alone as a separate provision or charter for children with disabilities. Thus, to comprehend the rights of children with special needs, one must examine the provisions of the Convention as a whole and not become focused on Article 23 alone.

Many of the Convention's articles are readily apparent in their support of inclusion. Article 2 prohibits discrimination based on disability, article 6 requires assurance of development of the child to the maximum extent, article 3 indicates the best interests of the child shall be a primary consideration in all actions concerning children, articles 9, 10 and 18 emphasize that children should not be separated from their parents, and article 30 recognizes the right of the child to participate fully in the culture of the community. Articles 28 and 29, which are specific to education, imply clear support for inclusion in education through requiring that States make 'primary education compulsory and available free to all', that different forms of secondary education be 'accessible to every child', and set as the purpose of education 'the development of the child's personality, talents and mental and physical abilities to their fullest potential'.

The Convention, in brief, insists that children must be seen as individuals with rights, views and feelings of their own. Every child has a right to respect, dignity and consideration of his or her views and best interests. Taken together, its provisions concerning the family, the community, the right to social integration and personal development constitute and justify a right to inclusive education, including, *inter alia*:

- the right of the child to attend his or her community school
- the right to live and study with peers of his or her own age

- the right to have access to the same curriculum
- the right to participate in leisure and extra-curricular activities
- the right to make choices concerning his or her learning, such as the selection of the learning environment best adapted to his or her needs
- the right to have access to available support, of whatever form, if and when needed
- the right to live within his or her family.

The Salamanca Statement, issued by the World Conference on Special Needs Education (UNESCO 1994), provides further support to this human rights perspective. It asserts that inclusion and participation are essential to human dignity and the enjoyment and exercise of human rights. Both the Convention and the Statement thus give international authority to endorsing the principle of inclusion as a human right.

The spirit guiding the Convention is that children with disabilities are, first and foremost, children like all other children. Logically, as recognized in the Preamble, the more vulnerable the child, the greater is his or her claim to protection. At a minimum, a child with a disability or other special condition has a right to a treatment equal to that accorded to other children, including the right to attend the community school and participate in all its programmes and activities. And in fact, he or she may make a valid claim to additional services and resources in order to promote a greater equality of educational and social outcomes.

The evolution of special needs education

It is useful to distinguish between the situation in industrialized and developing countries. While the experience of the former has had an impact on the latter, the differences in prevailing attitudes, circumstances and practices remain significant.

Industralized countries

In industrialized countries early efforts of provision for disabled people focused on care and protection, which were very medically dominated, and usually overseen by the medical and social services. Special institutions, separating individuals completely from their families and communities, from which education was absent were created. Emphasis was on diagnosing, sorting and labelling individuals with different types and degrees of disabilities. For a long time the focus of service planning, provision and staff training remained on the individual and his or her deficiencies, while relatively little attention was given to obstacles imposed by social institutions and attitudes. The involvement of the regular school system in the education of those with recognized disabilities was generally quite limited. In fact, many 'progressive' countries prided themselves on sparing children with disabilities the stress of competing with 'normal' children in regular schools. Equally, parents were left out of this equation.

Related thinking began to change in the late 1960s and the 1970s. This was prompted by both social and educational factors, including the mobilization of parents demanding equal rights to education for their children, support for the normalization movement first expounded in Sweden, the civil rights movement in the USA, and the anti-institutionalization movement in Italy.

By the 1980s new legislation emerged entrusting education authorities with responsibility for educating children with various forms of disabilities, and the doors of the regular school slowly began to open to them. Moreover, persons with disabilities drew inspiration from the climate of protest that spread through societies at the end of the 1960s and began to demand a dominant voice in the decisions that society made concerning them. They did not want sympathy or charity; they wanted to be heard and, above all, to be included. Education and other programmes were no longer to be judged on how successfully they sheltered people, but on the opportunities they provided for participation, empowerment and full inclusion in society.

Developing countries

In developing countries the situation was both different and in many ways more favourable. Indigenous societies never adopted the Western practice of excluding persons with disabilities by bundling them into asylums and later into specialized schools. Kisanji (1998) argues that indigenous customary education 'was based on strong family ties, the value of the individual person, co-existence and survival'. It was a pervasive form of education available and accessible to all community members, without distinction. It took place throughout the community and throughout the day: the life of the community was, in fact, its curriculum. Anyone present was included. Through colonial relations, Western practices inevitably had an impact on non-Western societies. Specialized schools were established in most countries, but their coverage was limited by both the strength of tradition and the low levels of educational investment prior to independence. However, in the first years of their independence, many developing countries copied Western models and drew upon Western expertise and technical assistance to establish such institutions. Fortunately, as the lessons learned in the West travelled, this trend has now been arrested in most countries and the principle of inclusion is reasserting itself in education.

Presently, the major problem in providing inclusive education of quality in the developing world is a serious shortage of resources: teachers, learning materials, adequate buildings and, in many countries, a complete absence of support systems of any kind. The extreme shortage of trained teachers poses a serious problem for all students – and especially for those who require special attention of any type. Many teachers have less than a secondary education. Classes of 50 or 60 students are common and classes of over 80 or more students are not unknown.

Thus, while the developing world has fewer psychological barriers to inclusive education, and has lessons to teach in regard to the use of students as peer teachers and the practices of learning by doing, it has extremely serious resource constraints that make it difficult to cater for individual needs. The developed world must give priority to the development of its overall education systems with special attention to the education and training of teachers. Within teacher education, attention should be given to ways of managing learning in large classes made up of highly diverse students that permit a higher degree of individual attention and help.

Toward inclusion

Inclusive education has grown in influence in an increasing number of countries It involves a fundamental rethinking of the meaning and purpose of education for all children and young people, and the part that schools play in the life of the community. Inclusive education is about a school for all, a school where everyone belongs, is accepted, supports and is supported by his or her peers and other members of the school community.

The orientation toward inclusion is clearly presented as the guiding principle of the Salamanca Statement and Framework for Action (UNESCO 1994). Article 2 of the statement stipulates that regular schools with an inclusive orientation are:

> ...the most effective means of combating discriminatory attitudes, creating welcoming communities, building an inclusive society and achieving education for all: moreover, they provide an effective education to the majority of children and improve the efficiency and cost-effectiveness of the entire education system.

Inclusive schools have to operate supportive classrooms and programmes that include and meet the needs of everybody; the biggest challenge is to maximize the participation of all learners. However, to do so requires genuine changes in all aspects of the school's programmes – curriculum, pedagogy, organization, assessment, staffing, school ethos and school support.

Economic aspect

From an economic point of view, the inclusive school has everything to recommend it. Unit costs are far lower than in specialized institutions and, by facilitating the integration of people with special needs into society, these schools can achieve long-term economies on social costs. While these potentials exist, the actual social benefits and economies will depend on how successfully the school fulfils its role in providing effective education and good educational management.

From rights to obligations and responsibilities

Obligations of parents

The active involvement of parents is at the heart of efforts to achieve schools that are effective and inclusive. Both the Universal Declaration of Human Rights and the Convention on the Rights of the Child recognize the rights of parents to guide and be involved in the education of their children (see particularly the Preamble and article 2). Thus, the rights of parents are well established both in international instruments and in the national laws that inspired those instruments or were derived from them.

What are the obligations that accompany these rights? Among them is the duty of the parent to care for, protect and promote the well-being and development of the child entrusted to them, thereby making them the partner of the school. To fulfil this role, the parent needs honest, accurate information and positive suggestions for action. Additionally, the parent should be an important source of information and insights about the child, including his or her needs and aspirations, hopes and fears, abilities and challenges. The parent, in brief, has to be a full and respected partner in the education of the child.

To assure a successful partnership between a parent and the school, the parent must be involved at all stages of the planning, implementation and evaluation of the education of their child. This could be facilitated through helping parents develop their capacities for wider participation in their child's education and for asserting their rights and their responsibilities. For parents of children with special needs, the obligation to be well informed and, where needed, guided by professional opinion in the decisions they make concerning their children assumes particular importance.

Parents also have an obligation to be effective advocates of the interests of their child. This may mean making the child's interests known to others and, in some cases, mobilizing the support that the child requires. Additionally, parents should consider participating in the development and activities of parent associations and advocacy groups of those with similar interests to work toward improving the education of their children and children in general.

Obligations of teachers and schools

> The challenge now is to formulate requirements of a 'school for all'. All children and young people of the world...have the right to education. It is not our education systems that have a right to certain types of children. It is the school systems of a country that must be adjusted to meet the needs of all children. (Lindqvist 1994)

This quotation expresses the prevailing thought and philosophy that informs the quest for inclusive education, yet most of the world's schools are still inadequately prepared to meet successfully the challenge of adapting education to the needs of all children. What, then, must be done to correct this situation and who must do it? There are a number of factors and patterns associated with successful inclusive schools that suggest the steps that need to be taken. They are related particularly to the characteristics and conditions of teachers, the organization and leadership of the school, including the role of the head teacher, and the curriculum of the school.

Teachers

The success of inclusive schools depends, above all else, on the attitudes, commitment and competence of teachers. One factor contributing to the slow development towards inclusive schooling has been and continues to be the belief on the part of teachers that the education of children with special needs is 'special'. The terms 'special education' and 'special teachers' has made this area so 'special' that it has been seen as a field only for very qualified specialists, of whom there are very few in developing countries, and maybe an excess in industrialized countries. There is too much mystification around the skills required and who can acquire them. What is needed is for all teachers in all classrooms to feel confident in working with all children, no matter in what shapes or conditions they come.

The role assigned to resource teachers with expertise in special needs education is also important, but inclusive education cannot be built on their efforts alone. Their help and encouragement can be of critical importance if they are used as resources for assisting and advising classroom teachers. However, if they are given primary responsibility in or outside of integrated classes for a group of children considered to have special needs, experience suggests that it will impede progress towards authentic inclusion. One set of barriers, segregated classes, will simply have been replaced with another subtler set of barriers, segregation within classrooms. Avoiding this pretence at inclusion requires knowledge of how to address and respond to the diversity of needs, not only knowledge of 'traditional special education' but also knowledge of how to manage diverse classrooms, how to encourage and nurture participation, how to adjust the curriculum and allow individual students to have the time each needs to master particular learning tasks. The success of inclusive schools depends upon the involvement of all teachers and staff working with a sense of common purpose to support the learning needs of all children. This must be supported by the conviction that special needs education incorporates proven principles of sound pedagogy from which all children may benefit and the assumption that a considerable range of human differences are normal, thus requiring that teaching be adapted to the needs of the child.

An essential underlying assumption to this vision is that child-centred schools are a training ground for a people-oriented society that respects the differences and dignity of all human beings. To implement this perspective, teachers must achieve supportive professional development, such as mastery of new and/or improved methods and practices, an awareness of the issues at stake, and a moral and social commitment to the education of all children as an essential step in the development of an inclusive and participatory society. To establish these conditions, there is a continuing need for effective pre-service and in-service training of teachers to enable them to view student differences positively, manage diverse classrooms, assess needs, individualize teaching procedures, adapt subject matter, use developing technology, and assure relevance to child and societal interests. Additionally, inclusive schools call for a stronger sense of teamwork and partnership among teachers, parents and the community, which must be supported by teacher education and facilitating school conditions.

School organization and leadership

Schools will be most successful if the entire institution is defined to support and assist all students and teachers to meet established goals for learning and teaching effectiveness. The organization of support services plays a critical role in achieving successful operation through inclusive schools. Today, special education support is defined not as a placement or separate programme, but as a system of support provided to address the learning needs of some students. Successful inclusive schools provide both supportive services for children with special needs and the opportunity to have full membership in the social and learning context of their peers.

In accomplishing these inclusive and supportive conditions, it is the quality more than the quantity of services that requires priority. Rather than directly aiding one or two students with special needs, emphasis should be given to having specialized teachers work with classroom teachers to develop approaches that will enable such students to be included in normal classroom activities. Additionally, services should be organized so that school managers, including teachers, will make flexible use of personnel and resources, develop new resources, apply child-to-child help and increase the involvement of parents in serving student development and learning.

The role of the head or supervising teacher is fundamental to this process. They have an important influence on the culture of the school through the management strategies they use and the values and beliefs their action encourages. It is essential that those selected for this role be committed to and explicitly and implicitly behave in support of a philosophy and policies that facilitate the necessary climate herein described.

Achieving the goals of inclusive education calls for leadership of a high order. This is expected in the head teacher, but it requires more than direction by a single individual. The collective will of the school community and the system must be applied to make inclusive education work. Indeed, the most essential skills of leadership are team building and the development of a shared set of purposes and values that enables communities to come together and strive to achieve common goals. In the case of inclusive schools, the unifying goals and beliefs are: that every child can learn; a commitment to enabling every child to do so; an openness to new approaches, even if they run the risk of failure; an awareness that it is not only students who must learn, but also teachers and the system as a whole; and a commitment to excellence and to continuing improvement through staff development and participation.

Curriculum

A curriculum and system of instruction to meet the challenges of inclusive education allows for:

- students with extraordinary gifts and talents to move at their natural learning rate
- students who progress slower than the average to move at the best of their ability (while still being part of the exciting content of the themes and lessons)
- students with specific learning challenges to receive creative and effective support to maximize their success.

Various additional supportive elements deserve consideration. Continuous assessment of learning with appropriate student and parent involvement is one. It may be strengthened in some cases by use of student portfolios rather than traditional exams because they demonstrate the progress of each child toward the goals that have been set for him or her, rather than sorting students. Porter (1994) suggests a number of other dimensions that characterize inclusive schools:

- special educators in the role of resources for serving all students and teachers within a school
- multi-level instruction to provide greater flexibility in matching learning tasks to student abilities and needs
- cooperative learning, peer tutoring and support groups to provide greater assistance and encouragement to students
- collaborative problem-solving
- continuing staff development.

Obligations of the community

Inclusive schooling has to concern, be valued by and draw upon the good will and resources of the entire community. Even when school is in session, students spend the majority of their time in their homes or elsewhere in the community. They also seek their futures in the community. The community, if it truly seeks to promote an inclusive society, has a moral obligation to support inclusive schools, to believe in and celebrate diversity and equality.

Support calls not only for silent approval, but also for the active participation of non-governmental organizations and other forms of voluntary organizations, which can be effective in promoting community support. They possess specialized knowledge, which they can individually and collectively apply to action aimed at achieving the inclusion and participation of all.

Advocating and promoting the rights of children, especially those with special needs, is a civic duty and obligation incumbent upon all citizens and the community as a whole. Furthermore, community-based programmes, which are designed and run by community participation and support, provide proof that communities can be effectively mobilized to support children's rights and development. Decentralization and local area-based planning enhances greater involvement of communities in development that affects children's everyday lives and allows for resources to be used more effectively at the community level. Successful community mobilization and participation can be an important source of moral and material support for inclusive education.

Obligations of government

The Salamanca Statement (UNESCO, 1994) calls upon governments, *inter alia*, to:

> give the highest policy and budgetary priority to improve their education systems to enable them to include all children regardless of individual differences or difficulties; adopt as a matter of law or policy the principle of inclusive education, enrolling all children in regular schools, unless there are compelling reasons for doing otherwise; establish decentralized and participatory mechanisms for planning, monitoring and evaluating educational provision for children and adults with special educational needs; and encourage and facilitate the participation of parents, communities and organizations of persons with disabilities in the planning and decision-making processes concerning provision.

These recommendations are intended to establish interlinked systems of support upon which inclusive community schools can be established and thrive. Government – the organ through which the collective will of the people is expressed – has an obligation to ensure that effective support systems are available to assist and sustain the institutions that serve the people, including the necessary overall policy framework and financial support. Governments must ensure that adequate means are available to support teachers in their professional development and that the education system as a whole is in harmony with the aims of that training.

The favourable worldwide trend towards decentralization does not change the essential and inherent responsibility of governments to ensure, directly or indirectly, that all citizens have access to education suited to their particular requirements and needs. Government policy speaks to a wide range of important issues and concerns in education: the design of school buildings, the levels of equipment and learning supplies, staffing levels and qualifications, the availability of technical aids (such as Braille) and much else. Some of these requirements and services have a direct impact on schools. Others are less apparent but also important: the provision of expertise in a wide range of professional and management skills, research and development support, policy formulation and review, and public information services. The critical point is that essential support services must be made conveniently available to all schools. Equally, schools and communities should have an active voice in defining the types of assistance needed and evaluating their effectiveness and impact. Government can render an important service to schools through policies that encourage their autonomy and promote the active participation of parents and community organizations in their educational processes.

Resources

Resources are crucial to the development of education and to it becoming more inclusive. Where resources are placed and how they are allocated must be considered in this context. If resources are targeted to specific children, the responsibility of the school as well as the classroom teacher is blocked, but more importantly the child will tend to be isolated. The channelling of funds for separate committees, specific agencies and ear-marked for specific children is one way of maintaining the present rupture within the system. If we believe that schools can and should serve a heterogeneous population of students, provision will have to be made for support services at the district and local levels.

Obligations of the international community

The international challenge to education is only partially understood by knowing that nearly all of the more than 100 million out-of-school children in the 6–12 age group reside in developing countries; millions of them are children with special needs. Even more dramatic are the facts that in developing countries: enrolment in schools is concentrated in the first or second primary grades with high rates of grade repetition – many children probably derive little benefit from that experience; schools are over-crowded and under-equipped; untrained or under-trained teachers must often cope with 60 or more students per class; and basic equipment and supplies are in critically short supply. It is evident that the first priority for inclusive education should be assuring that all children have a school to attend and a good chance of obtaining at least a basic education. The countries with the highest number of out-of-school children tend to be the poorest. There is clearly an enormous need for the international community to accept its obligation to provide assistance in a manner that reaches those in greatest need and supports their efforts to build a sustainable future. The Salamanca Statement (UNESCO 1994) makes a strongly justified appeal to the international community, including a call for an exchange of experience among countries – and especially with and among developing countries – to ensure that lessons learned and progress gained in one country in the struggle to achieve inclusive education may benefit all countries.

A societal commitment

The required response to the challenges and needs described herein is not to be found in a set of technical tasks left to the professionals. Indeed, nothing could be further from the mark. As UNESCO's Director-General, Mr Federico Mayor, has rightly noted:

> Special needs education cannot advance in isolation. It must be part of an overall educational strategy and, indeed, of new social and economic policies... What is required is a commitment and political will to bring about change – change in human attitudes and behaviour and the modification of development strategies. Through Education for All, it should be possible to enable all human beings – including the disabled – to develop their full potential, to contribute to society and, above all, to be enriched by their difference and not devalued. In our world constituted of differences of all kinds, it is not the disabled but society at large that needs special education in order to become a genuine society for all.

Inclusion – a question of values

Inclusive education needs to be seen within the broad, ever-changing social, political and cultural context. Inclusive education is ultimately a question of values and beliefs. In a democratic society, policy is to some extent a reflection of what the majority of the people value and want, and the compromises they are prepared to make. Equally, education is dependent on values, traditions and existing organizational settings and cannot be understood solely in terms of the structural changes or resource allocations made to schools. The issue of inclusive education provides an opportunity for raising serious questions about the kind of society we desire and the nature and role of schooling within such a society. The choice for inclusive schools is a choice for communities and societies that accept, respect and welcome all persons.

Note: This material was originally presented in *Prospects*, vol. XXIX, no.2, June 1999, which has given its permission here.

References

Canada Department of Education (1994) *Best practices for inclusion.* New Brunswick: Department of Education-Student Services Branch.

Centre for Educational Research and Innovation (1997) *Implementing inclusive education.* Paris: Organisation for Economic Co-operation and Development.

Centre for Studies on Inclusive Education (1997) *Inclusive education: a framework for change.* Bristol: Centre for Studies on Inclusive Education.

Clark, C. *et al.* (1997) *New directions in special needs: innovations in mainstream schools.* London and New York: Cassell.

Kisanji, J. (1998) 'The march towards inclusive education in non-Western countries: retracing the steps.' *International journal of inclusive education 2,* 55–72.

Lindqvist, B. (1994) Citation in *Final report. World Conference on Special Needs Education: Access and Quality, Salamanca.* Paris: UNESCO and the Government of Spain.

Porter, G. (1995) 'Organization of schooling: achieving access and quality through inclusion.' *Prospects 5,* 2, 299–309.

Porter, G. (1997) What we know about school inclusion. In OECD, *Implementing inclusive education.* Paris Organisation for Economic Co-operation and Development.

Skritic, T. M., Sailor, W. and Gee, K. (1996) Voice, collaboration and inclusion. *Remedial and special education 17,* 3, 142–157.

UNESCO (1994) *Final report,* World Conference on Special Needs Education: Access and Quality, Salamanca, Spain, 7–10 June 1994, Paris: UNESCO.

CHAPTER 7

Achieving Respect for Children's Views in Education

Roles for adults and children

Mary John

> British Schools remain depressing places for those sympathetic to the rights of young people and committed to their extension. During a decade and a half in which a torrent of legislation has sought to re-shape the administrative structure, ethos and content of our education system, it is impossible to isolate a single reform, clause within an Act, or ministerial directive designed to extend the capacity of young people to influence or exercise some measure of control over their own education. (Jeffs 1995, p.25)

So wrote Tony Jeffs taking stock of the research on children's educational rights in the UK in the mid-1990s. Is there any reason to believe that this picture has changed for the better in the years since then and is this problem unique to the UK?

The role of adults

Children's educational rights are not determined solely by legislation but rather by practice, that is by practices which respect children's personal agency. The views of adults in bringing about such changes are pivotal. Pressure from young people themselves is not enough. Robert Chambers put his finger on this as the crucial fulcrum for change in introducing a collection of papers on children's participation, pointing out that 'if we as adults can only change our views and behaviour, children will astonish us with what they can do, be, become, and how in time they can make the world a better place' (Chambers 1998, p.xviii). So the role of the adult educator can be as a catalyst for important changes in the way in which pupils are treated in institutional settings.

How much have adults themselves changed their views over the last few years on children's right to have a say in their education? The UN Committee monitoring the implementation of the UN Convention may provide an important yardstick here. Articles 12 and 13 of the UN Convention on the Rights of the Child make it clear that the child has a right to express a view and have that view taken into account in any matter that concerns them. When matters of educational provision are at stake this involves, of course, not just the child's voice but also the adult listener. These articles about children's participation are the most challenging because they require adults to start to re-think the powerful positions they have held in relation to providing for children. Listening and hearing, however, are not always one and the same when children's views are being sought or expressed. Minnow puts this well:

> ...power exercised in silence, is even less likely to know restraint; for silence, whilst sometimes eloquent, can seldom challenge. Language accompanying power enables the powerless to challenge power. Without language, and especially *without language recognised by the powerful,* those who would challenge or resist power are quite disabled. (Minnow 1987, p.1904; my italic)

So the tasks, if children's views in education are to be respected, are to find the means of enabling adults to listen and to recognize what the young mean, intend and are asking for.

At a formal level there have been a number of international activities aimed at educating adults about children's rights. The European Union set up a multi-national partnership under the Socrates Programme to develop a training kit for educating adults about children's rights. Countries as diverse in political, economic and cultural history as Greece, Finland, Germany, Estonia, Cyprus and the UK have all participated in the production of these materials (EU 2000). The kit is aimed at people working with children in Europe and adopts a training of trainers model.

Some contributors to the present volume have been participating in producing multi-media educational materials for adults based on the implications of the United Nation's Convention on the Rights of the

Child (UNCRC). These have an international focus and are aimed at professionals and practitioners working with children. This work has been directed by Professor Stuart N. Hart at the Office for the Study of the Psychological Rights of the Child at Indiana University–Purdue University at Indianapolis, USA, and has drawn specifically on experiences from Belgium, Brazil, Canada, Mexico, North America, Norway, and the UK. It has been informed by a network of ongoing work around the world and continues to extend this network and its information base. There is also the course on Children's Rights run at the Centre for Children's Rights, University of Ghent by Professor Eugeen Verhellen (Verhellen 1996; 1997) which keeps academics, professionals and practitioners aware of particular projects, research and activities which are developing this critical relationship between adults and children in various settings. These are but three examples of work currently going on around the world aimed particularly at consciousness-raising *amongst adults* about children's rights and in particular children's participation. Such work recognizes that before children can be in a position to claim their rights adults need to become more literate about the whole issue of rights, children's rights, about executing rights and the provisions of the UNCRC specifically. In the light of this they may need to re-think their established views and practices.

Young people and society

If we consider in detail the development of specific work within one country we become aware of some of the problems that are presented by trying to introduce a fairly novel agenda with children as significant players in the decision-making processes within established educational institutions. It was clearly going to be challenging for both adults and children. The nature and quality of the relationship between them becomes all important. In the UK over the last few years, it did seem as if the climate were ripe for change. Adults were beginning to respond to the gauntlet that had been thrown down by the UNCRC.

The 1990s has been a time of growing concern not just in this country but in the industrialized world as a whole that today's young people were opting out of society. Such apparent nihilism in the young had led to questions about the nature of an education system that resulted in such disengagement. Several examples of young people's behaviour had fuelled these worries and sharpened the debates about education. One has been the dismay of politicians of all parties that young people of voting age (which is 18 in the UK) had not voted, and young people generally seemed disillusioned with mainstream politics. Moreover, cases of criminal activity by young people, given the full media treatment, led to panics that young people were not being educated as morally responsible people. This precipitated the Prime Minister's 'Moral Crusade', with proposals to give new powers to the police in dealing with young miscreants. The education system and the family came under closer scrutiny. 'Villains' were identified in family circumstances with single-parent families coming in for unreasonable amounts of attention. 'Failing' schools were also put under the microscope.

The work of Demos, an independent UK think tank, in their report 'Freedom's Children' (Wilkinson and Mulgan 1995), which was a study of the generation born in the 1960s and 1970s, painted a picture of a generation that had apparently inherited unprecedented freedoms in relation to choosing their own lifestyle, relationships and career, to a degree that would have been inconceivable in the past. This study, drawing extensively on the British Household Panel Study and MORI (1994) and Socioconsult, revealed:

> this generation is the most educated ever: 90 per cent of 16–24 year old women have qualifications compared to barely half of 35–55 year olds. There is a steady shift towards what some commentators call 'post-material' values. Our map of British values shows how values are fragmenting as younger age groups move towards more 'modern' values such as autonomy and authenticity. (Wilkinson and Mulgan 1995, p.11)

They go on to refer to their findings that for this generation 'politics' has become a 'dirty word' (p.17). They state that this sort of disconnection has been observed in other European countries but has evoked a more serious response in those countries than in the UK. Political disconnection is seen by them to generalize to broad social disconnection, having found in their sample that over a third of 18–24 year-olds take pride in being outside the system. They are, nevertheless, concerned about many issues: environment, AIDS, jobs and most of all animals. This one might contrast with the position of young 'flower-power' people of the 1960s who were concerned with the global issue of 'Peace'. Now '...over half of under 25 year olds register as profoundly disconnected from the system, and a growing number of "underdogs" are now prepared to bite back – we call them the underwolves.' (Wilkinson and Mulgan 1995, p.17). In summarizing, Wilkinson and Mulgan say: 'New freedoms have brought far richer life opportunities, especially for women. No-one wants to give these away. But the hard task now is to define a sustainable framework for freedoms, and a better balance between choice and commitment' (p.19).

So the relationship between adults and young people needs, it seems, to develop a certain degree of inter-subjectivity and understanding of how young people came to feel the way they do about society.

What it means to be young

In emphasizing the need to develop a balance between choice and commitment Wilkinson and Mulgan draw our attention to characteristics which some have claimed are a fundamental part of being young. Michael Ignatieff (1998) questions whether the idea of 'belonging' is, in some sense, anathema to any sense of freedom amongst the young, and notes a crisis of identity around these tensions in late modernity. What it means to be young is something we have to have some hold on if we are to find a way forward to respect young people's views in their education.

In academic terms, James and Prout (1990) noted that at the turn of the last decade there was a crisis in the study of childhood, which they attributed to the inadequacy of previous frameworks. They asserted that 'any complacency about children and their place in society is misplaced, for the very concept of childhood has become problematic during the last decade' (p.1). The argument goes on to observe that the increase in consciousness, during the 1980s, of the profound differences in the realities of children's lives and experiences (a consciousness facilitated by the global media) has precipitated a crisis in the sociology of childhood and spurred on the recognition that each culture defines childhood in terms of its own set of meanings and practices.

Have we within our own culture in Western industrialized countries managed to articulate a meaningful definition of childhood and youth? Sharon Stephens, whilst agreeing with James and Prout's observations, takes us further in suggesting a more radical explanation of the crisis in the study of childhood. She feels such crises, constructions of childhood, the experiences of children and the sociology of childhood 'are related to profound changes in the now globalised modernity in which "the child" was previously located' (Stephens 1995, p.8). She goes on:

> Many of the authors exploring the world system, I would argue, are still operating in terms of distinctions between political economy and culture, the public and the private, that are themselves in the process of profound transformation ... It is also crucial for child researchers to rethink their own studies in the light of social and historical macro-perspectives if they wish to understand the explosion of concern about children's rights and to anticipate new risks to children and childhood that would otherwise go unrecognised. (p.8)

It seems, therefore, our understanding and conceptualization of children must take a more macro-perspective

The cultural context

Young people are not always at the periphery of the culture, by their own choice as their social disengagement would suggest, but are sometimes at the very centre of it. One of the ways which captures some of the transformations of globalized modernity, in which our children's views are indeed very much respected, is that dubbed 'Kinderculture' (Steinberg and Kincheloe 1997) which relates to the corporate construction of childhood. In the various papers in their collection they paint an alarming, if not terrifying, picture of the way in which media culture is affecting children and young people. It even seems that their lives are in the hands of media capitalists who are re-defining and re-shaping these young minds for their own purposes. They boldly depict media-made children and the post-modern family. In alerting us to the deleterious effects media culture is having upon children and through their useful and scholarly analysis of the dangers media pose for children, the research of Steinberg and Kincheloe and that of their colleagues suggests ways of countering such dangers. They see as a core issue the use of power. They suggest that:

> Unfortunately, Americans are uncomfortable with overt discussions of power. Such unease allows power wielders to hide in the recesses of the cultural and political landscape – all the while shaping cultural expression and public policy in their own interests, which may conflict with those of less powerful

> social groups such as children. (Steinberg and Kincheloe 1997, p.7)

They go on to develop the theme of power, building on John Fiske's (1993, p.11) use of the term 'power block', indicating that he emphasized that this concept 'can be better understood by what is *does* rather than what it is'. They describe the 'power wielders in America' who are not simply a category or class of human beings but rather, as in 'power block', the ways in which such social formations – in this case corporate America – hold special access to various resources (e.g. money, information, cultural capital, media and in this case the purchasing power of children) which they use for economic gain. So corporate America in Steinberg's and Kincheloe's view has become very skilled in schooling children's, and young people's desire. In this sense the 'power wielders' use their power to educate and manipulate the consumer behaviour of young people.

Steinberg and Kincheloe see that the way to counter this power is to develop a critical pedagogy of childhood 'aware and unafraid of childhood desire connecting it to children's efforts to understand the world and themselves' (Steinberg and Kincheloe 1997, p.2). Thus, reading has to include teaching young people to 'read' their own culture and deconstruct it. There are resonances here with Paulo Friere's assertions many years ago that a critical childhood education is interested in the knowledge and intuitions children bring to school. Children are steeped in and knowledgeable about the corporate and media culture that surrounds them. If we are fully to achieve respect for children's views in education then we have to understand this consciousness, their world, their desires and their perceptions of their own power in that world. This leads us to new forms of learning, a realistic appreciation of contemporary childhood and new partnerships of adults and children learning from each other.

Children and power relationships

Dorothy Rowe (1991) has suggested that power is about getting other people to accept one's own view of reality. Indeed, adult corporate America, as described in *Kinderculture*, has defined children's realities for them. Yet, in common with the rest of the developed world, the education system has resisted acknowledging this shaping and colonization of the child's desire. The role of the critical childhood professional might be seen as involving assisting children in the development of what John Fiske calls 'affective moments of power evasion' (1993). Such 'moments' do not constitute the ultimate expression of resistance. Nevertheless, harnessing existing critical and interrogative abilities in, for example, re-reading Disney films around gender issues and viewing with a detached eye the 'messages' given out by Ken and Barbie can be seen as assisting children towards self-assertion. Reading their own culture educates them towards resistance and confidence in and a valuing of their own views of reality. Surely this is what our role as educators attuned to children's views and the culture in which they are immersed should be about. This requires adults to be far more tuned in and aware of the knowledge and attitudes children bring to school.

There have been educational initiatives in the interests of sustainability that have ensured that children's and young people's views of reality have shaped the ways in which adults have been challenged to re-conceptualize the world. These have been effective in transforming power relationships between old and young. If we go to the other side of the world we can find such counterpoint in which children are valued in quite a different way – not for their consumer power but for their own individual insights into the society in which they live. An example is to be found in the work undertaken by the Barefoot College in Rajastan, India, with the children in the Night Schools (O'Brien 1996; John 2000).

The Barefoot College has tackled the problems of large-scale illiteracy amongst the villagers in Rajastan. They have provided for the children, whose daily work in the fields forms a vital part of their family's survival, night schools where they can learn to read and write and achieve functional literacy after their day's work. The thinking in teaching these children has gone beyond this immediate goal to include their involvement in the democratic process in imaginative and powerful ways. From the night schools, children, once they have achieved a certain degree of literacy, can be elected to become members of the Children's Parliament, responsible for overseeing a variety of essential services, facilities and activities in a large number of villages in a section of Rajastan. They elect, from amongst their number, a prime minister and ministers for health, education, women etc. These child ministers are serviced by adults acting in the role of civil servants. The details are fascinating, but what concerns us here is that the child members of parliament visit the night schools throughout this quite extensive area to monitor activities and to investigate complaints. They are responsible for appointing teachers and can if the need arises fire them too. The philosophy behind children's involvement in this way is that children will inherit the world that is being created so they should be involved in all the decisions that affect their communities and the well-being of these villages. This not only gives them a full involvement in democratic processes and the responsibilities of power, but also exposes them to new ideas and new points of view and the challenge of 'listening' themselves. In rural India the caste system still has quite a hold; yet these children, through the elections to the parliament, hear other points of view and as part of the campaigning are able to think through the merits and flaws in particular perspectives. They are not in the grip of corporate brainwashing. They moreover inform their elders and families about new ways of thinking. One could see this as the reverse thrust of socialization in that it is the children who are introducing the adults to new ways of thinking and being.

Remarkably the Barefoot College, through careful planning and systematic dissemination of information, managed to achieve a high level of support for the involvement of young people's parliament in the running of village affairs. Certainly children's views in education have been honoured and valued in this setting by their communities. It has involved the commitment and vigorous support of adults and a vision of how a society should be. The Barefoot College has been operating successfully in a number of fields for 25 years. It started with the provision of wells in the villages and the training of villagers as maintenance personnel, then through the manufacture and installation of solar panels as a source of power to replace the labour intensive collection of kerosene for cooking and lighting. The idea was always to make the villages self-sufficient and independent of urban aid. In later years they started through their education system to concentrate on the sustainability of the village populations. Ownership and responsibility for the means of survival by every member, young and old, was key. In so doing they put children in a powerful position in relation to the education process. They were not the mere recipients of a transmission process controlled by adults. They became aware of the importance of their commitment to quality, relevant education for rural sustainability and resourcefulness.

Children's education in the UK

In working towards achieving respect for children's views in education we have to have some grasp of their place within society. The Indian children were joint contributors to their family's economy and so had a 'place' within the family and their community. In the UK, since the ratification of the UNCRC, various ideas have been developed to engender a climate in which young people might feel that their views were important and would be valued. The setting up of the Children's Rights Development Unit, with its team of young advisers, was one such activity that has had a number of important spin-offs that have empowered young people.

Nevertheless, the sense of disconnection and disenchantment amongst many young people still persists here. In looking at the roots of this, the trail has led back inevitably to the family, to school and to practices there. Gerrison Lansdown (see Chapter 2), the first director of the Children's Rights Development Unit, emphasized the wider political context, pointing out the importance of a representative democracy that extends beyond governments to the full participation of all citizens:

> ... And for children and young people, who are explicitly excluded from the formal democratic processes, participative engagement is the only means through which their agenda, priorities, concerns and experience can inform and influence the political agenda. For the most part, the question of listening to children never arose, and if it did it would usually be countered with the views that they are too young, too immature, too inexperienced to play any effective political role. (Lansdown 1999)

To contrast this position with the situation in Rajastan is to make one wonder what is so very different about children in these two countries, or indeed adults in their relationships with children. Is respect for children and their views missing? As has already been pointed out, the UNCRC made it clear that children's views on matters that concern them should be heard and taken seriously, and that children have a fundamental right to express such views. The Convention has, in its very essence, participatory democracy, which includes children. Whilst the Convention was ratified in the UK in 1991, many of its provisions have yet to be incorporated in national legislation. Practices in relation to children and young people since the vision presented by the Convention was acknowledged have been very slow to change as evidenced, for example, in discussions still continuing about corporal punishment and the incarceration of young offenders and in controls over the educational process.

In education there are critics of complacency and retrogressive perspectives. Rhys Griffith (1998), in defining what he considered to be the characteristics of the ideal global citizen ('critically reflective, morally autonomous and socially active' (pp.193–194)), sees these characteristics as typical of those of an educated person, and goes on to examine how citizenship is ignored or even suppressed in schools. His study was based on 5 years' research in 97 educational establishments, which involved interviewing pupils about existing methods of teaching citizenship, and experimenting with independent learning projects. He concluded from this research that the emphasis in the curriculum was on the perception of the child as a passive vessel for accumulating knowledge. The result of this, he believed, was that conformity is encouraged rather than an enquiring, active and exploratory disposition, which is essential to the global citizen of this new century. This has had its effects in that large numbers of children in this country vote with their feet by staying away from school, some of them because they feel that the school curriculum is boring and irrelevant and the school regime repressive and out of touch. Others have responded with disruptive behaviour at school. A growing number of children are permanently excluded from school and truancy is increasing at an alarming rate. The Save the Children Fund Report (SCF 1999) 'Respect! A report into how well Article 12 of the UN Convention on the Rights of the Child is put into practice across the UK' reveals that education is a major source of complaint, and that the issue is largely that children are not listened to. The pupils have no say in how the school is run and feel they are not respected. Research on a similar theme by the Institute of Education in London University (Alderson 1999) reinforced this dismal picture of disaffection, powerlessness and oppression. Griffith (1998) makes proposals as to how the present system can be adapted to promote greater participation among pupils and, by these means, greater independence and flexibility. The whole strategy involves the reassessment of power relationships and how power is wielded in educational institutions.

Focus on the potential of education for the development of young morally responsible citizens had sharpened during the mid- to late-1990s. Most notably, citizenship education was being explored as a possible future inclusion in the National Curriculum. This seemed to herald an agreement on the part of interested adults that young people needed to be taught to become more involved and more active in democratic processes and in their community. On the face of it this would seem to be a way forward. It could be argued, however, that such a focus arose from a concentration on the measurable outcomes of education rather than on the nature of the processes themselves. The cynical saw this as a response to increasing unrest and disaffection amongst the young, attempting to ensure that the exit behaviours from the education system were pro-social rather than otherwise. The new Labour Government's commitment to citizenship education led it to set up a working party to take a grip on the issues, with a remit to provide advice on effective education for citizenship in schools. The Report of that group, 'Education for Citizenship and the Teaching of Democracy in Schools' (QCA 1998 – commonly referred to as the 'Crick Report' after the Chair Professor Bernard Crick), recommended that citizenship education must be included as an integral component in the National Curriculum. The recommendations, however, fell far short of expectations. They also fell within the frame of treating the child as the passive vessel for accumulating knowledge, which Griffith abhorred.

Gerrison Lansdown (1999), in summarizing her critique of these recommendations, based on her experience at the Children's Rights Development Unit and her own determined commitment to children's participation, said:

> ... The report acknowledges the importance of the ethos and organisation of schools in creating an environment in which children experience active citizenship... These proposals are welcome. However there are issues which are not addressed by the report.

Lansdown goes on to list what she saw as three major omissions. First was the need for political change. She felt that the onus for change should be as great, if not greater, for adults than for children and young people in dealing with the problem of disaffection and withdrawal from the political processes by the young. Second, she felt the report does not demand in any way that the school environment is made more democratic:

> How indeed can you teach democracy in an undemocratic environment... Yet the Crick Report explicitly rejects the idea that

> legal reform to require all schools to introduce democratic structures is necessary.

Finally she feels that the need to respect the contribution of children and young people is not emphasized enough by the Report that constructs the process of learning as one way:

> There are numerous examples of the capacities of children, even when very young, to provide mediation and peer counselling, to interview prospective staff, to evolve behaviour policies. These initiatives are not merely a learning process for children to help them evolve as responsible adults. They are approaches to creating school environments which learn from and build on, the strength of children.

She concludes:

> Democratic schooling offers a win-win outcome. Although many teachers are threatened by the prospect of conceding more power to pupils, there is ample evidence that it leads to more motivated and engaged children, less staff/pupil conflict, and greater skills in communication, listening, negotiating and peaceful conflict resolution.

Democratic schooling is often misperceived as involving relinquishing power and so becomes associated with anxieties about loss of control by the teacher and those in authority. Griffith (1998) has pointed out that to think of democratic practices this way is to misunderstand the real transformations of power that he feels are involved in which both teachers and pupils benefit from a real partnership in the learning process. It is important to understand how children themselves can, given the chance, contribute to the creation of democratic institutions.

So far, in thinking about how we might achieve respect for children's views in education, we have concentrated on the changes that need to occur in adult–child relations and the power balances therein. This has been advocated on the basis of pointing to contrasts between Rajastan and schools in the UK. The UK is by no means atypical of other Western industrialized countries where economies, market forces, performance indicators and quality control have all taken their toll on the relationships between adults and children at school. There are examples of good practice. Despite the setbacks in the UK some schools have set up School Councils, some local authorities have set up Youth Councils (Towsend and John 1997) working with young people to understand the child-impact of some of their decisions. The police, social services and health authorities have variously initiated projects to work more closely with young people, relating to them, listening to them and negotiating shared realities.

Relationships within the peer group are also vitally important. Respect for different views between children can contribute to their understanding of relationships and indeed their grasp of the micro-politics of the school. For them to be assertive in putting their own points of view they need a platform of constructive alliances within their peer groups as well as adults committed to hearing their points of view. It is to child-to-child relationships that we now change the focus of our attention for examples of good practice in achieving respect for children's views in education.

The role of the peer group

Changing focus from a macro to micro view of education, the model of good practice discussed here is based on a small-scale evaluation project (Taylor and Burden 1999) on the effectiveness of a form of social inclusion in schools known as 'Circle of Friends'. This approach is a means of facilitating and encouraging inclusion in the school and classroom. In Canada and the USA, where the approach originated (Pearpoint, Forest and Snow 1992; Perske and Perske 1988), it had been used to support the inclusion of children with disabilities in the mainstream schools as well as supporting adults with disabilities in the community. In supporting children with emotional and social needs this approach is:

> essentially based upon a systematic approach, whereby the context in which a person is functioning plays a key role in that person's behaviour and subsequent experiences. In particular, the power of the peer group in affecting the child's behaviour is acknowledged. The aim is to mobilise this force to support and encourage the child to have an increased range of choice in their behaviour and responses and to experience the positive gains of being an accepted member of a social group. (Taylor and Burden 1999, p.3)

Looking at the detail of the approach, initially a child is identified who would benefit from the backing of a Circle. This support from the immediate peer group is seen as holding the potential to reduce the child's challenging behaviour and/or experiences of victimization, enable the child to deal with problems as they arise and to gain some insight into their own behaviour and open up more choices to them. It also, of course, helps the child to make friends. Once the child has been identified then a discussion with the child's class about creating a Circle usually takes place, a discussion facilitated by someone not directly connected with the class in question. This is the one stage of the process where the focus child is most usually not involved, although the issue of whether or not they wish to attend the class discussion will have been carefully discussed with them and the final decision have been theirs. The ground rules are discussed and agreed, the context of the problem explored, empathetic understanding developed and the class's help enlisted in seeking to find a positive solution. Positive elements of the problem are identified before focusing on difficulties, followed by an exploration of how the child might be feeling. Ideas are then exchanged about how to support the child and change the situation. Volunteers are then requested to make up a special support peer group of six to eight children who will meet on a weekly basis with the class teacher and the focus child to take stock of how they think and feel things are developing and plan for the following week. There is usually no shortage of volunteers for the support group. It is stressed that the problem is a whole-class problem and not just that of the child. Group responsibility for it is encouraged. The facilitator of the class discussion takes great care to communicate respect and care for the focus child.

The work proceeds with full honest sympathetic discussions of the perceived problem that leads to positive action plans and commitments from all concerned to see these through. The formal life of the Circle ends, usually after about a half a term, when there is a general feeling within the group that there have been significant improvements in the situation, natural good friendships have been developed and the focus child feels confident about functioning well without the weekly meeting. Ending the Circle properly is seen as just as important as starting it, so there are still a few more meetings before the final closure which may again be facilitated by the original consultant who started it off. Circle participants are, as part of this process, encouraged to reflect upon the wider implications of what they have accomplished.

What became clear from this small-scale evaluation study of four classroom groups of different age levels in two urban schools is the important role that is performed by such groups and the significance of the social interactions within them. It is not simply a matter of the relationships between the children. The attitude, skill and confidence of the teacher responsible for introducing and facilitating any social intervention such as this is vitally important. It was clear that there was a need for careful preparation within the school and within the class group, and specific in-service training for teachers. Whilst the evaluation study, which was the first of its kind, was small it was intensive and detailed. Large-scale studies would not be appropriate for evaluating 'real-world' interventions of this kind.

> What is needed instead is a cumulative series of small-scale in-situ evaluations of single case-studies employing an ethically grounded, replicable research methodology. Only in this way will a body of knowledge be collected which will apply across a wide range of different contexts and circumstances. (Taylor and Burden 1999, p.1)

Six issues which Taylor hypothesizes (1997) are central to the evaluation of the success of Circle of Friends have been identified. These include empowerment, honesty, belonging, belief in change and positive alliances.

The study yielded some general conclusions relevant to the theme of achieving respect for children in education. It was clear that friendships were vitally important to children and that when these go awry the effects on behaviour at school and outside can be profound. The inability to articulate feelings of unhappiness and confusion which can arise may lead to completely inappropriate behaviour. Initially there is a tendency for teachers to interpret such baffling behaviour by a within-child, within-family model. It is essential for teachers to receive support in setting up a Circle of Friends so that they can move from teacher to facilitator role. Children need to be listened to and discuss issues seriously and also need the help of high quality facilitators if they are to develop their pro-social skills. The approach needs time and concrete plans as well as intentions. There is strong evidence that this technique can have an extremely powerful influence on the development of pro-social behaviour in both individual and groups of children across the whole of the school age range. There is a caveat, however:

> It would be extremely difficult, perhaps even impossible, to run an effective Circle in a school which was not committed to the democratic ideal and the development of citizenship in its students. Without an active commitment to values such as

> honesty and empowerment, it is possible that a Circle may be used as a repressive means of social control. (Taylor and Burden 1999, p.1)

The attitude of the teacher, the classroom climate and the whole school ethos is therefore important in the success of the Circle approach.

Throughout this chapter there has run an argument that at the fulcrum for change in valuing children at school is the way in which power is exercised. A strong message emerging from the Circle of Friends research is that schools would benefit from creating greater opportunities for children to feel powerful in bringing about positive change. It makes clear that children can be trusted to assist in the understanding and resolution of each other's problems and as yet they have not been sufficiently respected as a crucial resource in this respect. The Circle of Friends provides a microcosm of possible relationships that could, following a similar model, be built across the entire school. This might involve stepping outside traditional roles to enhance and facilitate communication. It would be useful to find out what the long term effects of this sort of re-structuring at a micro and macro level might be and to see in what way both children and teachers feel their views of themselves and their usual behaviour was changed by participation in such a project.

Conclusion

We have a long way to go to respect fully children's views in education. What could have been a breakthrough nationally in citizenship education has been disappointing. There are outcrops of activities, some of them imaginative and providing models for further work: some effective schools councils, children's newspapers; children's lobby groups; developing parliaments and parallel regional young people's administrative councils and work on school relationships, some of them specific such as Circle of Friends described above. Much has still to be achieved to coordinate and learn from these activities. The shift in emphasis in the practices of professionals working with children has often been subtle but has marked a deepening regard for children's agency and power and an emerging respect for children's views in the education that is theirs.

References

Alderson, P. (1999) *Civil rights in school.* ESRC Research Report. Swindon: Economic and Social Research Council.

Chambers, R. (1998) Preface to V. Johnson, E. Ivan-Smith, G. Gordon, P. Pridmore and P. Scott (eds) *Stepping forward; Children and young people's participation in the development process.* London: Intermediate Technology Publications.

E.U. (2000) Training Kit for Adults on Children's Rights.

Fiske, J. (1993) *Power plays, power works.* New York: Verso.

Freire, P. (1973) *Education for critical consciousness.* New York: Senbury Press.

Griffith, R. (1998) *Educational citizenship and independent learning.* London: Jessica Kingsley Publishers.

Ignatieff, M. (1998) 'Freedom and belonging.' In S. Orbach and M. Ignatieff (eds) *The age of anxiety.* Harmondsworth: Penguin Books.

James, A. and Prout, A. (eds) (1990) *Constructing and reconstructing childhood: Contemporary issues in the sociological study of the child.* London: Falmer Press.

Jeffs, T. (1995) 'Children's educational rights in the new ERA?' In Bob Franklin (ed) *Children's Rights: Comparative Policy and Practice.* London: Routledge.

John, M. E. (2000) 'Children's Parliament in Rajastan' in Audrey Osler (ed) *Citizenship and democracy in schools: Diversity, identity, and equality.* The ESRC Seminar Series on Human Rights and Democracy in Schools. Nottingham: Trentham Books.

Lansdown, G. (1999, June 18) *Human rights and democracy in schools: Preparing young people for citizenship through formal and informal education: marginalised and excluded young people.* Unpublished Paper presented as part of the ESRC Seminar Series: Human Rights and Democracy in Schools.

Minnow, M. (1987) Interpreting right: An essay for Robert Covern. *96 Yale Law Journal* 8, 1860–1904.

MORI (1994) *The moral values of young people.* MORI poll amongst 1200 young people aged 15–35 conducted on 18–22 August 1994. Reported on by M. Wroe (1994) 'Young and Adrift in the Moral Maze.' *The Observer*, 9 October.

O'Brien, C. (1996) *The Barefoot College...or knowledge demystified.* Paris: UNESCO.

Pearpoint, J., Forest, M. and Snow, J. (1992) *The inclusion papers.* London: Inclusion Press.

Perske, R., and Perske, M. (1988) *Circles of Friends.* Oxford Abingdon Press EU (2000) Training Kit for Adults on Children's Rights.

Qualifications and curriculum authority (QCA) (1998) *Education for citizenship and teaching of democracy in schools* (The Crick Report). London: QCA.

Rowe, D. (1991) *Wanting everything. The art of happiness.* London: HarperCollins.

Save the Children Fund (1999) *Respect! A report into how well Article 12 of the UN Convention on the Rights of the Child is put into practice across the UK.* London: Article 12 and Save the Children Fund.

Steinberg, S. R. and Kincheloe, J. L. (eds) (1997) *'Kinderculture': the corporate construction of childhood.* Boulder, Colarado: Westview Press.

Stephens, S. (1995) 'Children and the politics of culture in "Late Capitalism".' In Sharon Stephens (ed) *Children and the politics of culture.* Princeton Studies in Culture/Power/History. Princeton University Press.

Taylor, G. (1997) 'Community building in schools: Creating a circle of friends.' *Educational and Child Psychology,* 14(3), 45–50.

Taylor, G. and Burden, B. (1999) *The positive power of friendship: An illuminative evaluation of the Circle of Friends approach within the primary and secondary school phase.* Unpublished Research Report for the Calouste Gulbenkian Foundation.

Towsend, P. and John, M. E. (1997) 'Working towards the participation of children in decision-making: A Devon case study.' In B. Cohen and U. Hagen (eds) *Children's Services: Shaping up for the millennium. Supporting children and families in the United Kingdom and Scandinavia.* London: HMSO.

Wilkinson, H. and Mulgan, G. (1995) *Freedom's children. Work, relationships and politics for 18–34 year olds in Britain today.* London: Demos.

Verhellen, E. (ed) (1996) *Monitoring children's rights. Ghent papers on children's rights, No. 1.* The Hague: Kluwer Law International.

Verhellen, E. (ed) (1997) *Understanding children's rights. Ghent papers on children's rights, No. 2.* Ghent: The Children's Rights Centre.

CHAPTER 8

The Role of an Ombudsman for Children

Securing the child's right to education

Målfrid Grude Flekkøy

This chapter introduces the role of ombudsmen for children, particularly based on the experiences of the first ombudsman, followed by a brief presentation of similar models and an analysis of what they have in common. Focusing on an ombudsman's possible roles in securing the child's right to quality education, examples of issues raised by children illustrate how the ombudsman might handle such cases and how some of them could develop into issues of principal interest, affecting large segments of the school population. Finally future issues of particular interest are discussed.

What is an ombudsman?

'Ombudsman' is a Scandinavian term which has been adopted into English, possibly because there really is no adequate translation into English or any other language. 'Ombud' originally meant 'ambassador' or 'delegate', and was used especially to denote a messenger from the king to the people. In contemporary usage, the opposite is more nearly the case: it has become the word for a person or an office that deals with complaints from a defined, circumscribed group of people or individual members, speaks on behalf of that group and tries to improve conditions for individuals within the group as well as for the as the group as a whole. Often in a position of confrontation with authorities, an ombudsman serves as an independent, non-partisan agent, spokesperson, arbitrator or referee, ensuring that the ministries and others fulfil legislative purpose by suggesting measures for improvement. The effectiveness of an ombudsman, who has to be 'a strong figure...able to secure the attention of the authorities by sheer force of personality' may depend on the person having 'sufficient charisma, skill, and political stature and independence to carry out the office's mission' (Melton 1993). A public ombudsman, particularly one established by parliament, has particular responsibility in relation to the parliament, the ministries, and other levels of political and administrative authority, suggests improvement measures and seeks to increase pressure (often in collaboration with individuals or organizations) so that these authorities fulfil their legislative purpose.

An ombudsman has the power to investigate, criticize and publicize, but not to reverse administrative action or revoke administrative decisions. Confrontations with public authorities may be necessary from time to time, but often action takes place quietly, 'behind the scenes'. This means that much of the ombudsman's work must attract public attention, but often will be indirect and long-term, and also tailored to the needs of children in the country and within the cultural and political network in which they live.

Why an ombudsman for children?

Children as a group have their own particular needs, which must be respected and may require special measures. In addition children as a minority group have three characteristics, shared – in a democracy – by no other group:

1. Children have no influence on the choice of persons or composition of bodies responsible for decisions concerning or influencing conditions under which children grow up.
2. In contrast to children, adults have as well as the vote other means of swaying public opinion. Mass media provide channels through which adults can make their views known and provoke public debate. Organizations of adults also serve as pressure groups or lobbyists on the behalf of their members.
3. Legislation concerning the rights of children is still weak as compared to legislation governing the rights of adults. The main weaknesses are that the rights of children are often:

(a) indirect, i.e. the right is given to an adult (often the parents) on behalf of the child, or

(b) conditional, often in the sense that the right is only valid under certain conditions, e.g. that funds are available or that the parents are willing to cooperate to ensure the right of the child, or

(c) non-existent even in connections where adults, under very similar, even identical conditions, have clearly stated rights, and where there is really no reason why similar legislation should not apply to the younger generation.

In addition to all this, the proportion of the elderly in the population is increasing, in industrialized countries due to low birthrates, in some other countries due to high mortality amongst mid-life adults. While children today constitute 20 per cent of the Norwegian population, this percentage will be only 15 per cent in 20 years. In the political bodies, the adults who have the closest contact with the needs of children, e.g. parents (particularly of young children), are poorly represented. Even in Norway, where women have constituted 45 per cent of the Cabinet and over 34 per cent of the politicians in the Parliament, mothers of young children are unlikely to be a significant part of these groups. The elderly can not only vote, but also be elected. So there is reason to believe that the average age of politicians will go up and the support for issues concerning the elderly will increase. I do not say this to minimize the needs of the elderly, but to illustrate the need for strong voices for children.

A final point applies here. Ratification of the UN Convention on the Rights of the Child (CRC) (in all countries except Somalia and USA) requires a 'watchdog' on implementation of the Convention.

International developments

Following the establishment of the Norwegian office in 1981, a *national* ombudsman for children office has been established in Costa Rica, New Zealand, Iceland and Sweden, on the state level in South Australia, Austria and the Flemish and French parts of Belgium, on city-level in Vienna and Jerusalem. In Austria, efforts are underway to create an ombudsman on the federal level. In Israel the National Institute for Children has an ombudsman office for Israel, with a special representative for Palestinian children. In Spain legislation was passed in January

1996, according to which each regional Defensor del Pueblo is to have a Deputy Defensor responsible for children. In Guatemala, San Salvador, Nicaragua and Honduras an ombudsman for children has been established within an existing organization, often the Human Rights Commission. This is natural and logical, particularly since the Convention on the Rights of the Child is obviously a human rights instrument.[1]

Efforts to establish ombudsman offices are under way in other countries, e.g. the UK (possibly with independent offices for England, Scotland, Wales and Ireland, reflecting the differences in legislation concerning children in these countries). One of the most recent ombudsman for children has interestingly been established in Sarajevo, in June 1997, where a combination of three ombudsmen, under the public services ombudsman, represent the three main ethnic groups of Bosnia-Hersegovina. In Sri Lanka a countrywide humanitarian organization has started to work for the establishment of an ombudsman for children.

These developments illustrate the worldwide interest in the ombudsman concept. They also show that while the first offices were established in small, industrialized countries, modifications now exist in other countries, including developing countries. In some of these countries the political instability is high, the members of cabinet changing every few months. This is of course a problem, but perhaps also a compelling reason to establish some kind of permanent watchdog for children.

A variety of models are thus available for scrutiny by those contemplating such an office. This provides the possibility of finding a model that suits the political, geographical and traditional situation of the country.

What should ombudsman offices have in common?

In November 1990 the UNICEF International Child Development Center in Florence, Italy, organized a meeting of the then existing ombudsman offices and representatives of a number of developing countries. The purpose was to try to establish the principles which existing offices had in common, that were important to the efficiency of their work and to focus on possible obstacles to establishing similar services in other countries.

Although the models examined varied structurally, they were remarkably similar in their roles. In general terms, each was an *independent* body, created to defend children's rights, with the following functions:

> *To respond to complaints and/or violations.* This was viewed as a core function and the closest to the original meaning of the word 'ombudsman'. It was a means for individuals (in this case, children) to overcome a faceless, inhuman bureaucracy by having their grievances identified and pursued by a personal advocate. This function was variously described as 'to right individual wrongs', 'to humanize administrative relationships' or 'to serve as a watchdog against abuse'.
>
> *To influence legislation, policies and practices.* Particularly at national and sub-national levels, this function was written into the instructions of the public offices (i.e. 'To propose measures to strengthen children's safety under the law' and 'to ensure that legislation relating to the protection of children's interests is observed' were parts of the mandate of the Norwegian ombudsman). Similar provisions were stated in the mandates of the Costa Rican and New Zealand ombudsmen. It was agreed that the structure had to stand apart from, but be able to influence, government. In some countries this role was best accomplished by non-governmental bodies, in others it was inconceivable unless it was at least sanctioned by the government.
>
> *To carry out research or establish a database.* The systematic gathering of statistical and more in-depth information on the conditions of children and families was considered to be essential for establishing and monitoring good family policies and it was emphasized that this information should also include the views of children.
>
> *To review the performance of government and independent organizations from the point of view of children's rights.* It was suggested that monitoring of other monitoring structures would also be required and that a public ombudsman-type organism could not be expected to be responsible for government reports, but should keep these under review. (Flekkøy 1991)

The conclusions regarding guiding principles were summarized as follows:

- The monitoring structure should be a voice for children.
- As far as possible it should be independent in relation to political administration, legislature and political organisms.
- It should be financially independent.
- It must be as accessible as possible to the population, preferably including children themselves.
- It should be close to the decision-making bodies concerned with conditions that have an impact on children.
- It must work for, and within, networks at state and local levels, as well as at the non-governmental level.
- It should be legally established or in some other way given authority to carry out its functions.

Looking at these principles now, ten years of experience and several new offices later, the same main principles seem to apply. Different developments in different countries have further illustrated their importance.

The ombudsman and the CRC

Since the ombudsman has the power to investigate, criticize and publicize, but not to reverse administrative action or revoke administrative decisions, the ombudsman cannot in general *enforce* implementation of the Convention. The child's rights to survival, protection and development cannot be provided by the ombudsman, who, however, does have a responsibility for proposing measures that would secure or improve the conditions necessary to provide for these rights. The participation rights of the child may be somewhat different. These include the child's rights to adequate information (including information about the Convention and about the child's own rights), to voice opinions on and to take part in the decision-making process on issues that concern him or her. An ombudsman can certainly be instrumental in helping to provide information, but through the unique contact the ombudsman may have with children, the office can also act as a communications channel between children and the decision-making authorities, serving as a voice for as well as on behalf of the younger population. In this way the ombudsman may provide children with a possibility to make their views known and therefore perhaps have an influence on the final decision. A different aspect of this is the special (and strong) position the ombudsman has, based on the experience of and with children, to promote the importance of child participation, tailored to suit the evolving capacities of the child, in a democratic process in the families, in nursery-schools as well as in elementary and high schools, within their own organizations (e.g. Scouts or the local brass band), as well as in community planning of their neighborhoods.

The ombudsman and education

School-age children need to go to school, to acquire knowledge and skills they cannot get at home. They are eager to learn, glad to acquire new skills and thrive on responsibility, at a stage where rules and learning how to make them are of prime interest. Basic skills include reading and maths, although learning spelling and calculation may lose importance as computers take over. The use of language as a communication tool must be of paramount importance. Basic concepts should have been acquired in the pre-school years. In small families – and particularly when television is expected to substitute for *social* language learning or when experimental play possibilities have been seriously limited – children may come to school without basic concepts or even the words for ordinary things around them. In addition to the basic learning skills, children need facts and other information. But perhaps even more important in times when what is necessary information changes quickly, children may need knowledge about where to find and how to use whatever information they might need in the future. In addition to this, children need to learn social skills suitable for a world that is changing fast and is increasingly cross-cultural: tolerance, flexibility, creativeness and responsibility for others as well as for themselves. They need to know how a democracy works and how each individual can have an impact on the smaller or wider environment in which they live.

Cases for an ombudsman

School is one area in which children are at least as concerned as adults – and no wonder, since the children are the largest group of people in the school system, and a very eloquent group at that. Children's complaints relating to the school situation ranged from 16.5 per cent to nearly 25 per cent of the annual total of children's complaints, while adult complaints on the same issue comprised 11.7–15.7 per cent of the adult complaints. Children's complaints spanned a wider variety than adults', and were particularly numerous where conflicts with adults are concerned. The adults (teachers) in the school system complain to the Norwegian Teachers' Association; children complain to the ombudsman. (But the NTA and the ombudsman agreed on many of the basic causes for the conditions leading to complaints.)

Children have an everyday, first-hand and close knowledge about this segment of society. At least in Norway – they have no way (and no wish) to avoid it. Quite a few of the children's complaints led to issues of principal interest: why cases where pupils are the subject could be treated with less respect or care for the prevailing rules for public handling of cases than adult cases; why children themselves are treated in ways unthinkable where adults are concerned – examples of unreasonable lack of equal rights, discrimination or lack of respect for the person, regardless of age.

It must be remembered, however, that the ombudsman is a 'complaints office', so individual cases, while they may reflect more common problems and attitudes, should not be interpreted to reflect general attitudes or methods of teachers.

Other complaints reflect the attitudes of politicians, particularly when budgets are reduced or financing is otherwise insufficient, e.g. when proposals are made to close schools or cut down the number of classes. Difficulties with funding also had an effect on transportation and upkeep of buildings, as well as on the quality of school-books and other materials. One Norwegian statistician put it this way:

> Present-day children have 1½ years' less schooling than their parents had, (due to reducing the school-week from 6 to 5 days and the length of class-time from 60 to 45 minutes), but on the other hand can enjoy having the same books, even the same copies!

As one child put it,

> How can adults expect us to believe them when they say that education is the most important part of life, when the school-house is falling apart, the toilets and the heating don't work and the books are the ones my grandparents used?

New conditions, new school needs

Statistics show that increasing numbers of children no longer get pre-school social experiences at home. Both parents work. Therefore, children may need more adult supervision and care outside the home. More children experience familial split-ups, and all are exposed to the information and attitudes learned through the mass media, often contradictory to the values and morals of parents and teachers. When a new curriculum was proposed, the ombudsman criticized it for not taking the new needs and situation of children sufficiently into account. Nor was there any indication of the very important fact that children themselves are a very vital, dynamic element in the school, eager to learn, eager to cooperate, eager to share responsibility for each other and for the entire learning situation.

Physical working conditions

Physical conditions for children may concern conditions within the school property or the location of the school itself. Two girls told us that a garbage-plant was being planned next to their school (like the nursery-school planned between a garbage-plant and a housing area 'since the smell makes this area inhabitable for people'!) In other cases highways were built straight across school playgrounds, and paths for bicycles and pedestrians were lost when the road was rebuilt or expanded and traffic-lights, crossing bridges/tunnels were not built as planned.

> Three boys in Tromsø in northern Norway told the ombudsman office that plans to build a new wing to their school, connecting the main building and the building housing the swimming-pool, were now threatened due to the expenses involved. Realizing the special needs for considering the climate in that part of the country, the ombudsman turned to a climate expert, who pointed out that without the new wing, the playground would be impossible to use. The wing would protect the playground and provide an 'indoors-outdoors' area, in addition reducing the cost of heating the swimming-pool-building. On the basis of the ombudsman statement, the local authority decided to build the new wing. The case drew attention to the special requirements for play areas as well as buildings for children close to the North Pole.

A special problem area with regard to physical conditions concerns children with handicaps:

> Peter, when his class left the elementary school, was told that he could not join his class in their new school. Peter, the victim of a progressive muscular disease, was a wheelchair user, and the school did not have the necessary lift. The local authority decided that installing a lift would be too expensive. The ombudsman, pointing out the future need for a lift, asked the municipality to reconsider. This being denied, the story was, with Peter's permission, sent to the local newspapers. The Norwegian Association for the Handicapped reacted strongly, notifying the local authorities that a lift could be installed for less than five per cent of the calculated price. Then the lift was installed and Peter went to school with his classmates. The ombudsman asked the Ministry to investigate possibilities for helping to finance rebuilding of older schools to accommodate physically handicapped children and to circulate information on how best to do this.

Do rules and rights for adults apply to children?

In school, children learn about society's values and system of justice. Schools, by example as well as by teaching, demonstrate society's views on general human and equal rights. Indirectly, the school communicates society's views on the value of children – as individuals, as a group and as 'consumers' of the system within society which (in collaboration with parents) is responsible for developing the future adults of that society.

'It's not fair!' – or is it?

Many children complained of perceived injustice because the school had different rules for children and adults. Teachers were allowed to smoke or enjoy sweets (e.g. throat lozenges) in school, forbidden for children. Children had to go outside during recess, even in cold so severe that carpenters were not allowed, by law, to work on outdoor jobs, but the teachers stayed indoors, 'even though we are sure they could use some fresh air and some exercise too!'

Some of these problems were solved by the schools when the ombudsman notified the school of the complaint. Teachers are actually quite reasonable. In other cases the ombudsman asked the municipal authority to investigate the rules in the different schools, so that the differences between schools as well as between children and adults were at least minimized. A third group of complaints was answered by pointing out that there are differences between children and adults, and that some of the rules are actually good for the children, e.g. the rule against smoking, or the rule some local communities had, forbidding school-children to shop in school hours. This prohibition could have different reasons, e.g. that the children had 'junk food' for lunch instead of the whole-wheat sandwiches from home, or that they did not come back to school in time for lessons. Crowding or the suspicion of shop-lifting were, however, not accepted as good reasons by the ombudsman, since this would or should apply to adults as well. There were no grounds for discrimination on this account. Student councils very often managed to find out why the rule was there, negotiate for change if the reasons were unacceptable or if change in behaviour (e.g. coming back to school in time) could help, and try to improve the understanding of the rest of the student body if the rules were reasonable.

> Inger, ten years old, complained of a substitute teacher who had entered the class, the pupils silent and expectant, with the following remark: 'You should all know how lucky you are that I am here, because I know very well that this class is so impossible that no one wants to substitute here.'
>
> Berit (14) was accused, in class, of stealing, even though she was not even in school on the day the theft had occurred. The ombudsman contacted the teacher and suggested that an apology was due, in class, to which the teacher agreed.
>
> Knut (14) was accused of stealing his teacher's keys. When the keys were not found, the teacher went to the police, there being advised to drop the question at least temporarily, in the hope that the keys would turn up or the culprit confess (if there was one!). Instead the teacher took Knut and two or three of his classmates for interrogation at the police-station, without warning the parents and against the advice of several of his colleagues. The staff split over the handling of this case. About half of the teachers threatened to leave the school, saying they did not want to work in a place where pupils were treated as inferior to adults.

Feeling that the rights of the pupils to fair treatment had been infringed upon, they filed a complaint in the county school board and asked for an opinion from the ombudsman. The ombudsman agreed, pointing out that ordinary rules for fair treatment apply to young people and that the teacher (and the police) had broken the rules for police investigation of minors. The school board, partly based on the opinion of the ombudsman, criticized the handling of the case and demanded that the teachers, as a group of colleagues, find other ways of expressing and solving the interpersonal conflicts that had arisen during the case.

A group of 12-year-olds complained that immediately after a conflict (also of suspected theft) the bell rang for fire-escape practice. The class was told to go outdoors, without their warm clothes on. The teacher then told them that they would have to stay outside until the culprit had confessed – in minus 20 degrees Celsius. The class complained to the principal, who kept the entire class after school as punishment for 'opposition to the teacher'. The children then turned to the ombudsman, asking if group punishment was really legal – a difficult question. There is nothing in Norwegian law one way or the other. So this was actually a moral question – no less difficult, since group responsibility or group solidarity can be seen as a valuable social attitude. The ombudsman suggested that the children perhaps could solve this issue on their own – 12-year-olds are very fair and do not lack ability for moral judgments. If they could put pressure on the culprit to return the stolen goods, perhaps the teachers would be willing to drop the issue. The next question was easier: Would the teachers all have been punished if one of them had been suspected of some misdemeanour? Asked if they wanted a written statement, the children turned down this offer, wanting to try to solve the conflict on their own. No further action was then possible or advisable.

Eric, 13, was an unruly lad. His teachers, the school psychologist and the school social counsellor decided to transfer him to another class. But Eric did not want to move, so it was decided that he should be given a chance to improve during the following two months. The following day, however, when Eric came to school, his homeroom teacher immediately went to the principal and threatened to leave the school and not return until Eric was removed from her classroom. At this point Eric came to the ombudsman, who as a first step advised a complaint to the local school-board, on the grounds that rules for handling such cases had been broken. A complaint should also postpone carrying out the decision until the complaint had been investigated. The school authority, however, turned down the postponement, at which point the ombudsman for children asked the ombudsman for public administration to consider the case and give an opinion also in regard to the question of whether rules for handling cases and complaints of adults should also apply to cases of minors.

The ombudsman for public administration did not believe that the outcome of the case would have been different if the rules had been followed. But the school's administration, the local school administration, and the local school board were criticized on several points for faulty handling of the case.

Statements of the ombudsman for public administration carry a great deal of weight. Therefore, since the case also illustrated the lack of knowledge about the rights of pupils in the school system, the ombudsman for children asked the Ministry of Education to supply information about correct case handling in the Ministry's 'Handbook for the Norwegian School'.

Eric, who in spite of the support received from two ombudsmen, did not feel very welcome in his old school, asked for (and received) a transfer to a different school, a solution that turned out to be a good one for him.

Examples such as these demonstrate that even within the school system, children are treated in ways unthinkable or intolerable where adults are concerned. What boss, in working with an unknown group of employees, would expect cooperation if his opening statement expressed distrust of the group? Which group of adult employees would accept mass punishment on the mere suspicion that one of them had done something wrong? Would any adult stay in a situation, without even an apology, when evidently accused of a crime he or she had not committed?

Other issues were perhaps even more serious. Adult rights can be used against pupils.

> Paul was 14. In a conflict with his teacher, his teacher forced him against a wall and held him, calling for assistance from another teacher. Paul got very angry and hit the teacher. The teacher then called the representative of the local labor protection committee. Paul was expelled.
>
> John was eight years old and in anger threw a chair against the wall. The same procedure was used and John was expelled.
>
> Because the Protection of Workers Act says that if there is a threat to the safety of employees, work may be stopped until the threat is removed, Paul and John were defined as threats, expelled from school, and work was resumed.[2]

On the basis of several similar complaints, the ombudsman raised the following questions: Who should represent the pupil? Could this law really be used to expel children, denying them their right to education and fair treatment and to the help they need to treat the underlying reasons for their behaviour problems? What if their behaviour was really a reaction to a situation created by the teacher? Was it then fair to remove the child and not the teacher? Why does the Norwegian School Act have a whole chapter on the rights of teachers, who in addition, as employees of the municipality, are protected by the Protection of Workers Act, while no similar legislation exists for the children?[3] The State Workers Protection Control, the Ministry of Local Government and Labour and the Ministry of Education all answered that the law gave the school's elected representative the right to stop work in the classroom if a pupil threatened or physically assaulted a teacher.

The ombudsman then raised the issue with the Ministry of Education. Disciplinary problems must, the ombudsman stated, be solved within the rules and legislation of the school system, with early help from the psychologists and other helpers, so that situations leading to this kind of conflict could be solved and prevented. The Ministry maintained that while the Protection of Workers Act might be used in particularly difficult situations, the responsibility of the elected representative concerned the teachers only, while responsibility for the pupils must lie with the school principal. The elected representative therefore did not have the right to close schools or expel pupils.

This clarification, while important, caused reactions from the National Association of Teachers. The insufficiency of the clarification was demonstrated a year later, when a group of pupils had a conflict with their teacher, the school feeling that the solution must be 'making the children behave'. The pupils (and their parents) felt that the teacher's behaviour was at least partly the cause of the conflict. The elected representative was involved to protect the interests of the teacher, even though no physical threat existed. The ombudsman pointed out that with the use of the Workers Protection Act an entire school could be closed, and that this Act was not suited to solve interpersonal conflicts. The State Workers Protection Control then agreed: the Act could not be used to solve conflicts between employees or between employer and employee, but is aimed at the physical dangers of a working place.

The ombudsman pointed out that pupils have human rights that cannot be neglected. Behaviour problems of a pupil may be a signal of a more complicated problem in the classroom, in which the attitudes and behaviour of the teachers are important elements. Again the Ministry of Education and the Ministry of Labour clarified the position. The Ministry of Education stated categorically that the Protection of Workers Act could not and should not be used against or in a way harmful to pupils, the Act having no use at all in relation to pupils. The Ministry of Labour stated that while the Act could be used in principle for issues concerning pupils' behaviour in general, in no way could it be applied to the behaviour of individual pupils – the problems with whom were to be solved within the rules and procedures of the school system. The respect for the integrity of each pupil cannot be set aside, even in the interest of protecting employees' (teachers') rights.

Future issues for an ombudsman – school for learning democracy?

The availability of school is the first condition to enable children to participate in school settings. But many states have difficulties in providing even elementary education for all children. It is a fact that there is an unacceptable level of illiteracy, particularly amongst girls. States Parties are committed to providing elementary education, but it is also a fact that resources for this purpose fall short of need. The Convention does not offer an excuse to renege, but does give some leeway, namely that education shall be provided progressively. Still the question may arise of whether it would be better to provide some education for all children or more education for a few. If the latter is chosen, girls will more easily fail to get an education than boys. Such a decision would not be compatible with the Convention, with the umbrella article of non-discrimination (CRC article 2). So it would seem logical that when resources are scarce, the country must let the children share equally whatever is available, and make every possible effort to provide increased resources.[4]

If there are schools, some families may have the choice between alternative options. Many families do not have a choice, but can in some cases influence the education their child is getting. In some societies choice and influence are not likely, e.g. when the only education available is in Muslim schools. These schools may not offer a wide variety of ideas, but if the children did not attend them, they would forfeit learning the basic skills necessary for more learning: reading, writing and arithmetic. In other cases children receive their education at home, where there is always a risk (unless under some kind of public control) that the education will be biased one way or another.

Adult views upon children as future adults will naturally influence the goals parents set in bringing up their children and the goals society sets for its efforts for children. What goals the schools have, which values the school should teach, which potentials in the children should be cultivated and encouraged, which stemmed or discouraged depend on what skills present-day adults believe future adults will need and what qualities and traits they should have. The accelerating changes in society make it difficult to judge future demands. The difficulty of prediction increases because we realize that shaping the young entirely in our own image will hardly lead to a better world.

One goal of education is to train students for democracy. Therefore the content and methods of education should be considered in making the choice, i.e. allowing for the development of creative and critical thinking. This involves a respect for the student as a person, with educational methods that give honest reasons and answers. The student should (within reason) have the right to free expression (or non-expression), and self-sufficiency should be encouraged, in addition to offering a wide range of ideas and information. This raises some difficult issues.

For the individual child, as well as for the community, this is important because without a proper education, children cannot control their own destinies. The degree to which control is possible depends on the culture and the options available. But the ideal of education towards democracy may be valid even if there are various obstacles in different societies. And the Convention can be an important instrument.

The articles on education strengthen the overall participatory nature of the rights of the child. Article 28 sets forth the right of all children to an education, 'on the basis of equal opportunity'. In sub-paragraph 1b, States Parties take on the duty of encouraging 'different forms of secondary education' and to 'make them available and accessible to every child'. The implication of having various forms of secondary education is possibly to increase the choices available to all children. The choices, especially at the secondary education level, would entail participation by each child in the selection of her or his curriculum. Other educational aims would clearly be advanced by high levels of participation: information about vocational education; guidance about vocations; reduction in the drop-out rate. Further requirements, such as establishing discipline in a manner that is 'consistent with the child's human dignity' would also, if implemented in good faith, require input from the affected children. A reference is also made to increasing the use of 'modern teaching methods'; most modern pedagogy places heavy emphasis on student participation.

In discussing the goals of the educational system, as in article 29, much weight is placed on personal development and training for democracy. The entire article loses meaning in the absence of extensive participation by the students. How, one might ask, can a child develop her or his 'personality, talents and mental and physical abilities' without being actively engaged in decision-making? How might one imagine fostering the development of children's own 'cultural identity, language and values' and respect for the national values and for cultures different from their own without participation? How does one prepare children 'for responsible life in a free society' without participation?

One avenue to student participation would seem to lie in the student councils. Ideally the election of class representatives to a student decision-making body would be a true miniature democracy. But there are many obstacles on the way to this ideal. In some communities student councils do not exist at all. In others, the student council only includes delegates from the upper levels, and it is reasonable to ask why the younger ones are not there. The process by which representatives are chosen (not necessarily elected) can be questioned, as can the decision-making power of the student body. In some school districts representatives of the student council are members of a council consisting of parents, teachers and perhaps other school employees, and in a few the student councils of the entire community elect representatives to the school board, with or without the right to vote. When such things happen, we will often find as representatives students who are leaders in many connections. Even so, very few, if any, feel prepared to speak up. There are rarely ways in which the student representatives can get the views of the group they represent before the meeting or discuss upcoming issues or decisions with their peers.

Learning democracy in school should be part of everyday life. Small groups of children, guided if necessary by the teacher, can decide how to plan and carry out projects. Whole classes can function as a class council to discuss problems in the class, such as bullying or other destructive behaviour. Children of six or seven who make the rules for classroom behaviour usually come up with rules that are simpler to understand and easier to follow than adult rules, and the students feel more committed to them. Also, given responsibility for making the rules for keeping the classroom, school building and playground neat and clean, there is less damage and dirt.

Learning democracy, rights and responsibility in school is different from learning at home, because the group is often larger and the adults different. Chances for learning that the rights are respected for others are better in school than in the family. Being involved as a group, learning to listen to and respect others, enables children to understand implications of the decisions that are made and their impact on the group members. Thus, being listened to and encouraged to articulate views promotes development of social responsibility and understanding of the rights of others, probably mostly due to the confidence derived from the respect of the child's views, feelings and decision-making. Even making mistakes, particularly when based on a group decision, can be valuable elements of the learning process.

Teaching values in school

Participation is clearly implied in the discussion of the rights of ethnic, religious or linguistic minorities in article 30. Children are to be afforded the right, as earlier human rights treaties have done for adults, to join with others of her or his group to enjoy their culture, 'profess and practise' their religion, and use their own language. To realize the right, children, even at an earlier age, would be entitled to be informed of and to engage, with increasing choice, in activities in all relevant areas. But should this happen within school limits?

In connection with the child's right to freedom of religion, freedom of expression and freedom of thought, the question may be raised of whether or not schools infringe upon these rights if values are taught. In our view it would be impossible to conceive of an educational setting which does not in some way impart values, e.g. the value of knowledge or the ethic of learning.

The value of critical thinking for the development of democracy is undeniable[3] In accordance with the articles of the Convention, the intellectual rights of the child include the right to use and develop one's intellect, free access to information and ideas, freedom of beliefs, freedom of expression, i.e. many of the rights included in self-expression and participation rights. Since the Convention has been nearly universally adopted, we need no longer discuss whether or not the child should have these rights (unless we wish to amend the Convention), nor need we draw clear lines of distinction between the legal rights and the moral and philosophical ones. We may, however, need to consider how these rights are to be interpreted and exercised, in different cultures. As noted, none of these rights are as simple as they might seem at a superficial glance. The issue for discussion often concerns ethics and morals in general and religion in particular. The discussion of religious instruction can serve as an example of the necessity of viewing the issue with consideration of developmental stage and the effects of religious instruction on children of different ages. Also, social context needs to be considered. Children below the age of six or seven may have trouble understanding and accepting that people can have different beliefs and views. Religious instruction in the family will hardly be harmful, unless combined with fear or humiliation. But if the young child is subjected to conflicting views, e.g. that his parents believe in God while his beloved nursery-school teacher denies God's existence, the child may have a loyalty problem. Who to believe and trust? In some countries the parents can avoid this by choosing a nursery school that teaches their own faith. In countries where such choice is not possible, it may be better if the religious instruction of children is entirely a parental responsibility until the child can accept the existence of conflicting beliefs.

In many countries the question of learning religious values and traditions in school does not arise, because the school simply does not have this subject on its curriculum. In other countries, e.g. in countries with a State Church, the solution may be that the child does or does not stay in class when religious instruction is given. There are, however, problems connected with such choices; the decision is often left to the parents, even when the young person reaches the age when he or she has freedom of organization outside of school. The other problem is that younger children go to schools where religious instruction is not provided in lessons, in clearly marked slots on the timetable, making it impossible to provide alternative ethics instruction (if this is an alternative) or to enter or leave the class for the required time. On the other hand it may be difficult to distinguish clearly between religion and cultural values, particularly in cultures dominated by tradition as well as by practice of the religious expressions of one faith.

In other countries, with a multitude of different faiths, there can actually be no question of teaching one faith in the schools. This raises the distinction between religious instruction and religious indoctrination. The issue then becomes one of teaching general ethics, including tolerance and respect for the faith of others, but also a question of allowing religious expression, e.g. should individual or non-organized prayer in the school setting be allowed, or should religious groups be allowed to meet, and if so on school property or within school hours.

Examples of issues of self-expression in schools

School uniforms

In many school systems, particularly those stemming from the British, uniforms have been taken for granted. The idea of uniform dress at school was to erase socio-economic differences between students and create a feeling of solidarity. These arguments are still valid, if the values of equality and solidarity are ones to be communicated. But in view of the self-expression rights of children, the issue is being scrutinized anew. If choosing what clothes to wear is a way of expressing opinions or simply oneself, uniforms are debatable, even in countries that place a high value on self-expression.[4]

There can be little doubt that choice of dress can cause conflicts between parents and children as well as between children, with commercial pressure to buy certain brands and competition between young people as to who can and will wear what. Among elementary school-age children many feel that 'sameness', expressed through secret signs and codes, strengthens feelings of 'belonging' to a gang or group. They gladly wear Scout uniforms or the uniform of a sports team. In this sense, uniforms can be viewed as positive. In some school districts in the USA where uniforms have been introduced (e.g. California and Arizona 1995), administrators cite a better learning environment, increased school pride and fewer dress-related distractions. Violence in school seems to decrease. Parents have the option of transferring their children to other schools if they do not agree with the dress code. Trying a case in court (Arizona, as reported in the *Wall Street Journal*, 5 December 1995), the claim was that the uniform policy was unconstitutional (US Constitution); the court, however, refused to find that the school infringed on student rights to free expression. Being closed to the public, the school was not considered a 'public forum' where 'public opinion or sentiment' is expressed. Students could also express such sentiments in other ways, e.g. by wearing badges. No mention was made in these cases of whether or not the uniform policy also applied to adults/teachers. If not, it might be considered discriminatory. Nor was the decision-making process, with possible student participation, described.

It seems to me that this issue is not simple, but that if students participate in the discussion and decision-making, it may be resolved without infringing on their self-expression rights. Self-expression by dress will be possible after school hours, and students may (or may not) agree to uniforms in school. (Recently the student council of a Norwegian school decided to try black trousers and white tops as a uniform for a week and liked it so well that it will become permanent.)

Organizations within the school property

The rights to free association and freedom of speech can lead to the question of whether or not students should have freedom to organize in any way they wish on school property. Arguments for the positive view include reference to rights and also to the learning experience students can get through organizations. They can learn the rules for democratic decision-making or debate, as well as get information about the views and values of the group. On the other hand some groupings will conflict with values of the society, e.g. certain extreme political views or moral issues such as groups offering information that parents or teachers would prefer students to get elsewhere.

Encouraging student participation

Experiences from different countries are beginning to show that participation works, if the conditions are right. Children from the age of three demonstrate that they know how to ask for the floor, voice opinions, argue their cause, vote and take the consequences of the group decision, in the daily 'morning circle' of nursery school. Sadly these skills have been forgotten at age ten, but when re-learned, grade-school children can canvass all the classes of all the schools of a municipality for suggestions, appoint representatives to present the final suggestion of their school, debate with representatives of the other schools, vote and decide how to use a certain amount set aside on the municipal budget for the purpose of improving some aspect of their school environment. School student councils organize fact-finding about the traffic situation of their area, and drives to clean up not only the school area but also local buildings. Conditions for making such efforts effective include faith in the young people, respect for their ideas, really listening to their views, and making it very clear what the consequences of their activity will be. (One school in Australia was very disappointed when the local authority did *not* reinstate their school bus after the students had arranged a protest rally to protect it. They had not realized that their voice was but one amongst several – and in this case they were the minority.)

These are issues for an ombudsman:

- Informing society about the importance of child and youth participation.
- Clarifying conditions for child and youth participation.
- Collecting and desalinating practical examples of how participation can work.

These are demanding issues but not the whole list. In addition to all the other issues, an ombudsman for children must be concerned with improving conditions for children.

In developing countries an ombudsman might need to point out, explain and emphasize the benefits of education to the individual child, to groups of children (i.e. girls, working children, street children or children with learning disabilities) and to society, perhaps weighing these against the more immediate profits of working children. Long-term benefits for society include family planning or spacing, health issues and other advantages not always readily connected with education.

In industrialized countries the ombudsman role may be different. It may be aimed more at the content of education, curricula, values and, a more recent development, the need to implement in the schools the CRC, perhaps particularly the participation rights.

Endnotes

1 It is, however, as yet to early to say whether or not this solution is good enough, as good or better than establishing an Ombudsman for Children as an independent institution. Much would depend on the mandate of a Child Rights Commissioner and the administrative organization within the Human Rights Commission. If the Child Rights Commissioner serves as an assistant to the Human Rights Commissioner, the statements and opinions of the Child Rights Commissioner may be subject to the endorsement of the boss. If so, the effectiveness of the Child Rights Commissioner will depend on the person serving as Human Rights Commissioner. Also, if the Human Rights Commission is mostly concerned with violations of the human rights of the individual, the scope for the Child Rights Commissioner may be limited as compared with the mandate of an Ombudsman for Children. Issues that are unclear or difficult to define as a breach of human rights or issues that concern groups of children may then be neglected, particularly if the mandate of the Commissioner does not clearly include the option of investigating and raising class-action issues.

2 All case examples are published in Flekkøy (1991).

3 The Norwegian School Act can be obtained from the Norwegian Ministry of Education. The Protection of Workers Act can be obtained from the Ministry of Municipal Affairs.

4 The 'best interest' issue may also arise: If a child must work to survive or to provide for his or her family, is it then in the child's best interest to go to school and not work, or to work and forfeit education? In some cultures the working child is seen as being in a learning situation. Through participation in the tasks of adults, the child is acquiring skills that will be useful later. In yet other cultures the roles of particularly women do not include the knowledge acquired through school. An eduaction might even jeopardize the girl's chances for marriage and thereby threaten her future. In such cases arguments are made that formal education would not be in the best interest of the child. On the other hand, these practical and role-directed teaching practices can hardly cover the right to adequate education for critical and creative thinking, because the alternatives are not known to the young person.

5 For a more thorough discussion see Moshman, D. (ed) (1986) *Children's Intellectual Rights.* San Francisco: Jossey-Bass Inc., and Moshman, D. (1989) *Children, Education and the First Amendment.* Lincoln and London: University of Nebraska Press.

6 The value placed on self-expression can be questioned, when e.g. the right to carry a gun is included. School boards in the U.S. actually discuss whether students should be allowed to carry guns to school. To me this seems to disregard both the young student's need to learn to consider other human beings and the need the individual student as well as the group has for protection.

References

Melton, G. (1993) 'Lessons from Norway: The Children's Ombudsman as a voice for children 23, (3).' *Case Western Reserve Journal of International Law.*

Flekkøy, M. (1991) *A Voice for Children: Speaking Out as their Ombudsman.* London: Jessica Kingsley Publishers.

Flekkøy, M. (1991) *Models for Monitoring the Protection Rights of the Child.* Florence: UNICEF/Firenze.

CHAPTER 9

Facilitating Children's Rights in Education

Expectations and demands on teachers and parents

Eugeen Verhellen

This chapter addresses several basic issues concerning children's rights in education. These have serious implications for attitude changes, as well as development of strategies and methods.

Changing the image of the child and human rights[1]

For important historical reasons, children have been seen as 'future' performers of a prospective 'enlightened society'. This powerful definition, this social construct, of childhood had, and still has, enormous consequences for children and for those who relate to them.

This construction means that children are seen as 'not yets' (not yet knowing, not yet competent, not yet being). By strongly defining childhood as a 'preparation' period, a transition period, we have locked children in a limbo in which they must wait and prepare themselves to be future performers.

In recent decades, this adult-centric and adult-constructed child image has come under discussion and attack through the advocacy of a child's right to well-being based on human dignity. 'Respect for children as human beings' means that they are no longer perceived as mere *objects* of protection but as *subjects* – bearers of human rights – just as it should be for every human being. This new perception applies to the child as an individual (psychological) as well as to children as a social category: childhood as a permanent social class (sociological).

This conceptual switch in the child image is not that easy to implement and practise in daily life. In some ways, this challenge is new since we are not accustomed to treating children from a human rights standpoint. The UN Convention on the Rights of the Child (CRC) strongly promotes this human rights approach. Hereafter, three basic characteristics of the CRC are discussed: *comprehensiveness, binding force* and *universality.*

The Convention on the Rights of the Child

Comprehensiveness

Comprehensiveness is a feature that defines the CRC as a unique and indeed revolutionary instrument. Even the Preamble, which does not give binding principles, shows us the terms of reference on how to interpret the binding articles – emphasizing that the CRC is an integral part of the general 'human rights project' (i.e. the human rights movement).

The 'first generation' of human rights is about traditional civil and political rights; the 'second generation' deals with economic, social and cultural rights. For adults, these two generations of rights are protected by separate covenants,[2] while the CRC contains both generations in a single instrument. The CRC very clearly combines civil and political rights with social, economic and cultural rights to make them inseparable and without any hierarchical distinction. All rights are equally important and even interdependent – none can stand alone. This would be in breach of the spirit of the CRC.

This is a unique and unusual approach for governments, lawyers and other experts because they are used to reading and interpreting a convention article by article. In other words, the CRC enforces an active interpretation, a comprehensive and interactive reading.

Following this new approach, the CRC shows us a new potential direction for the overall human rights movement. Making standards for children's rights a reality, therefore, is a strong catalyst for a democracy of quality, based on respect for human dignity.

For heuristic reasons, while keeping in mind the indivisibility of the document, we can sub-divide the CRC for a closer examination. For example, looking at the CRC through the device of the so-called 3-P's (*provision*, *protection* and *participation*) is a very useful exercise.[3] Here, again, interdependence must be safeguarded – every right must be seen as inclusive.

Protection of the vulnerability and the dependence of children is guaranteed by the right to be protected from the choices and power of others: the right to life, survival and development (art. 6); the right to protection from abuse, neglect and exploitation (art. 19); etc.[4] The basic idea behind these protective rights is that children have the right to be shielded from individual and structural harmful acts and practices.

The child's right to *provision* includes the rights to information access (art. 17), social security (art. 26), the highest level of health (art. 24) and education (art. 29).

However, the most revolutionary part of the CRC is found among the articles on *participation* rights, which recognize the right of children to make certain choices themselves and to bring them in to dialogue with others: the right to express an opinion; freedom of thought, conscience and religion; freedom of association; protection of privacy (arts. 12–16). These participation rights bring children back into society by recognizing them as 'meaning-makers' – by recognizing their citizenship.

Legally binding[5]

By ratifying the CRC, States accept the legal obligation to implement the provisions of the convention (the *pacta sunt servanda* principle). However, States have the option of addressing this obligation through one of two theories: 'self-executing force' or 'non-self-execution'.

We speak about 'self-executing force' when domestic constitutional rules allow a treaty to have direct domestic effect. In a monistic system, by simply ratifying the treaty it becomes part of the legal system. Magistrates can apply treaties directly in the court. In a 'dualistic system', a clear distinction is made between domestic law and international law, with treaties being 'non-self-executing'. This means that an obligation undertaken under international law (for example, the ratification of an international treaty, like the CRC) takes effect in the domestic legal system *only* after it has been transposed into national law.

In other words, at the domestic level, States Parties that employ the constitutional provision of the 'self-executing force' are, therefore, bound via their courts to apply this strong provision for the CRC too.

Hesitations in this regard can weaken the CRC, since amending laws does not always guarantee that they are strengthened. Countries that have a clear dualistic system have an obligation to integrate the CRC into their national legislation.

At the international level, the Committee on the Rights of the Child (art. 43) monitors compliance with the CRC with an initial report two years after ratification and then via periodic reports (art. 44) submitted by the States Parties. States Parties must make their reports and the Concluding Observations of the Committee widely available to the public in their countries (art. 44, para. 6). This provision is a logical consequence of article 42, which obliges States Parties to make the rights contained in the CRC widely known to both adults and children. The great importance of this binding duty – both to report *and* to inform for an effective legal protection of children's rights – is obvious. And because of its periodicity, it is not just a single act but a sustainable process.

Universal ratification

In itself, and in the context of internationalization of the human rights project, the CRC has quite a long history. On 20 November 1989, after ten years of preparation, the United Nations General Assembly adopted the CRC without a dissenting vote. The CRC contains 54 articles, of which 41 substantive articles define the rights of the child and the obligations of States Parties ratifying the Convention. Unlike previous child rights instruments,[6] the CRC is a legally binding convention for the ratifying States.

The required minimum number of ratifications (20 – art. 49) was reached in less than a year, and the CRC entered into force on 2 September 1990. The speedy and massive response of the international community to the CRC is unique in the history of human rights. And this response has continued. Today, 191 States have ratified the CRC. Only Somalia and the USA have not![7] We have almost reached the stage of universal ratification, which again is a unique accomplishment in the field of human rights.

In conclusion, it may be argued strongly that by its comprehensiveness, binding character and near universality, the CRC is presently challenging the world with a geo-political social contract. However, we are only speaking about the very important phase of standard setting. Implementation and monitoring are the challenges before us now and they will not occur automatically. Since the CRC is a legally binding convention, children have the right to legal protection of their rights. As described in the next section, legal protection of children's rights is more than a simple judicial process.

Legal protection of children's rights

The CRC irrevocably closed the period of the mere *protection* of children and opened the period of legal protection of the *rights* of children. In other words, the CRC underlined the evolution of the child as a legal *object* to the child as a legal *subject.*

When speaking about legal protection of rights, one has to take into account more than just judicial procedures. Legal protection has some very basic requirements, including: [8]

- One must *have* rights.
- One must be *informed* about one's rights.
- One must be able *to exercise* one's rights.
- If necessary one must be able *to enforce* one's rights.
- There must be an interested community *to advocate* one's rights.

All of these requirements are *interdependent.* If one of them is not met, or is poorly met, legal protection is seriously jeopardized. As our child image is in transition, going through a process of deconstruction and reconstruction, these requirements are not self-evident when we discuss the legal protection of children's rights.

Children's rights education policy

Among the interrelated requirements for an effective legal protection of rights, children's rights education is key. Education cannot be restricted only to the area of school teaching. It covers a broad scope of activities in a much wider field of application.[9] Articles 17 (access to appropriate information) and 42 (duty to make the Convention known) are very clear in this regard.

Nonetheless, much of a child's learning takes place in the organized, formal school system. Consequently, education within the school system, as it is State-organized or State-supported, plays a central role in children's rights education policy.

Children spend a considerable part of their existence at school. School, as a socialization instrument, is therefore expected to be an adequate reflection of developments within society. Recent global social developments have created new needs. Education has to take these new developments into account or, at the very least, be aware of them. In ideal circumstances, education can even provide the stimulus for positive developments (the proactive approach).

Advancements in the concept of human rights go a long way toward explaining why the law is now a hot topic in education. Surveys and an increasing number of court rulings show that in many countries pupils are going to court to resolve disputes arising at school. This is a remarkable situation given that until recently education remained untouched by the law – since it was traditionally based on the absolute power of the teaching staff. A century ago, it would have been unthinkable for a pupil to appeal against the decision of a headmaster.

Because of the nature of the rights it confers, the CRC in many cases imposes obligations on States Parties. It also grants a number of general human rights to children. This impetus for children's self-determination demands new, important tasks of education.

Describing the relationship between education and the rights of the child is not easy. It is a relationship with many facets and problems that are not always immediately obvious. When a State ratifies the CRC, its implementation carries very serious consequences for the school system. Through ratification, three important tasks are imposed on schools that result in children experiencing their rights to education in different ways: rights *to* education; rights *in* education and rights *through* education.[10] These tasks exist side-by-side but, given the comprehensive nature of the CRC, are obviously interwoven. In daily school life, they are experienced by children as being interrelated.

The right to education

In various national and international legal instruments the right to education is recognized as a universal fundamental right in society. As mentioned before, the right to education was first stated in article 26 of the Universal Declaration on Human Rights (1948). This document, however, was not legally binding. Afterwards, the right to education was repeatedly confirmed in a number of legally binding international instruments. Article 13 of the International Covenant on Economic, Social and Cultural Rights, adopted by the UN in 1966, imposes an obligation on States Parties to recognize the 'right of every person to education'. In its articles 4 and 5, the earlier UNESCO Convention (1960) elaborates this right and deals more particularly with the principle of non-discrimination in education. Article 2 of the first Additional Protocol (1952) to the European Convention on Human Rights also affirms this right by stating, 'No person shall be denied the right to education'.

The CRC obviously reconfirms this right to education in two interrelated articles. Article 28 provides the means of enforcing it. The principles of equal opportunity, free access to education and the introduction of compulsory primary education are examples of subjects covered by the article 28 right to education. Article 29 contains detailed provisions concerning the aims and values involved: the development of the child's personality to its fullest potential, the preparation of the child for a responsible role in society, the development of respect for nature, mutual understanding and friendship among all peoples, and especially the development of respect for human rights and fundamental freedoms. Both articles therefore impose the obligation on States Parties to implement the CRC *directly* through their education policies.

In spite of the fact that during the second half of the 20th century significant improvements in raising the total number of pupils in primary education have been achieved, we are still confronted with the harsh reality that many children worldwide are excluded from their right to education. It is estimated that around 130 million children (two thirds of them girls) are deprived of their right to basic education.

There is an assumption that this only concerns developing countries. However the picture needs more nuances. At first glance, most Western industrialized countries seem to live up to the obligations imposed by the above-mentioned international instruments. And yet a considerable number of problems regarding the right to education have arisen and the number of court cases at the domestic and international (European) levels is on the increase. It would be impossible to deal with all these problem areas within the confines of this article, but a few examples will illustrate their complexity.

First of all, many doubts have been expressed about the concept of 'every person', which can be regarded either as a negative reference to the principle of non-discrimination, or as a positive reference to the democratization role that can be played by education. Various studies have demonstrated the existence of inequality in educational opportunity for certain categories of people. Access to education may be free – but that is not the end of it. Although free access means there are no school fees, it does not mean there are no other (sometimes quite substantial) expenses for all kinds of compulsory or optional activities. These extra costs may indirectly cause problems for certain people in asserting their right to education.

Moreover, there is a rather strange grants system (in itself an indirect recognition of the extra study expenses) in which the so-called 'Matthew effect'[11] (which benefits 'haves' over 'have-nots') plays an even greater part. Recent surveys have demonstrated that democratization in education is stagnating. There are far fewer children from the lower social classes in secondary and tertiary education. Phenomena such as drop-out, truancy, unsuitable curricula, etc. are related to the content and formal quality of education. All of this is directly adverse to the real aim of education, and therefore should be regarded as in conflict with article 29 of the CRC ('the development of the child's personality, talents and mental and physical abilities to their fullest potential').

The expulsion of children subject to compulsory schooling, or the refusal to enrol them at all, is also a focus of debate. These are incidents that occur regularly and have far-reaching consequences for children who cannot fight these decisions. The growing number of court cases involving pupils/students and the education authorities clearly demonstrates that the former have very little protection.

Rights in education

The fundamental human right to education must be guaranteed directly. However, the rights enshrined in the CRC also must be implemented indirectly by the school system. In other words, one of the first tasks for States Parties will be to clarify children's legal position in education to prevent breaches of children's rights (the reactive approach). In this regard one can think about the rules of discipline, the debate on corporal punishment and so on.

But there is much more to do from a proactive point of view. Articles 12–16 of the CRC contain important fundamental freedoms: the right to express an opinion; freedom of expression; freedom of thought, conscience and religion; freedom of association; protection of privacy. This clearly implies the introduction of the right to self-determination, which must also be implemented in the concrete daily school culture – human rights *in* education. Far too little thinking has been done on this subject and that work (i.e. respect for children) has yet to begin in schools.

To illustrate this assertion one need only to quote article 12, para. 2:

> For this purpose [to implement the right to freedom of opinion and to freedom of expression], the child shall in particular be provided the opportunity to be heard in any judicial and administrative proceedings affecting the child.

This is a clear reference to participation in school life. However, participation might be approached from different viewpoints. On one hand participation is seen as instrumental, as a means to improve the quality of the school as an organization or to educate pupils to become future good democratic citizens by learning participation skills.

On the other hand, and more importantly, participation has an intrinsic motive to recognize children as meaning-makers. In this sense participation is seen as a right in itself. In the long run, of course, it strongly affects the quality of democracy. But this is not the primary aim.

Rights through education

It is expected that the right to education and rights in education are crucial in order to improve democracy and respect for human rights in society. Therefore the comprehensive human rights project through its human rights instruments reflects also an inextricable third track: rights through education.[12]

The already mentioned UNESCO Convention (art. 5), and the International Convenant on Economic, Social and Cultural Rights (art. 13) clearly indicate that education in States Parties must aim at promoting respect for human rights. This is also in line with the spirit of the United Nations Charter and the Universal Declaration of Human Rights (article 26, para. 2), in that familiarity with human rights is the best protection against their infringement.

The Council of Europe Committee of Ministers has adopted recommendation R (85) 7, in which it urges Member States to firmly encourage education on human rights and their promotion and asks Member States to draw its recommendations to the attention of those involved in education. The recommendation contains many detailed suggestions to this end.

The most recent reaffirmation of the need for human rights education stated by the UN was the proclamation of the ten-year period 1995–2004 as the 'UN Decade on Human Rights Education' in its General Assembly Resolution 49/184 (1994). This resolution includes an elaborated plan of action, which urges governments and non-governmental educational agencies to elaborate programmes on human rights education.

It is not surprising that we should encounter the same idea in the CRC (art. 29, para. 1b). It even goes a step further, in article 42 which imposes the obligation on States Parties to make the principles and provisions of the CRC widely known to adults and children alike. Moreover, article 44, para. 6 requests States Parties to make their reports and the Concluding Observations comments of the Committee on the Rights of the Child widely available to the public in their own countries. It goes without saying that a permanent, large-scale information campaign about the CRC and its content is essential if it is to be implemented effectively.

It is equally obvious that education has a major responsibility in this respect. Spending an occasional hour or two at school on the subject of children's rights would obviously fall short of the obligations States Parties have taken upon themselves. Essentially, there has to be a shift in fundamental attitudes toward respect for children's rights. Theoretical teaching on the value of human rights and democracy serves very little purpose if those values are not also put into practice at the same time.

Apart from this shift in attitudes, we need changes in existing school curricula. Respect for human rights can be taught not only in history lessons, but in practically every subject. Teacher training will have to be adapted to this new task. There might also be specific training for regional press and information officers and the setting up of a specific information system. Finally, all kinds of educational aids could be designed (texts, audio-visual aids, educational games, exhibitions, etc.) to advance these objectives.

Conclusion

On the one hand it is very clear that education can act as a powerful catalyst to establish respect for human rights and therefore to favour the development of a democratic society.

On the other hand it must be obvious that the human rights project and the binding provisions in its instruments make demands on all actors in the school culture. Since we are now leaving the phase of international standard-setting and entering the phase of implementation, it is not surprising that almost no intentional, systematic, comprehensive programmes have been set up. Some governments, schools, teachers, parents and children are occasionally and partially dealing with it. However, these isolated actions are characterized by dramatically high commitment.

We must go beyond simply supporting these good practices. The challenge before us now is to set up intentional and systematic education policies from a human (children's) rights point of view.

Note: The material in this chapter was originally presented in *Prospects*, vol. XXIX, no.2, June 1999, which has given its permission for publication here.

Endnotes

1 For a more comprehensive explanation, see Verhellen, E. (1997) *Convention on the Rights of the Child. Background, motivation, strategies, main themes*, 2nd edn. Garant, Leuven.

2 The two treaties that were created to make the rights in the Universal Declaration of Human Rights binding are: the International Covenant on Civil and Political Rights and the International Covenant on Economic, Social and Cultural Rights.

3 Heilo, P.A., Lawronen, E. and Bardy, M. (eds) (1998) *Politics of childhood and children at risk. Provision – protection – participation.* Kellokoski, Finland: Eurosocial Report Series, no.45, Vienna.

4 There are numerous other articles that also protect the child from the acts of others, such as: articles 32–36, dealing with various forms of exploitation; articles 37–38, covering torture, deprivation of liberty and armed conflicts; article 40 on juvenile justice. Arguably, almost all of the CRC's articles deal with power relationships between adults and the child.

5 Verhellen, E. (ed) (1996) *Monitoring children's rights.* The Hague: Kluwer Law International.

6 The first international child rights legal instrument was the 1924 'Declaration of Geneva' adopted by the League of Nations. The second was the 1959 United Nations Declaration of the Rights of the Child. Neither of these instruments was legally binding.

7 The USA signed the Convention on the Rights of the Child in February 1995, but has not yet ratified. Somalia has neither signed nor ratified. States are not required to be Members of the United Nations in order to become parties to the CRC.

8 Verhellen, E. (1995) *Legal protection of children's rights. A framework for 'to be informed strategies'.* Luxembourg: European Forum for Child Welfare, Luxembourg Conference 'The rights of the child in Europe. Make them known – make them happen', pp.26–34.

9 See also: *Plan of Action for the UN Decade for Human Rights Education, 1995–2004,* Geneva, Office of the United Nations High Commissioner for Human Rights, n.d., p.7; Tarrow, N. (1992) 'Human rights education: alternative conceptions.' In: J. Lynch, C. Modgil and S. Modgil (eds) *Cultural diversity and the schools.* London: Falmer Press, p.21 (vol.4 of *Human rights, education and global responsibilities*); Lynch, J. (1992) *Education for citizenship in a multicultural society.* London: Cassell; Brock-Utne, B. (1994) 'Education about peace.' In D. Ray (ed) *Education for human rights, an international perspective.* Paris: UNESCO; Richardson, R. (1991) 'A visitor yet a part of everybody – the tasks and goals of human rights education.' In H. Starkey (ed) *The challenge of human rights education.* Norwich: Page Bros, p.5–10.

10 Verhellen, E. (1993) 'Children's rights and education: a three-track legally binding imperative.' *School psychology international* (London), vol.14, p.199–208.

11 The 'Matthew effect' is a metaphor derived from a Biblical reference. It means that those people who already have a lot (e.g. money, honour, etc.) get more and, as a negative effect, those who have little get less.

12 For more detailed information on key concepts such as citizenship education and/or human rights education, see:
The British Council, Citizenship education and Human rights education. Key concepts and debates, 2000.

CHAPTER 10

Respectful Learning Communities

Laying the Foundations of Human Rights, Democracy and Peace in the New Millennium

John Bennett and Stuart N. Hart

Introduction

These are extraordinarily dynamic times! New challenges and opportunities are emerging in our world at velocities and magnitudes never before recorded in history. Futurists such as Alvin Toffler (1971) or Francis Fukuyama (1999) speak of the 'acceleration of history' as the organization of our societies, forged by industrial production patterns, changes at an increasing speed, impelled by the information revolution. The mapping of the human genome promises even more radical change, as human science gains greater control over reproduction and even over life itself. In a situation where some of the most fundamental expectations and patterns of relationship are being altered, it is reasonable, in fact imperative, that persons and societies turn to shared values and to education of the young to achieve a sense of meaning and integrity in life.

In this chapter, some basic ideas about human rights teaching are considered, selected international visions for education in the 21st century are reviewed, relevant traditional and new educational values are clarified, future educational trends are described, and the significance of the Convention on the Rights of the Child is considered. The authors posit that the school of the future has enormous potential to realize the core values of the Convention and to assure their pervading influence on the human condition. The article ends with a proposal for initiatives to transform the transmission-of-content school into learning communities based on respect for the human rights of children, teachers and parents.

Basic orientations

Social reproduction theory and the nurture assumption

Social reproduction theorists provide – with somewhat different emphases – relevant and useful views on the issue of values. Parsons (1951) indicates that the core values in any society spring from wider economic, social and institutional arrangements. Though critical of the perspective, Bourdieu (1990) and Swartz (1997) underline the role of the family institution in establishing the base and likelihood of expanding 'cultural capital' through the values, experiences and opportunities that families provide to their children. In parallel, the significance of schools in forming the thinking, feeling and behaving of young people is given support in the views of Harris (1998), expressed in her book *The Nurture Assumption.* She concludes, from a credible review and interpretation of genetic and developmental research, that parents in general have little direct effect on the characteristics of their children, beyond the genetic pool they provide. They do, however, have significant indirect influence on the developing personalities of their progeny by virtue of the social contexts and resources they make available to children as they mature.

These theoretical positions indicate that the lives of children are powerfully oriented by the surrounding social environment. Any attempt to transform values within schools must take into account the deep influence exercised over the minds of children by social context, especially when reinforced by family or group culture. The education system would need to be a senior partner in any such enterprise, and the new values to be produced would need to be reflected not only in curricula but also throughout the school, in its organization and pedagogical practice.

Moral development

Attempts to advance commitment to and application of values must consider what is known about moral development. There is fairly widespread international support, including cross-national research, for the moral development theory of Kohlberg (Kohlberg 1981; Power,

Higgins and Kohlberg 1989). Kohlberg has proclaimed that both individuals and societies progressively evolve through

- *Concern primarily with survival and satisfaction*, while faced with control or danger from external forces or persons with power. This concern later becomes concern for reciprocal relationships with those with enough power to provide mutual advantage.
- *Investment in codes, rules and laws* that assure predictable systems of protection and satisfaction, which value adherence to a system of 'right' living, now and in the future. In this organization of values, all persons are assumed to have the same interests and deviants are challenged to comply, be punished or expelled.
- *Increasing appreciation for the diversity of individual and group experiences* through which respect for universal principles and democratic processes is ultimately to be achieved through individual choice.

Research has established the potential of this theory for application in schools to raise progressively the level of moral development of students. The theory has shown particular promise when its tenets have been instituted as the pervading ethos of a school community (Power 1992).

Human rights

The human rights movement exemplifies both the yearning for and progress toward establishing the fundamental rights of all persons. The combination of the Universal Declaration of Human Rights (United Nations, 10 Dec. 1948) and the Convention on the Rights of the Child (United Nations, 20 Nov. 1989) present a universal 'positive ideology' of persons. Their standards are translations of fundamental human needs and natural rights (Pappas 1983; Adler 1981) into a normative framework of respect for the dignity of each individual, for democratic principles, and for the full development of potentials.

While all the principles and themes of the Convention on the Rights of the Child can be related in some meaningful way to the topics of this chapter, its article on the goals of education is directly and powerfully applicable. It sets very clearly the expectation that education systems should move toward the development of respect for children and families, and for human and democratic rights in schools:

Article 29 [Aims of Education]

1. States Parties agree that the education of the child shall be directed to:

(a) The development of the child's personality, talents and mental and physical abilities to their fullest potential;

(b) The development of respect for human rights and fundamental freedoms, and for the principles enshrined in the Charter of the United Nations;

(c) The development of respect for the child's parents, his or her own cultural identity, language and values, for the national values of the country in which the child is living, the country from which he or she may originate, and for civilisations different from his or her own;

(d) The preparation of the child for responsible life in a free society, in the spirit of understanding, peace, tolerance, equality of sexes, and friendship among all peoples, ethnic, national and religious groups and persons of indigenous origin;

(e) The development of respect for the natural environment.

Perspectives on education in the 21st century

In this section, we shall briefly pass in review the positions of three major educational organizations with regard to education in the 21st century. The positions of UNESCO, the Jomtien/EFA Alliance, and Education International will be considered. It will be seen that these organizations, while trying to make education systems respond more adequately to the societal and economic needs of countries, conceptualize education increasingly in terms of human rights.

UNESCO's Commission On Education

The UNESCO General Conference of 1993, representing education ministries from nearly 180 countries worldwide, authorized the creation of the UNESCO International Commission on 'Education in the Twenty-first Century', chaired by Jacques Delors, the former president of the European Commission. The impetus for the creation of the Commission came from tensions, experienced in all countries, between tradition and modernity; between the expansion of knowledge and the capacity to assimilate and use it wisely; between the power of the burgeoning global economy and local needs; between the drive toward ever-higher qualifications and the need to maintain equality of opportunity. Of real concern to the Commission was:

> the major danger of a gulf opening up between a minority of people who are capable of finding their own way successfully about this new world that is coming into being and the majority who feel that they are at the mercy of events and have no say in the future of society, with the danger that entails of a setback to democracy and widespread revolt. (UNESCO 1996, p.51)

According to the Commission, this challenge should be met by ministries of education reinforcing their efforts to improve access to and the quality of basic education for all. The report of the Commission, *Learning: the treasure within* (UNESCO 1996) reiterated the United Nations position, namely that basic education, through the formal education system, is a fundamental right of each individual and all peoples, a passport to life and a fundamental guarantor of democracy. However, basic education must be seen not as a once-off period of education but as a foundational block of learning throughout life, which, according to the Report, will become a key characteristic of education in the 21st century. Education throughout life must be organized to avoid both the invidious 'selection by ability, (which increases the number of academic failures and the risk of exclusion), and the same education for all, which can inhibit talent'. Diverse paths should be provided through education systems to enable children, young people and adults to move smoothly from one stage of education to another. Lifelong education will become ever more necessary to allow people to upgrade or gain new qualifications to fit them for ever-changing job market conditions and, perhaps above all, to allow them 'to retain mastery of their own destinies' (UNESCO 1996, p.101).

Throughout the Report, the accent is placed on people *learning* rather than on credentials, important as these may be. Four pillars are proposed for the education of the future: learning to know; learning to do; learning to live together; learning to be. The latter goals are in keeping with the position taken by UNESCO since its foundation, namely, that education should aim not only to serve the economy but also to form 'whole human beings' (p.21). It is easy to see that this position is open to – even encourages – attention to children and to values in education.

The Jomtien/Dakar/EFA alliance

The Jomtien/EFA alliance came into being in preparation for the World Conference on Education For All, held in Jomtien, Thailand in 1990. Faced by ineffective schooling and mounting illiteracy in many countries, UNDP (United Nations Development Programme), UNESCO, UNICEF and the World Bank convened this key conference to stem the deterioration of education systems and to encourage countries, both individually and collectively, to adopt an action-oriented approach to reaching the goal of universal basic education. Basic education was defined as of at least four years duration, a period during which essential 'learning tools' (such as literacy, oral expression, numeracy and problem solving) and 'learning content' (such as knowledge, skills, values and attitudes) should be acquired. Both adults and children have a basic right to this minimal period of education, which was seen as a primary means of moving toward broad-based and sustainable economic development in all countries. Such education was required by human beings to survive, to develop their capacities, to live and work in dignity, to participate fully in development, to improve the quality of their lives, to make informed decisions and to continue learning (UNESCO 1990).

The conference focused attention on the basic learning needs of all human beings, on ensuring quality educational environments, on learning achievement in schools, and on the necessity of providing supporting policy and social contexts. In the follow-up to the Conference, significant progress was made in the enrolment of young children and girls in education. However, a realistic appraisal of the process would indicate that the commitments made by many countries that endorsed the Jomtien *Declaration and Framework* remained largely unmet.

Basic education and child labour in the world up to 1997:

- Seven African countries enrol less than 40% of primary aged children in school (Botswana enrols 94% of boys and 99% of girls in primary education).
- In India, 87 million children are not in school.

- Child labour is a significant problem in 74 countries in the world, and forced and bonded labour in 33 countries.
- Child prostitution is a problem in every continent, including 12 out of 38 European countries, 8 out of 18 Latin American countries and 10 out of 28 Asian-Pacific countries.

Source: *Education International Quarterly*, 4, 4, 1998

To some extent, this failure has been outside the control of ministries of education, which are confronted in many countries by intractable problems of poverty and population growth.[1] Hence, the UN followed up the Jomtien Conference with a series of world summits[2] committed to development and poverty eradication, with a clarion call throughout for quality basic education for women and other neglected majorities, as a primary means of fulfilling this commitment.

Since Jomtien, the work of the founding alliance continues unabated. Reinforced by the UN summits of the 1990s, the alliance has been broadened to engage many other key agencies in the international community, a wider range of government ministries, funding agencies, civil society and private partners. New educational themes and mechanisms are emerging, such as expanding early childhood care and education; reinforcing autonomous management systems for schools; using the new education technologies effectively; supporting teachers more practically and technically in their work; and engaging a broader set of actors in educational planning and practice.

A new assessment programme of the progress of nations in education has also been put into place. Six years after Jomtien, a first mid-decade review was made in 1996 at Amman, for which countries were invited to document significant progress and shortfalls. A new assessment has just occurred at The World Education Forum in Dakar, Senegal, 24–28 September 2000, to mark the 10th anniversary of Jomtien. This culmination of the UNESCO-led review of the UN's Decade of Education for All included consideration of individual country assessments and some regional surveys and thematic studies on education issues. The Forum reaffirmed the vision of the World Declaration of Education for All established at Jomtein, and recognized that, while progress had been made during the decade, the status of realizing the education needs and rights of youth and adults was unacceptably poor. A Dakar Framework for Action was constructed and participants committed to 'achievement of education for all (EFA) goals and targets for every citizen and for every society' (World Education Forum 2000, p.1, in UNESCO 1999) and to 'ensuring that the learning needs of all young people and adults are met through equitable access to appropriate learning and life skills programmes' (p.2).

It is perhaps the emphasis on human rights *to*, *in* and *through* education that is most innovative in the Dakar approach. The Convention on the Rights of the Child is cited in the Dakar Framework and education is identified as a fundamental right. Additionally, education is identified as 'key to sustainable development and peace and stability within and among nations' (p.1) and the importance of 'responsive, participatory and accountable systems of educational governance and management' (p.2) is emphasized. Education is recognized not only as a right in itself, but also as clearing the path to a whole series of other human rights. The Dakar Framework sets the expectation that the EFA goals and targets will be met no later than 2015. However, one would be more reassured were actual mechanisms put into place to make the right to education a reality in countries or, if in schools, the Convention was promoted strongly by ministries of education as a founding text for educational relationships.

Education International[3]

Education International, the international congress of teacher unions, based in Brussels, is the organization that is powerfully placed to introduce a practical recognition of rights in education. In 1999, it had 294 affiliates in 152 countries, representing 23 million members. A major goal of the organization is to expand and improve the quality of public education worldwide. In addition to its contributions to the theory and practice of the various branches of education, Education International insists on the promotion of democracy, social justice and equality through education. It is a staunch supporter of UN programmes, e.g. EFA (Education For All), the Convention on the Rights of the Child, the eradication of child labour and indigenous education. It has initiated a number of worldwide campaigns such as *Quality Public Education for All* and *Education for a Culture of Peace*.

In recent years, Education International has turned its attention increasingly toward human rights in education. It points out that many of the basic principles affirmed in international instruments are not met in national education systems, including the safety conditions of school buildings and equipment. Teachers also are poorly treated: they are often not consulted or are badly informed about educational reforms. In many countries, their conditions of work and salary conditions are deplorable. Little progress can be made in children's rights if teachers do not receive the respect their profession merits.

Above all, Education International calls attention to the plight of children who are denied the basic right to education, announced in article 28 of the Convention on the Rights of the Child. Over 125 million children, 60 per cent of whom are girls, have never gone to school. Another 150 million children receive schooling of such low quality or of disproportionate cost that they drop out of school altogether soon after they start. Not willing to let this injustice pass, Education International has joined in a powerful consortium of international organizations and national movements to launch a *Global Campaign for Education*. The Campaign intends to bring pressure on governments to fulfil their promise to provide free, quality basic education for all children.

To support this effort, Education International has undertaken to produce every three years a report, entitled the Education International (EI) Barometer, on human and trade union rights in education. The EI Barometer provides for each of the 149 countries and territories in which EI has a member organization, an overview of the situation with regard to the right to education, child labour and trade union rights of teaching personnel. The conclusions of the EI Barometer of 1998 are damning. Fred van Leeuwen, General-Secretary of Education International, described the situation as follows, as he presented the 380-page survey in Brussels: 'Millions of children in the world are deprived of an education, child labour is on the increase everywhere while the education budgets of many countries are being cut' (*EI Quarterly* 4, 4, 1998).

A notable feature of Education International's approach is its support for the Convention on the Rights of the Child. According to the EI announcement of the *Global Campaign for the Right to Education*[4] (Education International 1999) the Convention not only affirms the right *to* education of every child but also announces certain rights *in* education.

> The Convention broke new ground in getting governments to agree that the right to education goes beyond the right to a seat in a classroom. It calls for education that builds tolerance and

> equality, and enables each child to develop his or her fullest potential. Schools serving poor and minority groups too often abuse children's dignity, stifle their abilities and promote intolerance and prejudice. In these cases, fundamental reforms are urgently needed to engage children, teachers and parents in creating a better system. (Education International 1999)

Values in education

Values in traditional education systems

From our account of the above education initiatives, it is clear that human rights is becoming a powerful issue in education and that the conviction of having rights will eventually enter into the self-concept of children. It is not certain, however, even if human rights were taught regularly in schools, that the effect of such teaching would be great, as the core values of traditional schooling may not reflect a modern view of children's rights, although the Convention may be reflected in the curriculum. Systems secrete their own values and behaviours through their purposes and their physical and social organization. This 'hidden curriculum', the unintended learning agenda of schools and organizations, is often far more powerful than formal teaching.

The history of public education in 19th-century Europe is that of a movement toward universal primary education and socialization by the state. As education became a central policy objective for the industrializing countries, the state gradually took over educational institutions from communities and charitable foundations. State school systems were, however, very different in character to the local initiatives of charitable groups. They were national in their outreach and expressly directive in content and method. The primary school appropriated children from family and community culture, aiming to transform them into literate and disciplined workers for the new industries, then in full expansion. The common school movement in the USA, during the same period, was partially motivated to combat prejudices against the new minorities formed through immigration and was intended to overcome diversity of backgrounds and inculcate and achieve support for the common culture (Butts and Cremin 1953; Cremin 1961).

In addition to teaching literacy, elementary science and mathematics, the primary school also had a high moral and national aim. National history and language and the moral foundations of citizenship were inculcated to young children, sometimes in direct opposition to local culture and tradition. In those circumstances, states often tolerated and sponsored parallel education systems, generally religious in nature, as long as the essential aims of public education were met. Most often, however, public education had the full support of parents, who were pleased to send their children to school, seeing literacy and formal instruction as a necessary entry requirement into the world of salaried employment.

Supported then by society and families – and in this matter, culture has a profound influence – school organization and its unspoken values were to shape generations of children for over a century. Relationships with teachers were deferential and/or hierarchical, based on a strict differentiation between adults and children. Children were taught to compete with each other, as teachers and examinations evaluated them, as individuals, on their cognitive capacity to reproduce an external body of knowledge. Familial mixing of ages or expression of emotion or individuality were discouraged in favour of organization according to cohort, standardization, long hours of listening and a focus on cognition. In short, the traditional organization of schools instilled in many children acceptance of hierarchy, passivity and respect for external discipline. Yet, it should be signalled that the 'hidden curriculum' was often mitigated by more social, humanistic or child-based approaches, e.g. in many schools, a purely external approach to discipline was often transformed by inculcating in children and adolescents a sense of personal responsibility and solidarity with group values. Frequently, too, good teachers inculcated the importance of learning, perseverance and good work habits[5], and organized extra-curricular activities, including sports, that allowed children to value their individuality and the importance of teamwork.

In more recent decades, the conscious socialization role of the school has weakened, while its technical knowledge production role has been reinforced. The ideological nature of the 19th-century school has been undermined by the decline of state religions, the debacle of European nationalism in the first half of the twentieth century and more recently, by growing multi-culturalism. Practical considerations, too, such as the growing numbers and diversity of pupils, and pressures to include scientific and technical subjects in the curricula, have led schools to concentrate on academic achievement. Faced with the bureaucratization of large schools, with unfavourable staff–pupil ratios, and with student indifference or even hostility to ethical issues, many teachers are tempted to confine their role to one of formal instruction. They have become reluctant – except in some countries where the critical study of literature, citizenship and philosophy is part of the curriculum – either to orient young adults or to help them examine values and behaviour.

Hence, a hierarchical ordering of relationships and a transmission model of knowledge are still central features of education systems, although a considerable diversity of values may be found in the educational content taught in different countries each with its curriculum reflecting a unique history, culture or set of institutional arrangements. Yet, across nations, the common core values of traditional schooling mentioned above – passive learning, individual achievement, deference to hierarchy, submission to external discipline – are still to be found, generated by school tradition, linked to the purposes of a fading socio-economic environment. These values are not necessarily those that are found in official curricula, but they can be identified by close observation of school organization and teaching methods.

A new education paradigm reflecting new values

In recent decades, a new education paradigm is emerging, seeing education not just as a preparation for employment but as lifelong, not just as transmission of formal knowledge products from older to younger people, but as co-constructed knowledge, validated by teachers and learners together. The new education paradigm has many attractive features: lifelong learning, education for civic participation, equity and social cohesion, learning by doing and learning in teams; the school as a learning community.

Lifelong learning for all

To achieve the goal of lifelong education for all, the OECD education ministers proposed in 1996 four strategies:

- To strengthen the foundation periods of lifelong learning. In addition to primary and secondary school reform, a new accent should be placed on early childhood education and care, which was seen not just as liberating women to enter the labour market but as the period in which positive attitudes to learning and schooling are laid and reinforced, especially in young children from disadvantaged backgrounds.

- To promote coherent links between learning and work.
- To rethink the roles and values of all institutions – including government – which provide opportunities for learning, and support the growth of other formal and non-formal arrangements for learning.
- To create incentives for greater investment in lifelong learning and training, by individual users, employers and providers, as stable funding is a necessary condition for quality provision and access.

In principle, rising education levels would be a key to future economic prosperity, civic participation in society and greater social cohesion. Ongoing education, over the whole of a person's life, would help many citizens to take a more enthusiastic and informed attitude toward participation in the democratic process, both nationally and locally (Gelpi 1997; McLaughlin 1994). In addition, the offer of retraining opportunities and the reintegration into the workforce of poorly qualified adults would compensate for the diminishing pool of labour that many industrial economies were experiencing.

Although it is recognized that a quality supply of education opportunities can sustain demand and in many instances even stimulate it, it may not be sufficient to motivate the potential users of lifelong learning provision. Among the ways to address this issue must be an emphasis on positive educational experiences when children are very young. This will demand change in many schools, which are still characterized by rigid structures, relationships and practice. Schools of the future will need to encourage children, adopt child-centred teaching methods and devise appropriate strategies to support non-academic children, if the opportunity to return to an educational environment is not to be a source of fear and anxiety. The changes involved will favour a human rights approach to children and an emphasis on social cohesion measures at the level of the school.

Toward equity and social cohesion

The search for equity and social cohesion is evident in much contemporary education policy. In the view of governments, a central purpose of education systems is to provide qualified human resources for the economy *and* to ensure to societies a necessary degree of cultural and social cohesion. Countries today cannot afford to ignore the issue of re-integrating children who have not reached minimal standards in school or who have dropped out before acquiring a reasonable foundation of basic skills and competencies. On the one hand, a combination of structural and technological change have led to great complexity of economies, with a parallel need to raise educational standards. Having a well-prepared and flexible work force has become necessary if countries are to remain competitive in the globalizing economy. On the other hand, the costs of social exclusion, unemployment and delinquency are now so great that strenuous efforts are made to retain children in school and give them a fair chance of having a qualification which can ensure future employment. Yet, significant disparities in educational achievement among social groups and individuals remain, and have become even more evident as the duration of schooling increases.

What have been the strategies proposed by governments to resolve the unforeseen effect of reproducing, or even exacerbating, inequality through education expansion? Some of the strategies proposed fall within the responsibility of ministries of social welfare and lie outside the scope of this paper. Yet, mention must be made of programmes that encourage social integration through creating networks, institutions, policies and relationships that enable people to act together, create synergies and build partnerships. Coleman (1988) has shown how social capital can influence directly the education of children, for example, when strong community support for local schools exists.

Education strategies have tended to concentrate on the school itself, although some social capital formation measures, such as outreach to communities, are now undertaken to prevent school failure and drop-out in poorer neighbourhoods. Strategies have been formulated to impact at individual, institutional and social-group levels (OECD 1998). Pupils with learning difficulties are increasingly offered more effective assessments, individualized aid and instruction, career guidance and orientation through the educational maze. At the institutional level, there is a move toward more effective schools with high expectations of children. Head teachers have been retrained to provide real leadership, to organize active classrooms and encourage teachers to work in teams. Renewed attention is given to transitions to ensure that successful passages are being made: between early childhood programmes and the first year in primary school; from primary to the lower secondary entry year; and in the crucial transition from school to work (OECD 1999a).

At the social level, governments have set up priority educational zones with targeted educational programmes toward children 'at risk' of educational failure. There is still some doubt about the effectiveness of targeted programmes, but if undertaken with energy and creativity, much can be achieved, especially if outreach from schools to parents and communities is practised intelligently. A human rights perspective is useful in building consensus around such measures. A few fundamental principles can call attention to the citizenship aspects of schooling, viz. respect for difference; solidarity of the older or brighter pupils with the younger or weaker ones; the responsibility and right of everyone, including teachers, to give and receive respect.

Learning by doing, learning in teams

Toward the end of the 20th century, the world's economy moved into globalization, that is, the core activities of the major economies – innovation, production, finance and corporate management – began to function on a planetary scale, in real time and with little reference to either physical or cultural space (Carnoy, M. in OECD 1999b). Multinational companies may be head-quartered in Switzerland, raise capital in New York, have research laboratories in Germany, keypunch data in India, outsource clerical work and call centres to Ireland, run production units in Asia, Latin America or Morocco, and sell worldwide. The globalization of different functions is made possible by the micro-electronic revolution, which has created in the space of 20 years, worldwide infrastructures in information processing and telecommunications.

Because of globalization, business companies today demand a 'flexible' organization of work that allows rapid response to changes in demand. Core work, around policy, strategy or management, is conducted continuously in multi-task teams, while production or service delivery is often sub-contracted or achieved through part-time or temporary labour. Hence, there is a transformation of the labour market, with part-time jobs, flexible working time and self-employment on the rise in all countries. The new shape of the labour market and the work profiles required by companies will presuppose a capacity in children and adults to learn new processes quickly, to have sufficient self-confidence to change, to learn how to build up networks, both emotional and knowledge-based, that will allow them to cope with change and uncertainty.

The adaptability of companies to complex and changing market conditions requires in turn new assessments of knowledge, its acquisition and use. According to van Aalst (1998), in the decades to follow, 'knowledge will be increasingly produced within companies'. This knowledge is not content-dominated, as content can be assessed quickly once one knows where to find information. What counts is to be able to create meanings, concepts, principles and methods within the company that are capable of solving problems as they arise and that can carry the company toward its goals. Key company assets are, therefore, team intellectual assets, with the focus on 'knowledge worker', 'knowledge management', 'networking' and 'organizational learning'. The capacity to learn is the key, to be able to respond to new situations, to deal effectively with unwanted social and organizational effects, to innovate, to consult and network, to communicate what one is doing and its results. To enhance teamwork and common purpose, the company's priorities are discussed and agreed by all employees. At the same time, with the purpose of preserving creativity and motivation, the relevance and quality of one's work is determined by the individual.

If education authorities wish to maintain some coherence between school organization and the new demands of business organization, then schooling and the relationship to knowledge, as we know it, must change. Curricula, at least in the early years, will demand less the acquisition of discipline-based subject matter than the practice of multi-faceted cognitive and social skills. Learning by doing and learning in teams will become the norm. The school community will be assessed for the amount and quality of learning it generates rather than the amount of content assimilated. For this reason, and for the sake of equity and social cohesion, care will be exercised within the school to mix within teams children of different background and abilities, and, across the educational system, to ensure that schools in poorer neighbourhoods should have at least equal facilities.

Teachers will be key actors, as significant change can only be produced if teachers support the concept of knowledge as co-construction and learn to master the many new methodologies implied: team teaching, skills-based curricula, varied learning pathways for different pupils; new assessment policies; the imaginative use of technology; the opening of schools to resource persons. The basic building blocks of traditional education will not be neglected, such as the acquisition of adequate levels of literacy and numeracy, but in parallel, children's motivation will not be neglected. Learning will be made relevant to their interests and developmental stage, and the progress and involvement of each child carefully documented.

The school as a learning community

As we have seen, recent education research suggests that the banker/transmission model of knowledge and the rigid hierarchical relationships of the traditional school are becoming ineffective. Within schools, a sea-change is taking place, as education moves from a transmission of knowledge model to one of learning together and of constructing meaning in teams. Team learning and team skills (social capital building) contribute most to company knowledge and economic performance, as the analysis of excellence and competitiveness increasingly shows (van Aalst 1998). If applied to schooling, it implies a new relationship to knowledge, to teaching and learning, and to the underlying value system of the traditional school. The transformation can be encapsulated in the notion of the school as a learning community.

The term 'learning community' has been much used during the last 20 years, particularly within the school improvement movement. In general, and this is the meaning we would privilege, it is used to place an accent on the two elements that compose it, namely, on 'learning' and 'community'. The word 'learning' is used to underline the fundamental nature of education, which is drawing out what is already there, that is, the child's innate desire to learn and to socialize. In order to learn with delight, to be involved, children need other children, a stimulating environment and a guiding adult, who will model and facilitate social and learning behaviours, in the best interests of the child. 'Community', with its notion of living together in relationships of consideration, trust and mutual help, provides an idea of the ethos that should permeate the learning environment. This ethos, we suggest, can be made explicit and complemented by specific allusion in school curricula to basic human rights principles.

The proposed learning community will reinforce the traditional strengths of education systems: the inculcation of discipline and solidarity, good working habits, perseverance and personal honesty. But many new emphases will emerge in the new learning communities.

There will be an emphasis on active, self-directed learning. It is clear that passive learning, listening and reading can increase stored knowledge and allow pupils to retrieve it during paper and pencil examinations. However, educational research evidence, particularly in the area of science education across beginner and advanced levels, indicates that knowledge gained through passive learning will give way to previously held superstitions and misconceptions if it has not been field tested (Osborne and Freyberg 1985; Nussbaum 1979; Schnekps 1988). Gardner's (1999) review of this research led him strongly to encourage active learning, involving the practical testing of ideas to determine their validity, and an apprenticeship model for learning, one that would team the young learner with the more advanced.

> Discussion of education has often been restricted to the cognitive realm, even to specific disciplines. Yet I see education as a far broader endeavor, involving motivation, emotions, social and moral practices and values. Unless these facets of the person are incorporated into daily practices, education is likely to be ineffective – or, worse, to yield individuals who clash with our notions of humanity. (Gardner 1999, p.11)

Attempts to advance moral development have produced additional evidence that the active involvement of the learner in dealing with real-life moral dilemmas is most effective (Power *et al.* 1989). Trends in recent years have supported 'discovery' and 'constructivist' models in learning, models which value and promote active learning roles in exploring problems and issues, finding and constructing meaning, drawing conclusions, and developing new understandings and applications (Biehler and Snowman 1999; *School Psychology International* 1995). In sum, progress toward democracy and human rights in education is not necessarily led by formal curricula that incorporate information or teaching about human rights.

There will be an insistence too on building creativity, fundamental skills and positive attitudes toward learning rather than on the transmission and reception of codified knowledge; on the capacity to work in teams, engage in networks and self-evaluate rather than on individual performance and external evaluation; on outreach to the community rather than on treating the school as a self-contained microcosm; on respect for others and a human rights approach, rather than on hierarchical relationships with teachers and a neglect of peer relationships within the school; on attention to the social capital and political requirements of education as well as to preparation of human resources for the economy.

Apart from these common accents, learning communities will differ widely from each other. They will be distinguished by the type of programme and ideals that are institutionalized by countries and schools, within their particular geo-cultural and socio-economic contexts. Some learning communities may privilege formal learning more than others and resemble, to a great extent, a traditional caring school. Others will be more innovative in their efforts to involve children and parents. Likewise, in their value systems, the same diversity will apply: one school may be consciously religious in its value system, another may take on a more neutral, pragmatic stance, while a third may stress a human rights approach or, for example, in situations of conflict, focus on a peace programme. Common features, however, will be present, e.g. respect for children and their freedom of choice; an accent on learning by doing and on constructing meaning purposefully with others; interdisciplinary approaches; an ethos of supporting children in their educational life-course as compared to the present characteristics of class teaching, discipline-based subjects, and external standards and evaluations.

The new learning community will not necessarily be easier for either teachers or children. Opportunities and risks will be greater than they used to be. Greater skills are demanded of teachers if they are to become successful role models, facilitators and team players rather than 'lecturers'. A consequence of this change of role will be heightened expectations of children: to take a lead, to participate more energetically and to manage their time. They will need to develop the habits of setting goals, planning their work, working together in teams and checking their own progress. As they progress through school, they will be expected to demand less coaching, less counselling and less correction of errors.

In addition, the school community will need to find a proper balance between the rights of children and their duties and responsibilities. A number of countries, in making the CRC known to adults and children, have taken on this approach, e.g. the African Charter on the Rights of the Child includes for each section, whether dealing with adults or children, a section on rights and a section on responsibilities. Hence, the

Conseil national des enfants in Mauritius has produced a little booklet where one can read such things as 'Children have the right to a good education. They have also the responsibility to learn and to respect their teachers.'

The new ethos of respect, equality, teamwork and social responsibility, we suggest, can be made explicit and complemented by specific allusion in school curricula or school projects to basic human rights principles. Although they need to be translated into simpler and more operational concepts, the following is a list of such principles that may prove helpful:

- Respect for the human dignity of all persons.
- Support for full development of potentials and valued competencies.
- Establishment of pro-social skills and non-violent resolution of conflicts.
- Establishment of democratic citizenship and practices.
- Opportunities for meaningful work, leisure and play.
- Interpersonal support.
- Sense of partnership and community.

There are also indicators and examples of progress toward achievement of a human rights learning community that may be helpful: [6]

- The existence of a school vision or mission statement to promote a culture of human rights through formal and informal teaching, learning, and interpersonal behaviour.
- A negotiated short code of rights and responsibilities for all school community members.
- Formal and informal systems and mechanisms of participation and consultation to include the views of each and all school community members in decisions about its nature and practices.
- Evaluation practices which emphasize school community-based authority and which promote peer and self-evaluation for constructive purposes.
- Pro-social and non-violent attitude, skill and behaviour support and existence.

- Acceptance and support for multiple learning goals, paths and timelines.
- Opportunities for and recognition of contributions to living well now and in the future.
- Existence and continuity of cross-generational collaboration and relationships.
- Self-esteem and mutual respect based on character, competency and accomplishments.

A multi-dimensional human rights project for schools

During the last two years the authors of this chapter have participated in the formulation of a multi-dimensional project to create and sustain school learning communities which would help establish human and democratic rights, respectful of the practices of individuals, communities and nations. A substantial amount of energy and vision was derived from organizational sources, the International School Psychology Association (ISPA), UNESCO, UNICEF and the Committee on the Rights of the Child.

This envisioned project will develop a programme of information and education to be used at national and local education levels to facilitate the creation and maintenance of human-rights-centred learning communities. The programme will include core resources that can be upgraded to serve as the basis for the development of a wide variety of additional resources. The initially set goals for the project are to produce:

1. articles and book chapters announcing, explaining and describing the project and its rationale, and inviting involvement in its evolving design and development
2. a book providing in-depth coverage of its historical and conceptual supports, conceptual and organizational models for implementation, and cross-cultural examples of successful programs expressing its values
3. a brief guide in pamphlet or booklet form
4. a resource compendium
5. video tape and computer-assisted educational modules to guide policy development, program design, community

involvement, educator preparation, program implementation, and evaluation and refinement

6. an accessible cadre of experts to provide assistance as needed.

The first five components of the expandable project will adhere to or include some of the following essential elements.

- Agreed conceptual frameworks in support of respectful school communities.
- The essential principles, standards and ethos of respectful school communities.
- Indicators or operational criteria for use in determining the nature and degree of respect for human rights within educational communities.
- Concrete examples of existing programs in schools and their educational communities that are successfully achieving respect for human rights for some or all members of the educational community. These examples will be drawn from diverse cultures, communities, schools and educational program types.
- Alternative educational community models respecting cultural and contextual diversity.
- A road-map of frameworks and strategies for the development, maintenance and enhancement of respectful school communities.
- Identification of and access to needed and available resources.

Fortunately, it is not necessary to start from ground zero in developing supportive interest in this project, and facilitating mechanisms for this initiative. UNESCO, the International School Psychology Association, and Education International have agreed to be partners in the development of the project. The involvement of other interested parties would be welcome. Child Rights Education-International,[7] a new distributed learning program, has agreed to be a primary channel for information about the project and for the presentation of its educational modules. The 2nd International Conference on Children's Rights in Education, to be held on 18–22 August 2001 in Victoria, British Columbia will give attention to the Child Rights Education-International and its progress in developing educational models.

Conclusion

The barriers to implementing a human rights approach in schools should not be underestimated, as old approaches to teaching and schooling stubbornly persist. Yet, there is ground too for optimism. Research shows that substantial respect for children's rights and a variety of good models for teaching and living children's rights in schools do exist (Scherer and Hart 1999). Though reports by States Parties on the educational articles of the Convention were, on the whole, disappointing, some nations, e.g. Denmark, report a high level of success in implementing children rights and democratic principles in schools (Danish Ministry of Education 1998). The notion that rights are important in education is also making ground, as the analyses of the positions taken by UNESCO, the EFA Alliance and Education International have shown.

Educational research suggests, too, that the banker/transmission model of knowledge and the rigid hierarchical relationships of the traditional school have become an ineffective response to the needs of the new knowledge economies. Within schools, pedagogical practice is changing, as education moves from a transmission of knowledge model to one of learning together and of constructing meaning in teams. Team learning and team skills contribute most to knowledge creation and economic performance, as the analysis of excellence and competitiveness increasingly shows, as the analyses of van Aalst (1998) and others cited above show. When applied to schooling, this finding implies a new relationship to knowledge, to teaching and learning, and to the underlying value system of the traditional school.

Endnotes

1 Ministries of Education in the industrialized world are not confronted by the same problems. Yet it is estimated that one in five adults in industrial countries cannot read or write a simple text, that is, a significant proportion of all populations are functionally illiterate.

2 Notably, the World Summit for Children in New York, 1990; the World Conference on Human Rights, Vienna, 1993, the International Conference on Population and Development in Cairo, 1994; the World Summit for Social Development, Copenhagen 1995; the Fourth World Conference on Women in Beijing, 1995.

3 Education International http: //www.ei-ie.org

4 Global Campaign for the Right to Education: global.edu.campaign@ei-ie.org

5 Unable to come to terms with the cognitive demands of the school, many pupils did not learn these habits but, demoralized, simply dropped out or attended passively until the law allowed them to leave.

6 In a Child Rights Education-International website module, it is planned to provide for each or selected indicators, examples of existing practices in different geo-cultural learning communities.

7 Child Rights Education-International is a distance learning project being developed to: (a) become a primary international system, resource and model for children's rights education; (b) support development of competencies necessary to achieve effective and responsible children's rights research/scholarship, education, advocacy, policies, and services within and across disciplines and nations; (c) serve as a catalyst and coordinator for public discourse to advance understanding and thinking on children's rights issues; (d) provide organization and management of expandable and accessible archival holdings on children's rights history, issues, research, standards and practices; (e) provide an international base of information, expertise and education to interface with, complement and serve national efforts to understand and advance children's rights; and (f) make maximum use of the developing communication technology of distance and distributed education, including interactive television via satellite and/or telephone link, internet websites, digitalized video recordings, CD ROM, email and telefax. It has a 27-member international steering committee. Its website is http://www.childrightseducation.org.

References

Adler, M. (1981) *Six great ideas.* New York: Macmillan.

Biehler, R. F. and Snowman, J. (1999) *Psychology applied to teaching* (9th edn). Boston: Houghton Mifflin.

Bourdieu, P. (1990) *Reproduction in education, society, and culture.* London: Sage.

Butts, R. F. and Cremin, L. A. (1953) *A history of education in American culture.* New York: Holt.

Coleman, J. S. (1988) 'Social Capital in the Creation of Human Capital.' *American Journal of Sociology, 94* (supplement), s95-120.

Cremin, L. A. (1961) *The transformation of the school.* New York: Knopf.

Danish Ministry of Education (1998) *Report of the International Conference on Children's Rights in Education.* Copenhagen: Danish Ministry of Education.

Education International (1998) *EI Quarterly*, 4, 4 (Brussels).

Education International (1999) *Global Campaign for the Right to Education.* Brussels: Education International.

Fukuyama, F. (1999) *The great disruption: Human nature and the reconstitution of social order.* New York: Free Press.

Gardner, H. E. (1999) *The disciplined mind: What all students should understand.* New York: Simon and Schuster.

Gelpi, E. (1997) *Education des adultes inclusions et exclusions.* Rennes: Atopie.

Harris, J. R. (1998) *The nurture assumption.* New York: Free Press.

Kohlberg, L. (1981) 'The future of liberalism as the dominant ideology of the Western world.' In L. Kohlberg (ed) *Essays on moral development: Vol. 1. The Philosophy of moral development: moral stages and the idea of justice.* San Francisco: Harper & Row.

McLaughlin, T. H. (1994) In D. Bridges and T.H. McLaughlin (eds) *Education and the marketplace.* London: Falmer Press.

Nussbaum, J. (1979) 'Children's conceptions of the earth as a cosmic body: A cross age study.' *Science Education 63,* 1, 83–93.

OECD (1998) *Schooling for tomorrow; overcoming failure in schools.* Paris: OECD.

OECD (1999a) *Innovating schools.* Paris: OECD.

OECD (1999b) *The role of human and social capital in sustained economic development.* Paris: OECD.

Osborne, R. and Freyberg, P. (1985) *Learning in science: The implications of children's science.* Auckland, New Zealand: Heinemann.

Pappas. A. M. (1983) *Law and the status of the child.* New York: United Nations Institute for Training and Research.

Parsons, T. (1951) *The social system.* London: Routledge and Kegan Paul.

Power, F. C. (1992) 'An apprenticeship in democracy: The just community approach to civic education.' *Curriculum* 7, 3, 188–195.

Power, F. C., Higgins, A. and Kohlberg, L. (1989) *Lawrence Kohlberg's approach to moral education.* New York: Columbia Press.

Scherer, L. and Hart, S. N. (1999) 'Reporting to the UN Committee on the Rights of the Child – analyses of the first 49 State Party Reports on the education articles and a proposition for an experimental reporting system for education.' *International Journal of Children's Rights,* 7, 349–363.

Schneps, M. H. (1988) *A private universe* [videotape]. Santa Monica, California: Pyramid Film and Video.

School Psychology International (1995) Special Issue: 'Lev S. Vygotsky and contemporary school psychology', 16, 2, 99–221. London: Sage.

Swartz, D. (1997) *Culture & Power: The sociology of Pierre Bourdieu.* University of Chicago Press.

Toffler, A. (1971) *Future shock.* New York: Bantam.

UNESCO (1990) *Jomtien Declaration.* Paris: UNESCO Press.

UNESCO (1996) *Learning: the treasure within.* Report of the UNESCO International Commission on 'Education in the Twenty-first Century'. Paris: UNESCO Press.

UNESCO (1999) *Draft Dakar Framework for Action.* Paris: UNESCO Press.

United Nations (UN) General Assembly. (10 December 1948). *Adoption of a universal declaration of human rights.* New York: UN General Assembly.

United Nations (UN) General Assembly. (20 November 1989). *Adoption of a convention on the rights of the child.* New York: UN General Assembly.

van Aalst, H. F. (1998) *Learning and schooling in the knowledge society.* Paris: OECD.

CHAPTER 11

Status and Prospects

Concluding perspectives

Martha Farrell Erickson

The diverse and challenging chapters in this book got their impetus from the groundbreaking International Conference on Children's Rights in Education, held in Copenhagen, Denmark, in April of 1998. The major purpose of that conference was to advance respect and support for children's rights and the full development of children through education. Broadly speaking, the conference addressed the rights of the child to, in and through education. Now, coming three years after the conference, this book represents a focused effort to capture current thinking on where we have been and where we ought to go in order to operationalize and fully implement the articles (and the spirit!) of the UNCRC as it relates to education. Both the Copenhagen conference and this book have emphasized the Convention articles that specifically address education (e.g. articles 28 and 29, and article 23 on children with disabilities). But the chapters in this book clearly go beyond those articles, calling on educators – both formal and informal – to embody the entire Convention in all we do with and for children.

Chapters by Mason and Cohen and Lansdown create the broad context for this discussion, laying out the history of children's rights (overall and, specifically, in education) and tracking recent progress in implementing these rights. Scherer and Hart and Fredriksson make a strong case for defining and using consistent international standards and more detailed reporting forms to assess accurately progress in implementing the Convention. Reminding us that all children have rights, Saleh addresses critical issues related to the full inclusion and involvement of children with special needs. She also urges that we understand special needs as residing not only within the child, but also in the circumstances and social conditions that define the child's life.

Several authors address the complicated challenges inherent in honouring children's rights to participation and self-expression. John writes of the importance of respecting children's views, even when we sometimes need to deny their wishes for their own protection. And she offers practical suggestions for mobilizing peers to help marginalized classmates learn to express their views without violating the rights of others. With a broad view grounded in the history of childhood, Verhellen calls for a new child-mindedness and acknowledges the new demands this will place on teachers, parents and other adults. With a focus on the here-and-now experience of children, he challenges our societal tendency to think of children as not yet fully human beings.

Recognizing the importance of teaching human rights through education, Bennett and Hart emphasize a new paradigm that moves beyond 'transmission of content' schools to dynamic 'learning communities', in which children construct their own learning in social groups defined by respect for the human rights of students, teachers and parents. Similarly, Power describes the exciting 'just community' model of education and proposes a more culturally generalizable definition of the developmental concept of 'autonomy', one that acknowledges interdependence and replaces narrow notions of independence with the concept of self-direction.

Drawing on firsthand experience as the world's first ombudsperson for children, Flekkøy demonstrates the potential of the ombudsman model for helping nations implement and monitor the UNCRC. Her real-life examples illustrate the complexity inherent in full implementation – and they offer helpful and hopeful examples of how difficult situations can be resolved through reflection and thoughtful action.

Throughout all the chapters in this volume, the authors help to clarify and elaborate on 16 themes that emerged from the 1998 Copenhagen conference. These themes were first articulated by the rapporteurs of the Copenhagen conference (Cohen, Erickson, Flekkøy and Hart 1999). As summarized in the remainder of this chapter, these sixteen themes can guide us in ensuring that all children have access to appropriate education, in which their human rights are fully respected, and through which they learn to exercise their own rights and respect and advocate for those of others.

Sixteen guiding themes

1. Each child is a bearer of rights

This overarching theme encompasses several concepts that are central to understanding children's rights. First, children are not passive beings – or objects, in Verhellen's terms – on whom we adults must confer rights. Rather, they are subjects who bear rights that should be recognized and respected by others. Rather than the 'not-yets' we often think them to be – that is, young creatures in preparation to become full human beings – children, no matter how young, are already fully human beings entitled to full human rights (Verhellen). Furthermore, children are more competent than we often acknowledge. As illustrated in the specific examples provided by Power, John, Flekkøy and other authors of this volume, when given a chance, children join effectively with adults as full partners in governing schools, shaping their own education, and resolving dilemmas that arise when competing rights come into play. In fact, in many cases the children are the teachers, which is perhaps the greatest lesson to be learned.

2. Education is a right

International standards, beginning with those in the Universal Declaration of Human Rights and continuing with subsequent human rights treaties, plus the activities of international bodies, combine to establish the right to education as a universal norm. Nearly all of the countries in the world have pledged to uphold the child's right to education under articles 28 and 29 of the Convention on the Rights of the Child. At the World Summit for Children in 1990, heads of State from approximately 80 countries signed the World Summit Declaration, which emphasizes the child's right to education. Education has come to be recognized as the key economic resource and determinant for social and economic inequalities between individuals and nations. The right to education has achieved universal support through legal instruments. But, as highlighted in this volume by Lansdown, Scherer and Hart, and Fredriksson, the gap between intentions and implementation is enormous. We have much to do to ensure that the stated commitment to a child's right to education is fulfilled in local, national and international practice.

3. Society's obligation

The Convention on the Rights of the Child, as international law, specifically obligates governments to provide a free primary school education for their young citizens, to make secondary and higher education available, to provide vocational information, to take measures to encourage school attendance, to ensure that school discipline is administered 'in a manner consistent with the child's human dignity', and to develop fully each child's potential. These and the other standards specific to education are included in the education articles of the convention (28 and 29). Additionally, all the other rights included in the convention are to be respected in and through education. For example, in accordance with article 2, a child should not be subjected to unfair discrimination while being educated, and simultaneously, the child should learn to deal with others similar to and different from him- or herself in ways that are not unfairly discriminatory. National, local school system, individual school, and classroom policy and practice should apply the standards of the convention explicitly and implicitly.

But the societal obligation extends well beyond the formal education system. As Power notes, much education occurs after school hours, so coaches and other extra-curricular leaders have an obligation to respect the rights of the child just as formal educators do. Fredriksson emphasizes the importance of a broad societal commitment to children's educational rights, and acknowledges the challenge of trying to achieve respect for children's rights in societies where adults' human rights are not yet recognized. And Saleh calls on the international community to provide resources to nations whose economies are a barrier to implementation of education for all children.

4. The purposes of education (article 29)

Article 29 provides the basic and long-range vision for the development of persons through education. It is the clearest statement in the Convention defining the 'best interests of the child' and, in truth, of society, in terms of child development outcomes. The various authors of this volume emphasize both the individual and societal (economic, social) benefits of education. In one specific and extremely important example of education's benefits for children, Fredriksson points to data showing that increasing access to education produces a dramatic drop in the exploitation of children as labourers.

Among the goals of Article 29 of the Convention on the Rights of the Child are development of: the child's personality; respect for human rights; respect for the child's parents, culture and others; respect for the natural environment; and preparation for life in a free society. Within these universal goals, there is room for cultural interpretation and values. For example, while some cultures place a high value on team action, others value independence of spirit. But all cultures view education as the primary medium for ensuring responsible citizenship.

5. Support for the child's participation and full development

Children have participation rights from birth. They need to learn how, when, where and in relation to whom these rights can be expressed. Research on the social competencies of children has indicated, in general, that their capabilities have been underestimated. They can make choices, express opinions and understand relevant information at an early age. Long-term, comprehensive perspectives are needed that support the learning of democratic principles and practices with applications beginning before the child starts grade school. Nursery schools and kindergartens have been able to establish basic democratic decision-making principles for children by the age of three or four. Young children in both formal and informal group settings have learned to take responsibility in areas important to the group, enhancing their own feeling of being worthwhile. However, these competencies often are lost by the time children reach age ten because they are not enhanced or used in elementary or secondary school systems. This may be because pre-school teachers generally learn about and emphasize the development of children, while secondary school teachers generally learn more about subjects to be taught and how to teach them. Teacher preparation will have to change to provide continuity in the development of participation and democratic process competencies. This volume abounds with specific examples of how to honour children's rights to participation and self-expression – particularly chapters by Power, John, Flekkøy, and Bennett and Hart. And the authors are clear that children's full participation places new demands on the adults who teach and care for them, new demands that are not adequately addressed by current approaches to teacher education.

6. Promoting the child's present and future quality of life

The meaning and fullness of life as a child should not be sacrificed to the possibilities of a future state of development. Honouring a child's rights means focusing on the quality of life here and now, as well as preparing the child for the future. Full actualization of each period of development must be ensured if full development and maturity are to occur in later stages. At each stage of development, children need opportunities to play, explore, experiment and imagine. And they need opportunities, consistent with their evolving capabilities, to do meaningful work and make meaningful contribution. Every moment of life is 'real' life. Children have a right to the present.

7. Schools must respect the human rights of all persons

Children's rights are important, but their importance must not be exaggerated to the point of suggesting that they are the only rights of significance, more important than anyone else's rights, or that they can be achieved regardless of whether the rights of others are respected. The 'golden rule', that we should treat others as we would like to be treated, continues to ring true. In the slang of today, the phrase 'what goes around comes around' expresses the wisdom of informed self-interest. Schools, and the broader formal and informal educational environments for children, should be places where there is respect for the rights of all persons – children, teachers, aides, clerks, administrators and parents. Such environments enable children to value themselves and others; such environments promote learning and growth for all. Such are the 'learning communities' described by Bennett and Hart and the 'just community' schools advocated by Power.

8. Education and learning in and beyond school settings

A child's rights to, in and through education extend well beyond the walls of the school building. Children are educated in the family, peer groups, organizations, the local community. And, increasingly, they are educated by media, including powerful and pervasive new technologies. Some values and skills can only be learned within the close-knit, long-lasting relationships of a family where children belong, regardless of how they behave. For example, this is where children learn how to solve or live with conflicts between people who they love and who are essential to their survival. They learn through how they are treated and they learn from watching how other family members (especially adults) treat each other. Some other skills can only be gained in relationships with peers. In peer groups void of adult interference, children learn the ground rules for making democratic rules and decisions, and the conditions for being included in or excluded from a group where membership is not guaranteed. In many countries, children learn through organized after-school activities, particularly sports – an arena in which, as Power points out, children too often learn lessons that undermine respect for human rights. In the broader community, all child-focused services and activities should be formulated and integrated in ways that protect the rights and serve the formal and informal education needs of the developing child.

9. Overcoming existing barriers to implementation

The most important factor in the failure to implement the child's right to education may be inadequate funding. Sometimes this failure is the result of government policy in which budgetary allocations place education at the bottom of the list of priorities. At other times, failures may be subtler. For example, there may be an adequate number of schools and teachers, but no transportation and/or inadequate supplies. Or, in cases where children must supply their own books, parents may be too poor to buy them, thereby leaving children unable to study properly. Other interfering factors may include individual or institutional gender bias (particularly against females); the competing need for some children to earn money or resources through work to survive and/or help support their family; undiagnosed disabilities of children; and inadequate teacher training, as discussed by several authors in this volume. As advocates work to help nations and local communities overcome these cultural, economic and practical barriers, we need to share what we learn with others around the world. As discussed elsewhere in this volume, new technology can help us share ideas and strategies; and clear standards and improved reporting mechanisms will allow us to ascertain progress.

10. Education and learning need to be reconstructed

The whole approach to learning and education needs to be reconsidered in the light of social, economic and technological changes. For example, in an age of veritable information explosion, the emphasis of education may have to shift to learning more about where and how to find relevant information when needed, rather than acquiring facts that may be obsolete by the time children leave school. In an age of global connectedness and dynamic career paths over the lifespan, creative thinking, flexibility, positive interpersonal skills, and appreciation of cultural differences deserve more support as basics of education for all children. Approaches described in the chapters by Power and Bennett and Hart are examples of this more dynamic approach, as are Danish classroom models showcased at the Copenhagen conference (Danish Ministry of Education 1998). Danish models, particularly the 'class teacher' model that fosters long-term relationships between children and teachers, also address the developmental importance of children's enduring, trusting relationships with caring adults. (Such an approach to schooling has special significance at a time when children's connections with parents and other adults are often strained by economic distress, work-life imbalance, and the erosion of community.) Overall, a more holistic and integrative perspective on school, education and learning should achieve closer collaboration between schools and parents, schools and community, schools and youth-serving organizations, and various other arenas for learning. Such changes will benefit individuals and societies.

11. Education must respect differences

There is no one right way to honour the educational rights of all children. Differences in individuals, cultures and contexts must be considered in choosing from the substantial range of good and effective educational conditions and strategies that can be applied. In many situations, educational opportunities are limited by disrespect or misunderstandings about cultural differences. For example, we heard in Copenhagen that children whose religions require that they keep their arms and legs covered have been erroneously excluded from physical education and sports activities when all that was necessary to allow participation was good communication and tolerance for optional dress. Poor school attendance has been misunderstood to mean lack of interest or disrespect for authority when children were simply following a traditional pattern of apprenticeship in their parent's occupation, a misunderstanding that could be reconciled through home–school cooperation.

Even within homogeneous ethnic, geographical or religious contexts, families and professional educators face great 'cultural' challenges in supporting children's rights. For example, in both developed and developing nations, the needs of the 'drop-out' or 'pushed out' student population must be addressed by cooperation between parents and educators. However, many parents are reluctant to even enter a school and talk to a teacher because of the negative experiences they had as students. What is needed are new and better ways to build partnerships with these children and families, beginning by working with people in ways that emphasize points of agreement and existing strengths.

12. Understanding the moral principles, realities and fantasies

The most common conception of the special needs child is the child that has an obvious physical or mental handicap. In a broader sense, special needs can also be applied to those children for whom circumstances have made school impossible: children who work in sweat shops, children who are sexually exploited, or children who are living in extreme poverty or in a state of war. As Saleh emphasizes in her chapter in this volume, any child may have special needs, short-term or long-term, at one time or another. Refugee children who cannot speak the local language and hospitalized children have special needs until these conditions change. Special needs can also vary in severity. A very short-sighted child will be helped with glasses and being seated close to the teacher, while a blind child will need special education and technical aids.

Many children with special needs can get what they need in an ordinary classroom, on condition that the necessary human and technical resources are provided. But inclusive schooling may not be the best option for all children. For example, deaf children will need to learn to communicate by lip reading or signing before they can learn in an ordinary classroom. Totally inclusive schools may be a disservice to some children, failing to support the individual child's development or right to learn. Respect for the parents' and child's right to choose is a related factor. If there is no choice, rights may be infringed. The best interests of the child must be the main consideration, requiring creative ideas, participation in decision-making and flexible solutions to provide properly balanced developmental conditions for each and every child.

13. Long-term cost-benefit analyses for setting goals and prioritizing resource use

There appears to be broad agreement that education is the best long-term investment that can be made in the life of a child and in the quality of life for a society. The authors of this volume make that point strongly in a variety of ways. Yet this maxim, broadly supported in the words of governmental leaders and societal planners, is rarely translated into action when priorities for expenditures are set. In a world of competing interests for financial resources, it is critical that the *belief* in education-as-investment be translated into *facts* about costs and benefits. Education leaders and economic experts should collaborate to determine cost–benefit relationships between financial support at various levels for education and the long-term economic impact on individuals and society. Such analyses can engage policy-makers – and their constituents – in using such information to guide decisions about resource allocation. This kind of research is likely to provide strong justification to increase funding to education and to reduce ill-advised cost-cutting, which ignores a long, predictable future of negative results.

14. Teacher preparation, parent education, and the ability of the child to educate

Rarely are parents engaged as full partners in the education of their children. Children are usually absent from the power base of schools. Although both teachers and parents communicate to students, the voices of children are seldom heard in a meaningful way. At the Copenhagen conference, Norwegian ombudsman Trond Waage made a vivid point that schools will be most effective if parents and children, as appropriate to their evolving capacities, become the second and third legs of the 'tripod partnership' of effective schools (Danish Ministry of Education 1998). But moving to such a true partnership demands new ways of educating and engaging all parties. As discussed throughout this volume, teacher preparation must be changed dramatically, not only as it relates to new ways of educating children, but also new ways of welcoming parents as partners in education.

Parents also need education to prepare them to be active partners in their children's education. Their role begins long before the child reaches the age of formal schooling. The growing body of research attesting to the importance of a child's relationships and learning experiences in the first three years of life demands this (Erickson and Kurz-Riemer 1999). New or prospective parents need solid, evidence-based information about how experiences even in the first months of life provide the foundation that allows a child to become a motivated, confident, persistent learner and a caring, responsible citizen.

To meet these challenges, we need to harness all available media to inform parents about, and involve them in, the ongoing workings of the school. Personal outreach can occur through home visits, neighborhood meetings, and student-produced newsletters written for parents. Additionally, families can be drawn into the school by transforming schools into the focal point of community life, a welcoming place for multiple generations to gather and engage in lifelong learning. Grounded in the understanding that everyone has something to teach and everyone has something to learn, such community learning centres afford an especially rich opportunity for children to become the teachers of their parents and elders.

Finally, with a long-term view to building a society that honours the human rights of each citizen, children should become full partners in educating themselves and others. In schools, we need to engage children as early as possible in being responsible for advocating their own rights and honouring the rights of their peers. We need to look for opportunities to engage older and same-age children as educators and mentors for their schoolmates.

15. Accountability must be ensured

Nations, governments, non-governmental organizations (NGOs), special interest groups and the general citizenry should assume that ratification of the Convention requires full implementation of the rights it includes. The good intentions expressed in words through ratification must be translated into actions that are sufficiently well designed and supported by the necessary resources. As illustrated dramatically in earlier chapters in this book, the gaps between intentions and reality are wide.

As Fredriksson elaborates in his chapter, international standards are a critical step toward ensuring accountability. And as Scherer and Hart describe, accountability can be increased through establishing accurate, comprehensive, open and 'user-friendly' information systems for the reports prepared by governments and NGOs for submission to the Committee on the Rights of the Child. Instruments for organizing and reporting data specific to education should be strengthened; the research of Scherer and Hart provides an important step toward that end. The rapidly developing new technologies of communication are important tools to meet this need. Ministries or offices of education and NGOs within each nation can use websites to provide all relevant information about their reports on the education standards of the Convention at both formative and summative levels. Such technology will enable us all to learn from each other's successes and challenges.

16. Rights require more than legal support

The United Nations Convention on the Rights of the Child is an international legal instrument. Nations that ratify the Convention either automatically include all its standards within the laws of their lands, or move through some process that progressively adjusts and adds to existing law to achieve the equivalent of the Convention's standards. Laws at the international, national and local levels help make clear the formal commitments of governments to the rights of the child and set forth the essential interpretations, provisions of support, criteria and accountability mechanisms necessary for implementation.

However, laws are not enough to satisfy the spirit of intent inherent in the Convention or the broader vision for children's rights that led to its creation and nearly universal adoption, and which will shape future evolving standards and their interpretations. Examples abound of the inadequacy of law in achieving its intended goals. The driver of a car exceeds the speed limit and ignores a red light at an intersection. A friend brags about cheating the government by not paying the required taxes. A very real discrepancy exists in many cases between standards of law and actual human behaviour, usually because prerequisite values or moral commitments are lacking. The spirit of the law will not be realized until such commitments are made.

The Convention sets a 'positive ideology of the child' in front of the people of each nation and the world by establishing that children are rights-bearing persons and by guiding associated values, attitudes and actions. To achieve the rights proclaimed by the Convention, organizations, agencies and individuals of all ages must progressively understand, accept, appreciate, commit to and act in support of those rights.

The cognitive, affective and volitional capacities of people across all sectors of society must be activated to respect the rights of children.

Particular attention should be given to ensuring that the interpersonal environments of schools manifest and foster a shared sense of 'moral imperative' to advance the human rights of children. School personnel are a society's institutionalized child rearers who complement and supplement the roles of parents and who are expected to act in the best interests of society at large. Schools should be expected to champion the human rights and welfare of children in order to be true to their human development purposes and to counterbalance the denial of freedom of choice inherent in compulsory school attendance. Human rights values and practices learned and lived in school can contribute significantly toward better human rights conditions in society.

References

Cohen, C. P., Erickson, M. F., Flekkøy, M. and Hart, S. (1999, June) 'An international conference and an open file.' *Prospects, vol. XXIX*, no. 2, 167–179.

Danish Ministry of Education (1998) *Report Of The International Conference On Children's Rights In Education.* Copenhagen.

Erickson, M. F. and Kurz-Riemer, K. (1999) *Infants and Toddlers: A Framework for Support and Intervention.* New York: Guilford Publications.

The Contributors

John Bennett (Ph.D.) is Special Advisor to the Organization for Economic Cooperation and Development (Paris) for policy review of national early childhood systems. Formerly he has been Director of Early Childhood and Family Education and Director of the Young Child and Family Environment Project for UNESCO and representative to the United Nations Committee on the Rights of the Child. His specialty interests have included research on the psychology of the young child and early childhood advocacy.

Brenda Light Bredemeier (Ph.D.) is Co-Director of the Mendelson Center for Sport, Character and Culture at the University of Notre Dame, Indiana, USA. Her specialty interests include character development and sports, sports psychology, moral psychology, moral education and gender studies.

Cynthia Price Cohen (Ph.D.) is Founder and Executive Director of ChildRights International Research Institute in New York. She is a legal scholar specializing in international children's rights law and on children's rights issues of indigenous peoples. She teaches International Law and the Rights of the Child at the University of Tulsa College of Law. She participated in the drafting of the United Nations Convention on the Rights of the Child and in the formation of the NGO Group for the Convention on the Rights of the Child. She has written extensively on the rights of the child and has received several honors for her work in support of the rights of the child.

Martha Farrell Erickson (Ph.D.) is Director of the Children, Youth & Family Consortium of the University of Minnesota in Minneapolis, Minnesota, USA. She is a developmental psychologist specializing in parent-child attachment, child abuse prevention and community-based approaches to strengthening families. She developed STEEP (Steps Toward Effective, Enjoyable Parenting), a preventive intervention program for parents and infants and she publishes and lectures throughout the world on early child development issues.

Målfrid Grude Flekkøy (Ph.D.) is a clinical child psychologist and specialist in child and adolescent psychology. She is currently Chief Psychologist at the Nic Waals Institute in Oslo. She was the first Ombudsman for children in Norway (1981-89). She has been a Senior Fellow for UNICEF and authored *A Voice for Children: speaking out as their ombudsman.*

Ulf Fredriksson is Education Coordinator for Education International, the international federation of teachers' unions, based in Brussels. He is a qualified primary and secondary teacher who has taught in schools in Stockholm, Sweden. He worked as a full-time official for the Swedish teachers' union (1983-93) and was its international secretary (1988-93). He is preparing his doctoral thesis on migrant children's reading at the Institute of International Education, Stockholm University.

Stuart N. Hart (Ph.D.) is Founding Director of the Office for the Study of the Psychological Rights of the Child at Indiana University Purdue University Indianapolis, Coordinator of Child Rights Education-International, a member of the leadership team for the Institute for Child Rights and Development of the University of Victoria, British Columbia, and Chairperson of the Children's Rights Committee of the International

School Psychology Association. His specialty interests include theory, research, practice and education in the areas of children's rights and the psychological maltreatment of children.

Mary John (Ph.D.) is a developmental psychologist. Now in early retirement, she is Visiting Professor at the University of Exeter, United Kingdom, where she formerly held a Chair in Education, and was Dean of the Faculty of Education and Deputy Vice Chancellor for Research. Her interests include children's rights, Head Start programs, and children with disabilities. She is the founding Series Editor for the *Children in Charge* series for Jessica Kingsley Publishers, of which the present volume forms a part.

Gerison Lansdown is a children's rights consultant. She was the founder director of the Children's Rights Development Unit, now the Children's Rights Alliance for England, established to promote implementation of the UN Convention on the Rights of the Child. She has published and lectured widely on the subject of children's rights.

Sandra Prunella Mason is Chief Magistrate of Barbados and Registrar of the Barbados Supreme Court. She was a member of the UN Committee on the Rights of the Child from its inception in 1991 through 1999, and has served as its Vice Chairperson (1993-95) and Chairperson (1997-1999). Her previous experience also includes being a private practice lawyer, judge, being in charge of Barbados' Juvenile and Family Courts, and being Barbados' Ambassador to Venezuela, Chile, Columbia and Brazil.

F. Clark Power (Ed. D.) is Professor in the Program of Liberal Studies, Concurrent Professor of Psychology, and Associate Director of the Mendelson Center for Sport, Character, and Culture, at the University of Notre Dame in Indiana, USA. He is past president of the International Moral Education Association.

Ann Marie R. Power (Ph.D.) is Professor of Sociology at the University of Notre Dame in Indiana, USA. Her specialty interests include sociology of education, sociology of the child, sociology of poverty and race, and moral education.

Lena Saleh is a specialist in child development, education and special education. She is a Fellow of the London Institute of Education. Previously, she has been UNESCO's Chief of Special Needs Education in its Division of Basic Education. She worked for UNESCO from 1978 through 1999. Her background of experience also includes being a college educator of teachers, director of a special school, and consultant to UNICEF.

Lukas Scherer (Ph.D.) is a child and school psychologist in Switzerland, representative of the International School Psychology Association to the NGO Group for the Convention on the Rights of the Child and a member of its Coordinating Committee and Chairperson for its Sub-Group on Education, Literacy and the Media. His specialty interests in include children's rights across all areas and particularly as they exist in education.

David Light Shields (Ph.D.) is Co-Director of the Mendelson Center for Sport, Character, and Culture at the University of Notre Dame in Indiana, USA. His specialty interests include character development and sports, moral psychology, moral education, and peace education.

Prof. Dr. E. Verhellen (Ph.D.) is Director of the Children's Rights Centre and Professor of Juvenile Justice and Juvenile Criminology at the University of Ghent in Belgium. He is co-founder and a member of the Board of the *International Journal of Children's Rights* and he is co-ordinator of the Erasmus-Socrates programme 'Children's Rights in Europe' and of 'Children's Rights Universities', a UNESCO participation programme.

Subject Index

Name Index